Action Research in Teaching and Learning

A practical, down-to-earth guide for those v ....ching and learning in universities, this book will be indisp............. .eading for those who would like to carry out action research on their c.. n practice. Lin S. Norton's concept of 'pedagogical action research' has come from over twenty years' experience of carrying out such research, and more than six years of encouraging colleagues to carry out small-scale studies at an institutional, national and international level.

This accessible text illustrates what might be done to improve teaching/supporting learning by carrying out action research to address such questions such as:

- What can I do to enthuse my students?
- What can I do to help students become more analytical?
- How can I help students to link theory with their practice?
- What can I do to make my lecturing style more accessible?
- What is going wrong in my seminars when my students don't speak?

Action Research in Teaching and Learning offers readers practical advice on how to research their own practice in a higher-education context. It has been written specifically to take the reader through each stage of the action research process with the ultimate goal of producing a research study which is publishable. Cognisant of the sector's view on what is perceived to be 'mainstream research', the author has also written a substantial theoretical section which justifies the place of pedagogical action research in relation to reflective practice and the scholarship of teaching and learning.

Lin S. Norton is Professor of Pedagogical Research and Dean of Learning and Teaching at Liverpool Hope University. She was awarded a National Teaching Fellowship in 2007 and continues to champion the importance of learning and teaching by extensively publishing in journals and books.

Action Research in Teaching and Learning

A practical guide to conducting pedagogical research in universities

Lin S. Norton

Routledge
Taylor & Francis Group

LONDON AND NEW YORK

First published 2009
by Routledge
2 Park Square, Milton Park, Abingdon, Oxon OX14 4RN

Simultaneously published in the USA and Canada
by Routledge
711 Third Avenue, New York, NY 10017

Routledge is an imprint of the Taylor & Francis Group, an informa business

© 2009 Lin S. Norton

Typeset in Garamond by
Taylor & Francis Books

British Library Cataloguing in Publication Data
A catalogue record for this book is available from the British Library

Library of Congress Cataloging in Publication Data
A catalog record for this book has been requested

ISBN13: 978-0-415-46846-6 (hbk)
ISBN13: 978-0-415-43794-3 (pbk)

To the three most important people in my life:
Bill, Chris and Heather. Thank you for everything.

Contents

List of figures

List of tables

Acknowledgements

I am grateful for the support and encouragement of Patrick Smith who, with gentle good humour, motivated me by acting as a critical and constructive friend throughout the writing of the draft chapters. Special thanks go to my husband Bill Norton who has not only been a co-researcher in some of the action research studies described in this book, but who has also helped me practically with the bibliography and proofreading. Finally, I would like to thank both the reviewers of my book proposal as many of their suggestions have been incorporated here.

Foreword

Professor Lin Norton has written a book which, in many ways, is unusual, if not unique, making for interesting and informed reading. Throughout, the tone is both light and accessible without being simple and it is imbued with a tangible commitment to the processes of learning and teaching, along with those dilemmas and ambiguities with which inhabitants of classrooms at all levels are familiar.

Even before the expansion of higher education, there have been many books concerned with effective teaching and enhancing student learning. Unsurprisingly, since such books tend to be written by academics, they adopt a traditional, research-based and informed stance towards the topics of learning and teaching, citing the same authorities and research findings as well as tending towards the theoretical at the expense of the practical. In a minority of cases the opposite is the case with authors producing highly practical advice and precepts intended to inform the novice teacher. With the former approach the danger is that the reader will struggle to understand and apply the discussions to the practical realities of their classrooms, whilst with the latter there is a danger of reducing the processes of learning and teaching to a menu of mechanistic, quick fixes.

One of the distinguishing features of Lin Norton's book is the balance it strikes between these two positions. It is written in a style and adopts an approach which renders it both accessible and informative, underpinning the discussion of practical, classroom-based issues and scenarios with a comprehensive knowledge of the fields of pedagogy and curriculum. This foundation of knowledge and experience, however, serves to inform and illustrate those practical issues which are set out and does not dominate them.

Lin Norton is not afraid of acknowledging the complexities and 'constructive ambiguities' (Lampert, 1987) of classrooms – there are few, if any, quick and easy solutions – however such ambiguities are only constructive if those involved in teaching and the facilitation of learning choose to accept them as challenges inherent in teaching and learning, viewing them as opportunities for personal learning and development rather than inconveniences distracting lecturers from their existing research commitments.

Throughout the book, pedagogical action research is used to foreground a deep concern with the processes of learning and teaching whilst being sensitive to the human and social aspects of those relationships and transactions, which originate in classrooms and often continue beyond them throughout adult life. Such an emphasis on the 'softer' aspects of learning and teaching serves to distinguish this book from many of its contemporaries; however, for those whose interests are rooted in the processes of learning and teaching, for teachers as well as students, it represents a significant addition to the field.

Reference

Lampert, M. (1985) 'How do teachers manage to teach? Perspectives on problems in practice', *Harvard Education Review*, 55 (2): 178–94.

Professor Patrick Smith
Buckinghamshire New University

Preface

Why are students not attending my lectures?
Why don't students read?
What can I do to enthuse my students?
What can I do to help students become more analytical in their writing?
How can I help students to link theory with their practice?
What is going wrong in my seminars when my students don't speak?
Why won't students use the library?
Why are retention and progression rates falling?
What can I do to make my lecturing style more accessible?

If any of the above issues resonate with your own experience then you are not alone. Most of us who work in an academic role in universities do so because we have a commitment to helping students learn, develop and grow. Yet sometimes this process does not always work as well as we would hope, as the list of questions illustrates. Our students do not appear as interested or engaged in the subjects we are teaching, they do not use the libraries, they do not attend our lectures or seminars regularly, and perhaps worst of all, retention and progression rates fall. Is this the fault of the students, the system, dwindling resources, the government's current agenda, or is it something to do with the way we are teaching or supporting their learning?

Of course, it is very likely to be a combination of all these factors, and more besides, but this book is concerned with teaching/supporting learning and what might be done to improve it through the process of carrying out pedagogical action research.

Many definitions of action research in the literature usually involve reference to the twin purpose of action with research and to it being carried out by practitioners rather than by outside researchers. Some of the definitions include references to action research being cyclical, collaborative and constructivist, depending on which particular school of action research the author owes allegiance. None of this, in my view, has to be overly complicated. The principle of pedagogical action research is very clear; it is to improve some aspect of the student learning experience. Put more formally, the fundamental purpose of pedagogical action research is to systematically investigate one's own teaching/learning facilitation practice with the dual aim of modifying practice and contributing to theoretical knowledge.

Pedagogical action research involves using a reflective lens through which to look at some pedagogical issue or problem and methodically working out a series of steps to take action to deal with that issue. As in all forms of research (pure and applied) the ultimate aim is to publish, but of equal importance is the imperative to change one's practice. As we go through the book, elements of this definition will be explored in greater detail.

My intention in writing this book has been to offer a practical down-to-earth guide for anyone who has a teaching and/or learning-support role in universities and who would like to carry out action research on their own practice. In the book I have made some assumptions about you, the reader. I have assumed that you are interested in the concept of researching your own teaching but that you are also concerned about fitting it in with all the other demands of your academic role. I am using the term 'academic' to include anyone in higher education who has a role in facilitating students' learning rather than to refer solely to those who are described as lecturers, tutors or university teachers, since so many personnel can influence and research the quality of students' learning.

In so doing, I hope to have provided a guide that is encouraging but at the same time does not attempt to gloss over the very real issues that doing pedagogical research in a university context can create. Throughout the book, I have adopted an informal personal style, drawing directly on my own experience in carrying out and promoting this type of action research. In this way, my purpose has been to illustrate how feasible action research is, even when you are hard pressed by other academic demands, and also to show you some of the pitfalls I have encountered along the way, so that you will, at the very least, be forewarned.

The book is organised into two sections: the theoretical and the practical, either of which can be read independently, so for those of you who are keen to get on with the practical aspects of doing an action research study, a good start-ing point is Chapter 5. If you already have a fair amount of experience with action research but would like some theoretical underpinnings, you may prefer to start with Chapter 1. In this first section, which includes Chapters 1 to 4, I make a case for pedagogical action research in higher education where there is still an uncomfortable divide between research and teaching, and where the former is more highly rewarded. I have spent some time on this as I have found that in the highly competitive academic research world, you need to be able to justify and defend any research activity which might not be recognised as 'mainstream'. In keeping with the overall aim of this being a practical book, I have incorporated some reflective questions in each of these chapters.

In Chapter 1, I begin with considering some of the pressures that face those of us who teach and/or support student learning in universities. This is important because we cannot carry out pedagogical action research in isolation since the very context of that research is inextricably interwoven with the work we do and the institution in which we do it. In Chapter 2, I move on to considering the relevance of being a reflective practitioner and in Chapter 3, I describe the scholarship of the teaching and learning movement and why, I think it is important. Chapter 4 is where I make the case for pedagogical action research. This chapter acts as a transition from the theoretical emphasis in the first section to the practical emphasis in the second section.

In this second section, I have written essentially a 'hands on' practical guide to enable you to carry out your own pedagogical action research study, with further resources suggested at the end of each chapter. I begin in Chapter 5 by describing how to get an action research study started, followed in Chapter 6 by a consideration of some of the more commonly used research methods. In Chapters 7 and 8, I describe some basic qualitative and quantitative analysis and then move on to Chapter 9 where I demonstrate some of the ways in which you can use or adapt existing research tools. In Chapter 10, I discuss ethical issues of carrying out pedagogical research and I end in Chapter 11 by suggesting how you can publish your findings and apply for research funding.

Throughout the book I have used the device of hypothetical case studies or vignettes to bring to life some of the dilemmas and decisions we have to make in carrying out our action research projects. This has also been a useful device to include illustrations other than those from my own experience as an academic psychologist, but I hope in reading them, you will have caught some of my enthusiasm and commitment to this type of research. I wish you the very best of luck in your own pedagogical action research journeys.

Lin S. Norton
2008

Chapter 1

Putting pedagogical action research into the university context

What are the pressures?

Introduction

Pedagogical action research, like all forms of research, requires time, commitment and resources in order to carry it out successfully, but in some university contexts it can be seen to be of little value compared to subject research, so the effort to do it may require more justification, more knowledge and a realistic appraisal of what it can and cannot achieve. In this chapter I write about some of the pressures and constraints involved in our ordinary working day lives as academics, in order to help you to offset them against the very real benefits of doing pedagogical action research. It is my intention throughout this book to portray an honest and robust case for this specialised form of research, and to champion it as a rigorous approach worthy to sit alongside other research approaches.

The university context

As university academics we work in a fast-changing environment, which puts competing pressures on us including the need to be excellent at teaching, research and administration. More recently, we have been urged to prepare students for employment and to be entrepreneurial in a global market. It is difficult when planning an academic career to know whether we should concentrate on just one of these elements, or be more reactive and adapt to the latest demand or trend, while attempting to keep the others up in the air, like a juggler, without having a predetermined career path. Compromises and sacrifices will inevitably have to be made and each one of us has to make our own choices. Knowing what some of these pressures are will help us to clarify what it is that we do want in the way of career development and job satisfaction goals. I am also hoping to show you how pedagogical action research might help you by serving several of these demands in a coherent course of action.

In describing the choices that face us, I am going to use a framework proposed by Fanghanel (2007), which she based on an interview study with

18 lecturers from 15 different disciplines in seven different institutions. I have found this framework to be a useful shorthand device for thinking about the difficulties that colleagues sometimes face when doing a pedagogical action research study. Fanghanel uses the term 'filters' by which she means influences that are fluid and have complex and differential effects on the choices we make and the extent to which we emphasise one filter over another. They operate at three levels of academic practice.

1. The macro level which includes the institution, external factors, academic labour and the research–teaching nexus.
2. The meso level incorporating the department (or equivalent) and the subject discipline.
3. The micro level meaning internal factors affecting the individual lecturer.

In order to illustrate this framework, I have drawn on the literature and also on five hypothetical vignettes showing how individual academics keen to take some action to address a pedagogical issue, dilemma or challenge are also faced with pressures specific to the higher education context. I have also inserted reflective questions so that you are able to relate the theory to your own practice and specific situation.

Identifying a pedagogical issue

When our students are not learning or performing as well as we would hope, it is all too easy to blame the rapidly changing higher education context, the government of the day's agenda, such as widening participation, employability skills, fewer resources, and so on. However true these pressures may be, they do not help to move us on in improving our teaching and assessment practice so that our students have a better and more satisfying learning experience. Whether we are relatively new to university teaching, or have had many years of experience, the chances are that each of us will have identified some aspect of our students' learning that we would like to change. Consider, for a moment, the following five 'cases'.

Angela: Inspired to improve feedback

Angela is a newly appointed lecturer in a department of classical studies. As part of her probationary year she has been attending a university learning and teaching course, where she has learned some interesting ways of giving effective feedback. Keen to incorporate these into her department, she finds herself faced with colleagues who are unconvinced that the new methods will make any difference to student performance.

Berit: Concerned by innumeracy

Berit is a part-time university teacher who has been working for eight years in a well-respected department of physics. She is sure that the levels of numeracy in the first year undergraduates have been dropping year on year, and is keen to do something about it for next year's incoming cohort. Berit is also aware of the constraints that being on a part-time contract poses to any intervention that she designs.

Charles: Confronted with an under performing module

Charles has been a lecturer in civil engineering for three years, coming from industry where he worked for over 20 years. He made the move to an academic post, because he wanted to pass on his enthusiasm for the profession to the next generation. Charles is particularly proud of a work-placement module, which he designed for third year students on the full-time three-year programme. Students love Charles' module and give it high satisfaction ratings but the head of department is concerned that their academic performance is markedly lower than in the other third year theoretically based modules.

Delyth: Adapting to needs of dyslexic students

Delyth has been in charge of a masters programme in contemporary crafts for several years, but is increasingly concerned with the number of dyslexic students attracted to the programme. She would like to set up some workshops for dyslexic students to help them cope with the subject specific demands of her course, but is aware that she might be treading on the toes of the university support services for students. This is a prestigious and influential central unit, which is a strong feature in all the university's publicity material.

Eric: Bridging the gap between theory and practice

Eric is responsible for the academic provision of the clinical extra mural studies on a BSc in veterinary medicine, which undergraduates take in their vacations and in their fifth year. Eric has noticed that students find it difficult to apply the theoretical knowledge they need for passing exams into the complex combination of professional skills that they need for clinical decision making. He decides to introduce an assessed personal development planning (PDP) module, which will run over the five years to address this deficit, but such a long 'thin' module does not fit in with the university's regulations.

These fictitious case studies have been drawn from real life situations adapted from case studies and projects supported by the Higher Education Academy Subject Centres Network, so hopefully they will contain some elements that resonate with your own situation. What they each have in common is a learning and teaching 'issue' set in a potentially problematic context. So far, I have tried to avoid the use of the word 'problem' as my much-respected colleague Professor Patrick Smith, who wrote the foreword to this book, pointed out that the starting point for pedagogical enquiry is not always a problem but a dilemma, an issue or something that catches one's eye or ear, arousing interest and curiosity. Bass (1999) makes the point that how we conceive and think about the very notion of a 'problem' appears to be different depending on whether it is in a research or in a teaching context (see Chapter 5), but as Smith says:

> The irony of this not admitting to having problems in relation to teaching and learning never ceases to amaze me – stepping out of the comfort zone and into the uncertain penumbra beyond it. Vygotsky's zone of proximal development is what we expect students to do every day, but somehow it does not apply to us.
>
> (Smith, 2008: personal communication)

I agree with him, and yet, this is a state of affairs that does persist. Reconceptualising the learning and teaching problem into a focus for systematic enquiry, however, is one way of liberating us from this straitjacket that we put ourselves into. It enables us to carry out research, which will have the benefit of enabling us to modify our practice, improve student learning and contribute to new knowledge. Because such enquiry does not take place in a vacuum, Fanghanel's tripartite framework can help us to identify where the pressure points are, and deal with them more effectively when carrying out our own pedagogical inquiry. In order to do this, I want to step back a bit from thinking about pedagogical action research per se and consider the context in which university academics work. In so doing, I cover a huge amount of literature and concepts about learning and teaching that I cannot possibly do justice to in one chapter, but interested readers may follow these up in the references provided.

The micro level of practice

I have reversed Fanghanel's framework to begin at the level of the individual, because this is where, I think, we all start in looking at our own situation, experience, values, hopes, fears and aspirations, particularly when starting out on a career as an academic in higher education.

Why do we work in higher education?

Most of us come into an academic career for a variety of reasons. For my own part, I was totally captivated by the discipline of psychology; I wanted to be a psychologist and a 'perpetual student' for the rest of my working life, so academe was the place I wanted to be. I do not recall, at that time in my life, my prime motivation being about wanting to teach, to pass on any wisdom or to help other people. That came later when the anxieties about being proficient and expert in the subject subsided and pedagogical issues came to the fore.

Of course one cannot extrapolate from a single academic's recollections, but what literature I have found tends to suggest this is a common experience (Entwistle and Walker, 2000; Martin and Lueckenhausen, 2005; Martin and Ramsden, 1993; Nicholls, 2005). Nyquist and Wulff (1996) described three main stages in our development as university teachers. We begin, they say, by being concerned with issues related to ourselves such as wondering whether the students will like us, and whether we will be sufficiently knowledgeable, called the 'self/survival' stage. We then move on to the 'skills' stage in which we are concerned with our teaching and assessment methods. Finally we turn our attention away from ourselves to wondering whether our students are learning anything, which Nyquist and Wulff called the 'outcomes' stage.

I am not suggesting that this is the path that all academics take, as for some a research career is more important and rewarding than a teaching-focused career. The current tension between the two has not yet been satisfactorily resolved, in spite of the Dearing report (National Committee of Inquiry into Higher Education, 1997) which called for professional training for university lecturers. This led to the establishment in the UK of the Institute for Learning and Teaching in Higher Education (ILTHE) later replaced by the Higher Education Academy with its emphasis on the student learning experience.

The current UK national emphasis on teaching 'excellence' is influential but monetary rewards are not comparable with those generated by the research councils, so promotion depends in many universities on research accolades rather than teaching accolades. However, the move to establish teaching-only institutions appears to have been largely, but not entirely, resisted. There are an increasing number of posts that are teaching only, such as Berit's case illustrates. For Berit, and for academics like her, the difficulty lies when working in a traditional research-active department where she is not expected to carry out research and where, if she proposed some pedagogical research, this probably would not be well received.

For those of us who are not in teaching-only posts, we still have to make a choice to become a 'teacher who researches' or a 'researcher who teaches', and in both cases we may well face scepticism about the value of pedagogical research. Even this is a simplification as the role of the academic is multi-faceted and includes, according to Falchikov (1993), being an administrator, consultant and counsellor, with responsibilities to students and to colleagues in the institution.

The pressures described at the micro level come from an ill-defined and constantly changing role where multiple demands and expectations are made of the individual, which are sometimes conflicting. There is also an expectation on lecturers to be an expert in some aspect of subject knowledge. This state of affairs is chronicled and debated in the higher education policy literature, but for our practical purposes, we need to be aware of these competing demands on our time and energy.

Reflective questions

1. Why did you come into higher education?
2. How would you describe your primary role?
3. Do other roles conflict with your wish to carry out pedagogical action research?

What are our conceptions of teaching?

Before considering this question, it is instructive to look at some of the research that has been done in this area. There is a wealth of phenomenographical research which describes how academics conceptualise teaching and which has resulted in a broadly accepted scheme of 'conceptions of teaching' (Martin and Balla, 1991; Martin et al., 2000; Prosser, Trigwell and Taylor, 1994). Conceptions of teaching are commonly found to fall into two main categories: teaching as information transmission and teaching as supporting students' learning (Kember, 1997), although there are many more subtle differentiations (Samuelowicz and Bain, 2001).

Teaching as information transmission

In the first conception, which has also been termed teacher centred/content oriented, academics see their role as knowing their subject and effectively imparting that knowledge to their students.

Teaching as supporting students' learning

In the second conception, sometimes termed student centred/learning oriented, academics see their role as facilitating the process whereby students actively construct meaning and knowledge for themselves.

The link between conceptions and teaching practice

There is also some research to show that there might be some functional relationship between conceptions and actual teaching practices, although this has been recently challenged, as often the research infers teaching behaviours from the conceptions that academics hold (Devlin, 2006; Kane, Sandretto and Heath, 2002).

Critiques of the conceptions of teaching research

Conceptions of teaching have also been critiqued as being too simplistic. For example, Malcolm and Zukas (2001) have argued that conceptions present an overly neat picture, which suggests that there is no such element as identification with, or resistance against, values or ideological frameworks. This means issues about power, and academics' room to manoeuvre within these other expectations are not acknowledged.

A further problem is that the terminology used in the literature is confusing, with terms such as beliefs, orientations and approaches sometimes being used interchangeably and often not defined (Kember, 1997).

Perhaps the most worrying aspect of the conceptions of teaching literature is that it has given rise to the assumption that learning facilitation conceptions are somehow 'superior' to knowledge transmission conceptions. Gibbs and Coffey (2004) used an early version of Prosser and Trigwell's (1999) approaches to teaching inventory, which measures the extent to which teachers' approaches are teacher focused and student focused. They make the point that these are independent scales, not opposite ends of a single scale, so good teaching may well involve high scores on both.

Nevertheless, in spite of some of the criticisms of the conceptions of teaching research, we can use it as a very powerful framework for challenging the status quo and bringing about change.

Reflective questions

1. What are your conceptions of teaching?
2. Can you think of any recent examples when you felt unable to put your conceptions of teaching into practice?
3. If so, could this be addressed in a pedagogical action research study?

What are our beliefs about students?

As well as our conceptions of teaching, we also have to think about our beliefs about students because this will have an impact on the way we think about an effective curriculum and the way we conceptualise quality teaching. If, for example, we hold views of students as demotivated, strategic, not able and so on, this may well cause us to adopt practices that are not always pedagogically sound. Fanghanel (2007) argues that this filter is highly agentic and susceptible to

> dominant themes in higher education such as … the widening participation agenda and generally held 'folk' beliefs about students' laziness, instrumentalism, inability to concentrate … .
>
> (Fanghanel 2007: 11)

Her findings showed that, for some of her interviewees, beliefs such as these led to unfortunate piecemeal consequences such as fragmenting lectures, or giving very short assignments in order to tackle what they believed were negative characteristics or attitudes in their students. In terms of carrying out pedagogical action research, such 'blame the students' beliefs may lead us to designing interventions that do not take account of the whole system of learning and teaching as propounded by Biggs (1994).

In his paper, Biggs described three main types of theory; the student based, the teacher based and the process based.

1. The theories that offer student-based explanations of learning draw on an individual differences approach based on psychology. The problem with this theoretical approach is that it can lead to a 'blame the student' model where the teacher is 'let off the hook'.
2. The teacher-based theories are those upon which current staff development initiatives and accountability depend, but again the problem is that they are another form of attributing blame, in this case 'blame the teacher'.
3. The third type of theory is the process based which, like information processing (again derived from psychology), is seen as separate to the actual learning context. Study skills training is a common example where students are trained to read more effectively and then are expected to transfer this skill to the learning of their subjects.

The point Biggs is making is that all three models of student learning assume a deficit; poor learning is seen to be due to a lack of something, either in the student, the teaching, or in something the students are trained to do. If we do this, he argues, our interventions may sometimes be successful but we are avoiding the 'real situation', which is that we are dealing with a complex system where the classroom is a subsystem of the institutional subsystem in which each acts and interacts on the other.

Changing one element of the system means other elements have also to change to produce a state of equilibrium. An illustration of this is shown in the case study devoted to Eric. He believes that students are having difficulty in applying their theoretical knowledge into clinical decision making. This is a 'blame the student' model of learning and leads him to assume that a PDP module will help them as it will enable them to reflect on their learning as they go through their five-year course (a process-based model of learning). If Eric was to see this as a systemic issue, it might lead him to think that his students might be just lacking practice in clinical skills, so reflective learning alone will not help them. A more integrated solution might be to undertake some revision of the curriculum for instance (a systemic approach).

Reflective questions

1. Does a systemic model of student learning resonate with your experience?
2. Can you think of ways of carrying out a pedagogical research study that are not based on a deficit model?

Having considered some of the influences that operate on us at a micro level, I now want to consider Fanghanel's next level, as this is probably the level that will most readily impact on any attempts we make to carry out pedagogical action research.

The meso level of practice

Fanghanel (2007) describes this level as having two filters: the department and the discipline.

What pressures does the department exert on us?

The department has a huge hold and influence over us and over the way we work. Knight (2002) argued that the academic department was the prime location for any educational improvement, a view supported by Ramsden (1998) who identified it as the key organisational unit in universities. Knight and Trowler (2000) carried out studies with 24 new academics in two Canadian and eight UK universities in 1997–1998, and found some common patterns of experience. These included very simple things such as academics being affected by the geography of the department and where their office or desk was in relation to everyone else's.

More importantly, perhaps, was their finding that new colleagues have to uncover departmental tacit knowledge, sometimes captured in the phrase 'that's the way we do things around here'. This tacit knowledge includes norms, discourse and value sets associated with assessment, teaching practices and research culture as well as our daily work practices. Knight and Trowler argue that tacit knowledge is acquired informally through discussion, observing colleagues and through professional practice, and that this is more powerful than any 'formal mechanisms' such as a mentor, induction programmes and so on. Trying to fit in with departmental mores can create stresses and tensions particularly for new academics who are trying to establish a role identity, professional knowledge and competence as defined by Eraut (1994).

Fanghanel makes the point that the department filter is highly influential where alliances and conflicts impact on academics' teaching approaches and where conceptualisations can lead to estrangement and isolation if you do not fit in. Angela's case study is just such an example of how it can be very difficult to introduce an innovative teaching or assessment practice, particularly if you are a new colleague faced with scepticism from 'old hands'. Departments can be very different, ranging from tightly knit single discipline-based organisations to much more amorphous structures where individuals might not know all their colleagues. This is a consequence of recent patterns of growth and fragmentation in higher education, where there has been an explosive growth in some disciplines and fragmentation into sub-disciplines, but this means that sometimes an individual finds it hard to feel part of a department or build a sense of identity. Even in tightly knit collegial types of department there may well be strongly contested notions of the subject, which lead to schisms and different concepts of teaching.

Departments will also hold strong conceptions of, and attitudes to, research and scholarship. In traditional research-orientated universities, departmental heads may insist on research output coming before teaching responsibilities, particularly where an academic's tenure is dependent on a specified number of publications a year. In such contexts, engaging in pedagogical research might be difficult to gain support for and a careful case has to be made for it being a research area in its own right. D'Andrea and Gosling (2000) say that combating such resistances is difficult but not impossible and suggest strategies such as providing opportunities for discussion about the values of pedagogical research to the institution, the subject and the students, and creating networks of staff sometimes from other departments that can form a critical mass in influencing others to join them.

This is one of the benefits of engaging in pedagogical action research, as one of its characteristics is that it encourages a collaborative approach. This particular strategy would serve Angela very well, as she has a ready-made network with her colleagues on the teaching programme who may well be interested in introducing innovative feedback practices. Because feedback is such a generic issue, she might also be able to draw in more experienced academics who see the need to improve this element of their practice.

Reflective questions

1. Is pedagogical research valued in your department?
2. Can you think of ways in which you can encourage colleagues to become interested?

What are the influences of our disciplines?

As well as the impact of the department in which we work, we also have to consider the influence of our subject discipline. This is possibly even more deep-seated as it most likely comes from our own experience as students learning the subject. Perhaps the best-known work related to disciplinary influences has come from Becher and Trowler (2001) who revisit the phrase first coined by Becher of 'academic tribes' in which disciplinary knowledge is the territory. Though, interestingly, Fanghanel says that disciplines are actually constructed by the academics themselves in terms of their own educational ideologies, and cites the example of one of her interviewees who taught chemistry and thought that this was a discipline that taught criticality above everything else.

The influence of the discipline on us is also affected by epistemological and cultural determinants, which can be hotly contested. In my own discipline of psychology, for example, there are very distinct approaches ranging from the 'hard' approach of neuropsychology, which is closely allied to biological science and is sometimes seen as higher status and more scientific, through to the 'soft' approach of social psychology which is sometimes seen as low status. Psychology is also very closely related to other disciplines such as biology, medicine, linguistics, philosophy, anthropology, sociology and artificial intelligence. This also makes a difference if your discipline serves other disciplines such as health or is subsidiary to the main discipline, such as sports psychology. This will impact on the status of the discipline. Another of Fanghanel's respondents says how tricky it is persuading medical students that psychology is an important part of their curriculum.

Neumann, Parry and Becher (2002) categorised disciplines on the two dichotomies of pure versus applied and hard versus soft based on Biglan's (1973) original classification. See Figure 1.1.

Looking at this figure, we can see four quadrants.

A Hard pure knowledge (e.g. Berit in Physics) is concerned with universals, simplification and a quantitative approach.
B Hard applied knowledge (e.g. Charles in Civil Engineering) is derived from hard pure knowledge but is concerned with applications such as mastering the physical environment and is aimed at products and techniques.
C Soft applied knowledge (e.g. Delyth in Contemporary Crafts) is derived from soft pure knowledge. It is concerned with enhancing professional practice and is aimed at protocols and procedures.
D Soft pure knowledge (e.g. Angela in Classical Studies) tends to be holistic, concerned with particulars and is likely to favour a qualitative approach.

Using this framework, Neumann and her colleagues analysed disciplinary differences in terms of the group characteristics of teachers as well as in terms

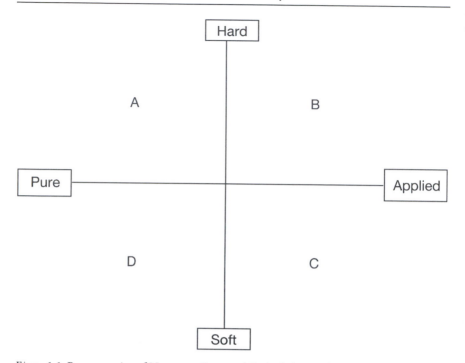

Figure 1.1 Representation of Neumann, Parry and Becher's (2002) description of disciplines

of their representative views of the curriculum, assessment, main cognitive purpose, types of teaching method and the requirements of students. What they found was that academics in hard pure and hard applied fields were strongly committed to research and less committed to teaching, which was generally seen as relatively straightforward and unproblematic. In both the soft pure and soft applied disciplines, a greater emphasis was put on scholarly knowledge that translates readily into teaching, but unlike staff in hard pure fields who were used to researching and teaching collaboratively, there was more emphasis on individualistic enquiry and not so much acceptance of joint teaching, except for the pure applied staff. Because the subject matter also tends to be open to interpretation and debate, academics in soft pure subjects spend more time on teaching preparation than academics in the other fields, and soft applied colleagues spend more contact hours teaching in a concern for coverage of theory and acquisition of practical skills.

Frameworks such as these enable us to see more clearly why it is sometimes difficult to relate to staff development and quality assurance procedures that sometimes seem to bear little relationship to either the subjects that we are actually teaching or how we conceive of research. Pedagogical action research fits the subject-based disciplinary context very well, but faces opposition from the pure subjects where disciplinary research is perceived to have the highest status.

Reflective questions

1. How do you see your academic identity in relation to the disciplinary framework proposed by Neumann *et al.* (2002)?
2. How is pedagogical action research seen in terms of your discipline?

We have now reached the final level in Fanghanel's framework.

The macro level of practice

This is the level that Fanghanel's (2007) findings suggest has the most filters impacting on how we conceive of, and approach, teaching and learning. Just to remind you, these are:

- the institution
- the research–teaching nexus
- external factors
- academic labour.

In this section I discuss just three of the four filters. This is because, for me, academic labour and many of the concomitant challenges or stresses that are related to working in universities can be pragmatically responded to by carrying out pedagogical action research. This is an essential argument that I develop throughout the course of this book, so I do not want to spend time on it here. Of the other three filters, I discuss them separately for clarity but each, of course, has an interactive effect on the others.

How do we respond to institutional policy?

While Fanghanel's respondents indicated that their teaching practices were directly related to their institution's policies, they also felt that some of these were not always pedagogically sound. Where the institution's influence was crucial was in its position on teaching and research. This confirms findings by Nicholls (2000; 2005) that academics will seek to develop themselves according to the rewards and promotions elements of the university structure. There was also evidence that although most of the interviewees endorsed their institutional mission, they did not identify strongly with their institution, owing their allegiance instead to their discipline (see also Becher, 1994; Gibbs, 1996; Healey, 2000), but as Land (2006) points out, this is not without risk. Disciplines, like any communities of practice can be inward looking and self-fulfilling and there can be schisms where new sub-disciplines emerge.

Where do we stand on the research–teaching nexus?

This is possibly the most current and critical of Fanghanel's filters as it impacts on the way we relate to our discipline, department and university in whether we see ourselves primarily as researchers or as teachers. This has a direct influence on our pedagogical philosophy, practice and, most crucially, on our students' learning experience. Yet the research–teaching nexus is an area that is hotly contested. Much play is made about the necessity of inter-dependence between teaching and research but this rhetoric is not matched by the reality, where universities tend to reward research over teaching. There appears to be little consensus about what the term teaching–research nexus or even research-informed teaching actually means (Healey, 2005) and there are several different ways of linking research and teaching, such as:

- ensuring that the content of courses is informed by staff's own subject research;
- teaching students about research methods;
- giving students experience of carrying out their own research or enquiry thereby giving them direct understanding of how knowledge is constructed.

One crucial, but not always mentioned, element is encouraging staff to undertake pedagogical research, which will improve their teaching and students' learning. This links to the scholarship of teaching and learning which is a growing movement as described by Kreber (2005). I discuss this movement in some detail in Chapter 3.

Perhaps the most influential paper in this area has been that of Hattie and March (1996) who, in their meticulous meta-analysis of 58 research articles using correlational analyses, found that the overall correlation between research and teaching was 0.06. They concluded that

> the common belief that research and teaching are inextricably entwined is an enduring myth. At best teaching and research are very loosely coupled.
> (Hattie and March, 1996: 529)

In a more recent review of the empirical evidence on the so-called link, Zaman (2004) found that

> research and teaching quality are not contradictory roles. However, we cannot conclude from the information at hand that the link is strongly positive ... though it is likely to be stronger at postgraduate than undergraduate levels.
> (Zaman, 2004: 5)

Hattie and March's research has been widely cited and used to suggest that funding for research and teaching in higher education should be separated, see, for example, the UK government's (Department of Education and Skills, 2003) white paper which was used by the government to make its case for teaching-only institutions. Commenting on how their original research has been misrepresented, Hattie and Marsh (2004) made the following observations about such an interpretation:

> Overall, we have consistently found that there is a zero relationship between teaching and research at the individual academic and at the department level. The greatest misinterpretation and misrepresentation of this overall finding is that it leads to the conclusion that research and teaching should be separated for funding purposes. This conclusion could meaningfully be made *if* the correlation was negative, but it is not. Zero means that there can be as many excellent teachers and researchers as there are excellent teachers, excellent researchers, and not-so-excellent teachers or researchers. Zero does not mean that there are NO excellent teachers and researchers. It could be claimed that universities have survived with a zero relationship, but that does NOT mean that all academics within those institutions are EITHER researchers OR teachers.
>
> (Hattie and Marsh, 2004: 1)

They go on to say that what is important is how higher education conceives of the relationship and how it then determines the policies to make such a relationship happen. At an institutional level this would involve determining what a university with substantial evidence of a research–teaching nexus would look like. Such evidence, they say, should include:

- selection and promotion policies;
- some specialists in research, but most academics being specialists in both research and teaching;
- courses where the material is up to date and includes the lecturers' research outputs;

and, that the success of academic programmes should be measured in terms of:

- the students' knowledge of current research;
- demonstrations of the research processes in the area;
- a demonstration of, and commitment to, the principles of research enquiry;
- an eagerness to (re-)search for more understanding of the area, which should be illustrated in the assessment of students' learning.

Hounsell (2002) also stresses the importance of viewing the nexus in the context of its institutional setting. He illustrates this point by describing how research-led universities may have outstanding research laboratories, library holdings and sophisticated computer networks, but access to these facilities may actually be denied to students, particularly those at under-graduate level as it would impede researchers' access to the same facilities. Similarly, the pressure on academics to be excellent in research may force them to neglect teaching, which results in first year undergraduates, in par-ticular, often being taught by doctoral teaching assistants rather than by the professors and researchers in the field.

Jenkins (2004) made the salient point that it is misleading to think of a single research–teaching nexus; there are many and they operate at the level of the individual, the department, the discipline, the institution and the national system. What Jenkins also does is to point out the importance of the perceptions of students about the link between research and teaching. He concludes that, while there is evidence that students value learning in a research-based environment, they vary in their attitudes, which may depend on the discipline being studied and their level of study. However, Jenkins also found evidence that research-based institutions and departments may not be effectively supporting students to get the most out of this type of learning, nor did he find much evidence to show an effect of research-based learning on students' intellectual development. Clearly, this is a filter, which is highly complex, multilayered and nuanced, but it is one that is funda-mental to our conceptions of teaching, our identity as an academic and our aspirations for career development.

Reflective questions

1. What are your beliefs about the teaching–research nexus?
2. Bearing in mind, the elements that impact on this concept, how do you think pedagogical action research might fit in?
3. In what ways might a pedagogical action research study benefit your students' learning experience?

How do external factors affect us?

According to Fanghanel, these relate to the interface between the university and external stakeholders that include regulatory and professional frameworks, and the big change there has been from academic freedom to accountability and transparency, as well as the need to take account of the agendas of employers and professional accreditation bodies.

Deem (2001) identifies four changes in universities in western countries that influence not only academics, but also the composition of the student body and the way we conceptualise the curriculum and research:

1. Globalisation, which she defines as the global spread of business and ser-vices as well as key economic, social and cultural practices to a world

market, often through multinational companies and the internet. This also means that universities are competing nationally and internationally for student recruitment and for research funds.

2. Internationalisation, which involves the sharing of ideas, knowledge and ways of doing things in similar ways across different countries. This has implications for how we support international students who bring with them diversity in social, economic and cultural backgrounds.

3. Managerialism, which is an ideology originating from contemporary business practices and private sector ideas or values.

4. Entrepreneurialism, where academics and administrators explicitly seek out new ways of raising private sector funds through enterprising activities such as consultancies and applied research.

Other factors include the effects of the change there has been from elitism to massification and to students as consumers (Van Valey, 2001). It also includes influences from higher education-related organisations such as:

- the Higher Education Academy and the Subject Centres Network;
- the Staff and Educational Development Association (SEDA);
- the Society for Research into Higher Education (SRHE);

and government agencies such as the:

- Higher Education Funding Council for England (HEFCE);
- Scottish Funding Council (SFC);
- Quality Assurance Agency for Higher Education (QAA).

Added to these is the dominance of information and communication technology. Students are now described as 'digital natives' and come to university with expectations of information delivery in multimedia formats.

This list is by no means exhaustive but what it indicates is a cumulative effect of imposing different and sometimes competing agendas on us in prioritising the work we do as academics.

What does all this mean for pedagogical action research?

Looking again at our five case studies using Fanghanel's framework, we can see that each situation is not only different, but the solutions could be equally as varied. Angela, for example, is faced with departmental pressures and sceptical colleagues, yet the vignette indicates that she sees her primary role as a teacher, but she is in a traditional department where subject research is favoured. She is on the first rung of the academic career ladder so has to make some hard decisions about whether she will devote her spare energies to researching her own area in classical studies or whether she will spend time on improving her teaching. In her case, seeking ways to improve feedback may serve both purposes. If she carries out a rigorous research study that indicates enhanced student performance, her colleagues may well be convinced and adopt pedagogically sound practices that might also save time. If the research is published, Angela has a second research string to her bow. It is a fact that many academics for all sorts of reasons have more than one area that they are active researchers in, so pedagogical action research can fit in well with building a research track record. Finally, she is adding to her CV as an active and committed teacher who is genuinely concerned to improve students' learning.

For Berit, the problems are different, as she is on a part-time contract where any extra work such as pedagogically based research would not be viewed or remunerated in the same way, as physics research. Berit, then, has to either persuade a full-time colleague in the department to take on the research or to seek some funding, which of itself is time consuming. Here there are no easy answers and Berit may have to decide that she will need to invest in terms of her own unpaid time if she is to make any headway with her idea of designing an intervention to improve the numeracy of first year undergraduates. Like Angela, if she can manage to carry out a careful and systematic piece of research that shows some appreciable increases in students' performance, then further pedagogical and personal benefits should flow.

Charles is faced with rather a different dilemma that involves him in a situation where his teaching effectiveness is under some scrutiny. At first glance, pedagogical action research does not appear to be a very practical solution, but consider for a moment what benefits might come of taking such an approach. It may, for example, deflect the head of the department from some of his concerns if Charles can present a proactive teaching-focused approach to the problem. The other advantage is that, rather than simply presenting a ready-made solution to the poor academic performance rates on his module, Charles is setting up a systematic enquiry into the possible causes, which would then give a reliable basis on which to take action. Of course, it may be that his head of department is not content to wait that long, but a pedagogical action research study would certainly provide a very positive and proactive response to a difficult but common problem.

Delyth has a somewhat different issue to contend with which is almost exclusively at the macro level of practice related to the filter of institutional policy. Delyth wants to provide subject-specific support for the dyslexic students who are taking a masters degree in contemporary crafts, but she will be faced with some delicate and possibly political manoeuvrings if she is not to alienate a prestigious central service that is clearly highly regarded in her university. What Delyth is doing is actually challenging the premise that the university has invested in, which is that students are best supported through a central unit staffed by support staff rather than by tutors within their own disciplines. Carrying out a pedagogical action research study to demonstrate the efficacy of her workshops is therefore extremely unlikely to cut any ice with senior management. She could, of course, acknowledge that this will be the case and accept the consequences, which happens to some academic researchers who are fêted outside their own university but practically ignored within. If she is more concerned with changing institutional policy, Delyth has a much bigger task to accomplish, but she may well decide it is worth doing. One of the fundamental principles of action research as proposed by Carr and Kemmis (1986) is that educational action research should be emancipatory.

In Delyth's context she has the opportunity to do research which may generate a new theory of practice, which in turn, could influence policy making not only in her university but also across the sector. A first practical step might be to invite the support staff in the central unit to join her in some collaborative action research perhaps to compare the two types of support. This case study demonstrates the capacity of pedagogical action research to be either small-scale or context specific or to be much more grand scale and contribute to theory building and policy change.

Finally, we have Eric's case, which has some similarities with that of Delyth in that he is faced with the macro-level filter of institutional policy but this is further complicated by the filter of discipline requirements. How can such a dilemma be solved with a piece of pedagogical action research? The short answer is that it cannot on its own serve such a purpose. For Eric, much work will need to be done with the department team on working on curriculum development, including close consultation with the university quality assurance unit as well as possible negotiations with the Royal College of Veterinary Surgeons (which is the UK regulatory body). However, this does not mean that carrying out an action research study would not be a valuable part of the longer curriculum development process. Eric would be able, in the first instance, to draw on the considerable literature that already exists on the potential effectiveness of PDP to see if that would influence colleagues. He could then design his own study, perhaps by incorporating an assessed PDP element into the clinical extramural studies, and seeing if it would have the desired effect of helping the veterinary students combine their theoretical knowledge with their professional skills, before he recommended it as a five-year module. In any case, providing some solid pedagogical research evidence would help Eric achieve what might have to be a long-term goal.

Summary

This chapter may not, at first glance, appear to link very strongly with the practical subject of carrying out pedagogical action research, covering as it does some of the theoretical and empirical research literature around learning and teaching in higher education. The reason why I have begun the book in this way is that I wanted to start by considering some of the elements that might impact on you, the reader, when you are thinking about how best to carry out a pedagogical action research study. Of course since each of us who work in universities has different backgrounds, experiences, perceptions and situations, I can describe only some general pressures. In so doing, I hope to have highlighted some that resonate strongly with you and perhaps triggered others that you might not consciously have thought of before.

Fanghanel's framework seemed a useful device to demonstrate some of the filters through which our perceptions are developed, and the hypothetical case studies have been added to illustrate how sometimes our action research efforts can be encouraged or subverted by the contexts in which we work. This knowledge is very important if you are to have the best chance of carrying out a pedagogical action research study that will influence and change matters to improve student learning.

Synopsis

- In this first chapter I have taken as my starting point the various pressures, demands and expectations that face those of us who work with university students, because until we reflect on the effects of these influences, we will not be able to make our pedagogical action research as robust or as influential as we would wish it to be.
- In discussing Fanghanel's framework, I have tried through the case studies to describe some of the more common contexts that readers will be familiar with and to explain how this may sometimes pose challenges and frustrations that cannot always be resolved.
- Throughout the chapter, I have posed some reflective questions to help you to think about your own values, experiences and ambitions. Even if you do not wish to engage with these natural pauses for thought, my intention has been to portray as honest a picture as I can of what undertaking pedagogical action research can and cannot do.

Chapter 2

Why be a reflective practitioner?

Introduction

Having described some of the complex issues and factors that face those of us who want to make a difference to the quality of student learning, I want to spend some time in this chapter thinking about why it is important to be a reflective practitioner. In so doing, I will draw on the extensive literature as well as from my own experience as it would be curious in writing a chapter about reflective practice not to reflect oneself. As a practitioner-researcher, reflection is, in my view, fundamental to the whole cycle of carrying out a pedagogical action research study, but the whole concept is conceptualised in many different ways for many different purposes.

In this chapter I will explore some of the more mainstream views of reflective practice and show how it fits with the cycles of carrying out an action research study. Some of the research I cite is about schoolteachers but I am perfectly comfortable with this for I believe that as a sector, higher education has much to learn from the other sectors. The studies are also not confined to those carried out in the UK, thus I hope to show how similar issues are not confined to one culture but are widespread.

What do we mean by reflective practice?

This is a term which has been somewhat overused in recent years, indeed Knight (2002) has some criticisms about what often has been an unquestioning and somewhat rhetorical use of the term, which is not surprising given its apparent simplicity and transparency. To be a reflective practitioner seems to be unarguably a good thing to be, but what does it actually mean? The term has come to us from the work of Donald Schön (1983) whose book *The Reflective Practitioner* is generally accepted as a seminal work. His argument was that, no matter what our profession, we all need to reflect as we will inevitably be faced with new situations or problems for which we were not specifically trained. Reflective thinking and Schön's concept of the reflective practitioner has widespread currency in higher education.

Much of this is due to the work of Brockbank and McGill (1998) who took up his ideas and argued that reflective practice should be seen as a core element of teachers' work, not as an optional extra. They said it has benefits not only to the teacher for thinking about how to improve their own practice but also for the students, as teachers will be modelling the reflective process for them. This latter point is important for reflection is not an easy thing to do and involves thinking of the hardest kind. John Dewey, the great American philosopher and educationalist eloquently describes it like this:

> reflective thinking is always more or less troublesome ... it involves willingness to endure a condition of mental unrest.
>
> (Dewey ,1910: 31)

Of course, some university academics are resistant to changing the way they have always taught or to examining their own practice, preferring instead to talk about their experience, their professionalism and connoisseurship (this last is often used in connection with marking practice). Experience is undoubtedly an important element but, of itself, is not sufficient. We demand that our students become lifelong learners, so why not ourselves? Sotto (2007) questions how we privilege experience by reflecting on his own experience of fifteen years as a learner and another ten as a teacher and wondering why he had not learned more:

> it was becoming clear to me that one of the main effects of personal experience is to corroborate for us what we expect to experience. In other words, it looks as if, once we have got used to doing something in a certain kind of way, our experience often has the effect of reinforcing the way we actually do it.
>
> (Sotto, 2007: 9)

Biggs (2003) illustrates this same point by comparing two university academics who both have been teaching for twenty years but one has twenty years of experience whereas the other has one year of experience repeated nineteen times. This is a telling way of distinguishing the academic who is a reflective teacher, learns by her mistakes and keeps improving, from the academic who is a reactive teacher who does the same things year on year and blames the students, or the institution, or gives some other reason, rather than examining her own practice.

This point about reflection challenging experience is a key one and will be revisited in the rest of this chapter.

Why is reflective practice important in the higher education landscape?

One of the dearly held and fiercely defended privileges of being an academic has always been the concept of 'academic professionalism'. In a thought-provoking paper, Nixon (2001) challenges a view of professionalism that is predicated on autonomy of the individual with its related concepts of self-regulation and the differential status of academic workers. Although Nixon does not explicitly mention it in his paper, I would argue that the concept of personal experience is also tied up with his view of professionalism. He argues that such a view leads to institutional inertia and that we have a moral obligation to rethink what we mean by academic freedom – whose freedom are we talking about – our own or everybody's?

Nixon argues that academic freedom if seen purely from the perspective of the academic, is inward looking and self-referential; it demands that we have the right to speak our own minds, decide our own interests and research agenda and teach according to those interests. It also extends to the sanctity of the department and the subject, but increasingly, such disciplinary boundaries are being eroded. (This is an interesting perspective on the departmental and discipline pressures discussed in Chapter 1.) Nixon argues not for the abolition of academic freedom but for a reorientation in which professional values and practices are used as freedom for all. It is not about a preoccupation with professional standards, instead it is about examining the values that underlie those practices. This seems to be a call for the necessity of reflective practice.

How does reflective practice relate to pedagogical action research?

As argued earlier, reflection, of itself, is not some magic formula that will necessarily translate our problematic practices into models of perfection and we have to be particularly careful that reflection does not merely confirm our experiences and personal beliefs and values. However, reflecting on practice as part of an action research cycle is essential if any enduring change is to be effected, because it involves some transformation from previously held assumptions to adopting a new framework. Action research enables us to reflect on our teaching in a systematic way (Parker, 1997). Reflective practice is inextricably related to continuing professional development which, in the current climate in higher education, puts us firmly at the centre of our own learning and self-development. The action research process encourages academics to take control of their own professional development by being active learners. Hannay, Telford and Seller (2003) argue that this is because action research:

- encourages teacher ownership of the change initiatives;
- encourages collaboration;
- increases teacher willingness to invest time in addressing problems;
- gives teachers a voice.

They used an action research framework in a Canadian school setting, as an alternative method of teacher appraisal, and found several benefits including significant shifts from:

- being an artificial process to addressing real issues;
- an event to a process;
- isolated to collaborative (which in its turn had benefits for the school by making individual tacit knowledge collective explicit knowledge);
- a concern with competency to that of professional learning.

In an American study, Seida and Lemma (2004) investigated the long-term effects of undertaking action research on teachers who completed masters programmes of which an action research study was a capstone project. Using questionnaires and interviews over an eight-year period, they found that 85 per cent of their teachers reported that they were currently reflecting on their teaching practices in a similar way to when they did their action research project. Of that percentage a small number claimed they were always reflective but many of the participants said that participating in action research had made them more consciously reflective. They also used the teaching strategies that they used in their action research projects but did not feel ready to do any more action research. This somewhat disappointing finding reflects the realities of doing pedagogical action research in a context that is not always supportive, as discussed in Chapter 1. Nevertheless, Seida and Lemma conclude that encouraging teachers to engage in systematic and sustained inquiry into their own practice is a useful way of developing the mindset necessary to deal with the educational challenges that face them on a daily basis.

In a similar study carried out in a university in the UK and in New Zealand, Staniforth and Harland (2003) investigated the potential of collaborative action research to support new academics as opposed to traditional induction days/workshops. Their findings showed that the early experiences of newly appointed academics were characterised by the stress of having to continuously deal with complex problems without much support and in which work pressures were significant. Generic induction programmes were seen to be ineffective either because of lack of relevance or inappropriate timing. Induction through departments was perceived as more effective but departmental practices varied widely. Staniforth and Harland concluded that:

> Intervention using collaborative research provides a genuine opportunity for newly appointed academics to validate and contest their tacit knowledge, challenge ideas and values and gain support for their immediate needs.
>
> (Staniforth and Harland, 2003: 89)

They went on to say that all their participants valued the potential of an action research study to provide a safe space, as well as being part of a social group drawn from different disciplines and cultures, and that collaboration was essential to them in establishing their professional identity. What the authors did not say, however, was whether or not engaging in such collaborative action research had a long-term effect on these new academics.

Such studies provide empirical evidence that action research and a reflective stance to our practice are closely linked, but what they do not do is to tell the whole story in terms of what individuals actually do when they reflect and what effect this has on changing their teaching practice. In order to do this I want to use the device of describing two scenarios, both of which are based on a mix of elements of real life situations.

David: Doomed to disappointment

David is an ambitious young lecturer in biology, keen to try out a form of problem-based learning with his first-year module in cell physiology, even though his more experienced colleagues in the department are openly derisory about such a method.

He persuades his head of department to allow him to redesign his module; he passes it through the necessary quality assurance processes and then proceeds to design an action research study.

In thinking about the basic 'issue' of how he will get students motivated to study in this new and untried way, David decides to use an established motivation questionnaire, which he will administer to the students at the beginning, the middle and the end of his module. He chooses an experimental design with quantitative analysis, as he is comfortable with a scientific way of doing research and formulates a hypothesis that students' motivation scores will steadily increase.

David is keen to present his findings to his department and to the whole university in their annual learning and teaching conference, as he is convinced that if he can present his colleagues with hard evidence that his method works, they too will be converted to problem-based learning (PBL).

To his immense disappointment, the results show hardly any change in increased motivation so he decides to abandon PBL as a method and goes back to a more traditional way of teaching. Having such a discouraging experience also makes him think, when reflecting on the whole exercise, that carrying out pedagogical action research is not really worth the time or the effort. Having his colleagues say, even if somewhat indirectly, 'I told you so' is a particularly bitter pill to swallow.

Karen and Jon: Gaining a new perspective on an old issue

Karen is a university librarian with several years' experience who is interested in why students did not appear to take readily to using electronic books and wanted the actual physical books to be on the shelves.

In a meeting of the library users' group, Karen asked if any of the lecturers might like to take part in a small action research study and to her delight, Jon, an associate professor of history expressed an interest. Jon had long wrestled with the problem of trying to get his students to read more and he had been hopeful that the accessibility of e-books would improve the situation, but he found that it had made very little difference.

Together, they pooled their collective experience and backgrounds, and discussed ways of carrying out a pedagogical action research study to find out why history students did not use e-books. Since neither of them came from a science, social science or educational background, they both felt a little uneasy with an 'experimental' design, but since Jon was very experienced in documentary analysis, they thought that a more narrative type of study would be appropriate. They also considered the ethics of Jon researching his own students so agreed that Karen would interview them and transcribe the interviews, leaving Jon to carry out a thematic analysis.

Their findings unearthed a number of factors that surprised them both:

- the students relied far more on Jon's recommendations than he had ever realised, so if an exact title was not available as an e-book, they would not look for an alternative;
- the access to e-books was more complicated than Karen had realised and counter-intuitive, so students often gave up too soon in the process;

  but perhaps the most significant finding was that:

- the interviewed students did not see the reading to be an essential part of the course, but an optional extra to the lecture material Jon provided them with.

Reflecting on this together, Jon and Karen realised that the issue was not as simple or as straightforward as they had assumed – it was a complex problem seated in the way the students actually understood the learning task that Jon had set them. Karen was intrigued by this and found some books on theories of student learning which they both read.

They presented their findings to the history department and to the librarians, as there were implications for both sets of professionals. They also resolved to carry out a second action research study using a joint 'intervention' lecture about the centrality of student reading to the course and a librarian-led demonstration and hands-on practice session with the improved access programme.

There are many differences between these two scenarios, but focusing on the issue of reflection, what is crucial is that David's reflection did not move him on in any way. He might, of course, have talked it through with another teaching colleague, but bereft of any underlying knowledge of theories of how and why students learn, he was unlikely to make any significant changes. His findings did not cause him to examine his beliefs about teaching and learning, nor did they cause him to question whether his actual research methods were appropriate to what he wanted to find out.

Interestingly, Karen and Jon were also not aware of the literature on student learning when they began their action research study, but their findings gave them a shock as neither had realised how students conceived of reading tasks before. Ultimately, both discovered the literature on deep and surface approaches to learning (Marton and Säljö, 1976) which was to influence their long-term practice in quite a profound way.

Another reason why their action research study 'worked' was the element of reflective practice that Karen and Jon were able to establish. They trusted in each other's professionalism and expertise and used that trust to draw on in order to develop a course of action designed to improve the students' learning experience. David, on the other hand, tried to reflect on his lack of success but without a colleague to discuss possible reasons he was unable to gain any insight into why his students were not motivated by the PBL method. Had he talked with someone who had a background in learning and teaching he might have been encouraged to think more deeply about what his students' expectations were and perhaps even used the presage–process–product model elaborated by Biggs (2003) from an original model by Dunkin and Biddle (1974), in order to analyse how students actually learn in novel situations such as a PBL context. This might have helped him to understand how a simple measure of motivation might be obfuscating a much more complex and nuanced stage in his students' learning development.

Another possible insight might have come from David discussing his findings with a staff developer (since many universities have some sort of central unit devoted to learning and teaching and academic development). Such a discussion might have led him to realise that creating a PBL module in a department that was fundamentally opposed to such a method of teaching was attempting something very difficult. It is a reality that when attempting to make any sort of change in an organisation, you need to acknowledge that there are some things which are under your control and some things which are not. In David's case, realising that students on his module were not going to go along with a different way of learning when all their other modules were taught and assessed traditionally, might have given him the insight he needed not to give up on his action research. For example, he might have proceeded in a small scale way by discussing students' expectations at the start of his PBL module and this, in turn might have led him to read more, research more and even begin to challenge the departmental pedagogical philosophy. This point about the 'larger aims' of pedagogical action research informed by reflection is taken up in Chapter 4.

Reflection as transformation of professional perspective

I have attempted by means of these two scenarios to demonstrate the different forms reflection can take and the different outcomes. Whereas Karen and Jon reflected together from different professional backgrounds and from engaging with some of the theory, David's reflection was done on his own. It was limited, as it did not take him further and instead acted as a confirmation of what his own personal experience had led him to believe, which was that something was wrong with the students' motivation. Unaware of any kind of pedagogical theory, which might have shifted his perspective on how students learn, his conclusion was to slide back into his former way of teaching.

Kember (2000) writes about the importance of what he calls 'perspective transformation'. He says that our professional practices can become so ingrained by often what are unconsciously held conventions that often we do not realise how these conventions may be constraining us from challenging existing practice and making changes. Kember goes on to argue that a particularly strong and deep-seated belief is a teacher's understanding of teaching that can, for many of us, be quite resistant to change. This is what has happened with David.

Gravett (2004) uses the term 'teaching development' from a transformative learning perspective based on Mezirow's (2000) transformative learning theory. This involves individuals gaining a critical insight and awareness into their own ways of thinking and assumptions. Insight, on its own, is not sufficient to effect change, so there must also be an evaluation of alternative ways of doing things (in this case, teaching) together with a commitment to make a change. This might be, perhaps, by synthesising some new elements with the old or, less often, by replacing a teaching method with an entirely new one. In either case, if the change is to be driven by a genuine transformational process, the individual academic will be able to justify her or his actions with a dependable knowledge base.

Real conceptual change or perspective transformation is, however, very difficult and takes a long time, which is why managerial, top-down approaches to improving teaching quality are hard to implement. At best, there is a grudging compliance with whatever is being offered as the latest teaching innovation, but no real ongoing long-term changes will be made. Gravett (2004) lists eight elements of what she calls transformative learning, based on the literature. To illustrate these, I have added my own examples in brackets.

1. It needs a trigger (problem/issue) that makes us aware that the way we previously thought and acted is not adequate to deal with this issue. (Students are not attending my carefully prepared lectures, which I thought were both stimulating and exciting.)

2. It engenders a feeling of disequilibrium or unease. (Are my lectures not that interesting? Am I a poor lecturer? What are lectures for anyway?)

3. There is a recognition and articulation of assumptions that are largely held unconsciously. (It is essential to cover the content when designing my courses.)

4. This is followed by a questioning and examining of our assumptions including where they come from, the consequences of holding them, and why they are important. (Is covering content what the curriculum means? If so, it means believing in the information transmission approach to teaching, which I am no longer sure I do believe in. Yet this is the way it is always done in our department; indeed, this is the way I was taught, so can there really be anything very wrong in it?)

5. There is a need for engaging in reflective and constructive dialogue in which alternative viewpoints are discussed and assessed. (I talk to my colleagues in the department who assert that lectures are the staple of the curriculum and the problem lies with this year's cohort of students who are not as able as previous cohorts. I am comforted but not entirely convinced by this explanation, so seek the advice of the staff development unit who introduce me to the concept of teaching as learning facilitation and suggest methods such as problem-based learning or experiential learning methods. I am quite shaken by this new way of thinking about teaching as it had never occurred to me before, but now it has been explained, it seems so obvious.)

6. Assumptions and perspectives now need to be revised to make them more discriminating and justifiable. (I now see lectures in a completely different way and while not ready to jettison them completely, I do feel able to revisit each one to make sure it fulfils my new learning-facilitation approach. This is the 'perspective transformation' that Kember refers to.)

7. The need to take action arising from the revised assumptions. (I am redesigning my courses to use lectures as spaces in which students become more actively involved in the topics I am presenting. I have been given so many suggestions by the staff development unit that I fear

the result might be a mishmash of innovative techniques which are exciting in themselves but which, if put together without an underlying pedagogical rationale, will possibly do more harm than good and confuse the students.

I decide to focus on using the personal response system (PRS), an electronic device where students use handsets in the lecture theatre and can vote in answer to a number of questions I pose to them. Not only will students enjoy being actively involved in this way, the technique will give me an on-the-spot way of checking their understanding about certain concepts, which I can further explain if it appears they do not understand. I am also keen to see if the PRS system will have an effect on student attendance, my original problem, as well as what I hope will be a more long-term effect on improved understanding, leading to better exam performance.)

8. The previous seven steps will build a sense of competence and self-confidence in our teaching role.

(I am wholly respectful of the way my colleagues teach, but no longer feel that I have to accept unquestioningly that doing things differently is not to be encouraged. I feel ready to be able to defend this point of view with some solid theoretical arguments as well as with some empirical evidence of the effects of my own experimentation with a new teaching method.)

(Gravett, 2004: 261)

Gravett goes on to say that taking these essential elements of transformative learning and applying them to teacher development fits very closely with an action research approach. In her paper, she describes a South African study designed to look at the effects of an action research project designed to assist a curriculum committee in designing and implementing an appropriate teaching methodology for the new curriculum they were in the process of constructing.

The action research project aimed to shift teachers' perspectives and practices from a teacher-centred, content-focused approach to a learning-centred dialogic teaching approach. Three institutions were involved and, of the three, two appeared to take well to the new methods but the third institution largely abandoned the new dialogic teaching approach. This, Gravett says, was caused in part by the lack of support and belief in the methods from the top. This study illustrates how action research can only be as effective as the support structures which underpin it.

Collaborative reflective practice and action research

Pedagogical action research may, then, be one way of giving us at least the opportunity to fundamentally question some of the things we hold most dearly. As Kember says:

Employing an action research approach does not guarantee a change in beliefs. Action research projects, though, do at least provide a mechanism for perspective transformation through regular meetings with participants.

(Kember, 2000: 32)

This is, of course, only true in action research studies which are collaborative. Woolhouse (2005) says there are two main benefits to doing research collaboratively:

- time (in terms of making time for the research and realising that development is not always instant);
- support from others (both within the action research group and the wider research community).

Support from each other is the advantage that Karen and Jon had, as compared to David who was working on his own. Woolhouse also says that working in a group is motivating. It allows for a number of different research experiences and perspectives to add to the overall project and may help to ensure that research and improvements continue, which is not always the case when working alone.

Kember likens collaborative action research to action learning, which was founded by Revans (1971) and initially used in industry but now is frequently used as a tool for training and problem solving in many different settings including education. The basic premise is that individuals (in a learning set which meets regularly) develop questions from their experiences at work, in order to find potential solutions through a cycle of identifying the issue and implementing a course of action, monitoring the effects, refining the action, retesting and so on. In this respect it is very close to action research. Kember describes collaborative action learning and action research as poles of an action spectrum where both have the same assumption that learning is predicated on active experience and improvements come about through cyclical processes. They also both share the practice of collaborative reflection. One of the great advantages of working together as opposed to working individually, according to Revans, is that an individual can only work effectively to solve those issues, problems or dilemmas over which that individual has some power to change. Collectively, the power is greater.

Where action research and action learning differ is that the former is a methodical, systematic and rigorous process of enquiry in which the results are disseminated for peer scrutiny, whereas the latter may not involve gathering data but relies instead on personal observations and reflections. While action research is almost always of necessity an action learning project, the converse cannot be said to be true of action learning, which does not have to involve systematic research of any kind. It can, however, be used as a preliminary stage to an action research study.

Stark (2006) has used action learning as an approach to professional development with a group of nursing professionals and educators (working in all three sectors). One of her main findings was that her participants from both professions found learning about learning was not only challenging but was painful because it related not only to professional development but to personal development. Indeed it is difficult to envisage how the one would occur without the other. Perhaps not surprisingly, some of Stark's participants resisted such reflection and their learning was limited, meaning that they reverted to the familiar way of doing things. This is what happened to David. Another main finding was that the action learning sets developed a clear understanding of their organisational cultures and how the complexities of organisations often makes any kind of change slow, but this also led to them having a much more realistic view of what could and could not be done, a recurring theme in this chapter.

The role of reflective practice in developing teaching and learning

Boud, Cohen and Walker (1993) define reflection as a generic term to describe the process involved in exploring experience as a means of enhancing understanding. Reflection is essential because it is the means by which experience can be turned into action.

Postareff (2007) says that a reflective teacher compares her or his teaching against experience and knowledge of educational theory. Her point about academics' knowledge of educational theory is a telling one and one which I explore more fully in Chapter 3.

Postareff goes on to say that reflection can take place at three points.

> Reflection can take place prior to (reflection for action), concurrent with (reflection in action) and retrospective to teaching (reflection on action).
>
> (Postareff, 2007: 18)

Hammersley-Fletcher and Orsmond (2005), in their study on peer observation and reflective practice, describe reflective practitioners as those who use experiences as opportunities to consider both their pedagogical philosophy and their practice. In their view, reflective practice involves the process of teaching and, crucially, one's own personal thinking behind it, rather than simply evaluating the teaching itself.

> It is, therefore, addressing the question of why as opposed to how and, most important, it is about learning from this process. Moreover reflective practitioners are involved in comparing the quality of their teaching against experiences and knowledge of educational theory.

Reflection, therefore, leads to self-knowledge, and this is important if not fundamental to the development of lecturers.

(Hammersley-Fletcher and Orsmond, 2005: 214)

Reflective practice can take many forms but can also be quite daunting if you have never tried it before and do not know where to begin. To help you with this process I have drawn on some suggestions in the literature of tried and true methods, see Appendix A.

What are the limitations of reflective practice?

To look at our own teaching and facilitating student learning, however honest we are with ourselves, does pose limitations. It is difficult to confront yourself and challenge beliefs and practices which have become valued routines, and, if you seek to change them, may be disruptive and uncomfortable (Day, 1993; 2000). We are unlikely to see our own weaknesses particularly if they are personal ones, so we need other people to tell us such things.

Very importantly, other people are sometimes our students but sometimes their feedback and evaluations can be affected by other factors. They want to be kind (or sometimes unkind), for example, or they are affected by their own preferred ways of learning and so do not readily take to teaching that does not fit with these preferences. Peer observation and professional buddying or mentoring systems can also be of help but only if there is trust between the two people involved and provided they share the same beliefs about what constitutes good teaching in their subject. This is why carrying out action research or action learning can be a useful way of minimising these limitations.

Reflective practice also requires considerable investment in terms of time and energy. In reporting on a year-long project in which a group of five lecturers explored their practice as supervisors of students preparing their dissertations, Burchell and Dyson (2005) write about the need for what they call 'reflective spaces'. By this they mean both the external dimension of time and an actual physical environment, which is separate from one's routine workspace, but also, the internal dimension of a space to dialogue with oneself and with others. They take the perspective of reflection using Schön's (1983) concept of 'surfacing', which essentially means making an idea or a thought more visible and available for inspection in a way that it was not before. They also use Boud, Cohen and Walker's (1993) view of reflection as a recapturing and re-evaluating experience through conscious attention. The focus is not on change or development in practice but on whether reflective spaces can promote a reflection on practice that lecturers do not normally use.

Burchell and Dyson's study explored these conceptions of reflection through interviews in which the supervisors actively contributed to the exploration of their own practice, and which the researcher used to produce pen portraits for each supervisor to help them reflect further through the perspective of another. Group meetings enabled the participants to focus their reflection in a systematic way and use reference points provided by others in the group when considering their own individual practice. The authors comment, however, that organising such group meetings in the face of other competing demands was not easy. They did not investigate whether the reflection led to any action, but claimed that it provided the potential for learning.

Finally, reflective practice and action research can be criticised as being too inward looking and concerned only with the 'here and now' of immediate practical problems in teaching and learning. Ledwith (2007) in a hard-hitting political paper argues for the kind of action research which is emancipatory, by which she means research which is committed to the practice of social justice with the intention to bring about social change. She says that such action research is not difficult.

> It simply calls for a critical gaze that sets current practice within the bigger picture, building theory in action and acting on theory.
>
> (Ledwith, 2007: 605)

By this she means that using understandings gained from research with individuals at the local level must be seen in the context of the bigger picture. In our case, in higher education, this would be within the department or support service, the institution, the sector, the government and beyond. Research, then, needs to encourage action, which is beyond the immediate and specific, to build alliances and networks that press for change.

Jon and Karen might want to take their research findings to other university history teachers, to raise questions about the way history is taught and learned, to think about the underlying purpose of history, to press for a new undergraduate curriculum for history and even further. Of course, this may well be too much for two individuals, nor may they hold such ambitious goals, but the point is that when research is published and disseminated, no matter how small and specific its original focus, it can be used by larger networks to inform and contribute to change on a grand scale.

Summary

Reflective practice is a complex and challenging element in improving learning and teaching, yet, as the literature shows, when viewed as an essential part of the action research process, it has the power to effect change that is transformational within the individual academic's psyche. A wise word from Smith (2008) cautions us not to overdo personal critical reflection, since it might be injurious to our confidence as academics and our sense of well being. If, however, we each learn to challenge conventional wisdom in our practice, this is outward not inward reflection and greater change can be made through networking, collaboration and collective action in the bigger context. This potential will be explored more fully in the next two chapters.

Synopsis

- In this chapter I have discussed some of the main reasons for the importance of being a reflective practitioner.
- In drawing on the literature, I have considered the different and sometimes contested views of reflection and reflective practice, pointing out that it is difficult and troublesome but is an essential part of the pedagogical action research process.
- While reporting on the research literature, I have also attempted to highlight the consequences of differing forms of reflection by using the device of scenarios.
- Throughout the chapter I have argued that reflection on its own is not sufficient to effect change; action must be taken and one of the most effective ways of making sure that there is an improvement in learning and teaching is to carry out action research which is reflective and which will lead to a modification of practice.
- Finally, I suggest in Appendix A some practical methods to get you started on reflecting on your own practice.

Chapter 3

Why engage with the scholarship of teaching and learning?

Introduction

The argument that will form the backbone of this chapter is that untried introspective reflection, on its own, might lead to erroneous thinking and consequent changes in our practice that are not necessarily beneficial. Alternatively, it might lead us to thinking no real change is necessary for it has confirmed for us that the way we do things is perfectly fine. Actively engaging with the scholarship of teaching and learning grounds reflective practice in a wider body of knowledge and experience, but there are many hurdles along the way. Persuading busy academics to get involved demands time and an institutional commitment to see teaching development as important as subject research development, and therefore, equally rewarded. For these reasons, top-down managerial approaches, as discussed earlier do not tend to work, but I will make the case that carrying out pedagogical action research is a practical way of enabling us to engage with the scholarship of teaching and learning.

A brief account of the history of the development of the scholarship of teaching and learning movement

The concept of the scholarship of teaching is attributed to Boyer (1990), whose work was subsequently developed by the Carnegie Foundation for the Advancement of Teaching. Boyer was unconvinced by the way that research and teaching were seen as being in opposition to each other, and by the way that reward structures in universities privileged the discovery of new knowledge through discipline-based research. In his view, other equally important aspects of academic work such as integrating, applying and transmitting knowledge were undervalued. To address this problem he suggested reconsidering the traditional meaning of scholarship, so that it should be recognised as residing in all aspects of academic work.

Boyer (1990) proposed four domains of scholarships:

1. the scholarship of discovery (which is the traditional concept of subject research);

2. the scholarship of integration (which involves making connections across the disciplines and placing specialities in a larger context);
3. the scholarship of application (which goes beyond the application of research by developing vital interactions where one informs the other);
4. the scholarship of teaching (which both educates and attracts future scholars by communicating the excitement at the heart of significant knowledge).

What Boyer was advocating here was that the scholarship of teaching should have its own status and recognition. Rather surprisingly, the concept did not appear to take hold as might be expected. This may be because the term itself is ambiguous and has not easily entered into pedagogical discourse.

One of the reasons why the scholarship of teaching is so ill defined, and perhaps not as readily recognised as other terms, may be due to the fact that it has developed differently in different countries, being much more readily recognised in the USA than in the UK. As Kreber (2002a) notes, in the UK the notion of professionalism in university teaching has taken hold, initiated by the Dearing report (National Committee of Inquiry into Higher Education, 1997) which translated into the establishment of the Institute for Learning and Teaching in Higher Education (ILTHE), which then later became the Higher Education Academy (HEA) and the 24 Subject Centres. In the USA, the Carnegie Academy for the Scholarship of Teaching and Learning (CASTL) was launched as a major programme of the Carnegie Foundation for the Advancement of Teaching.

Conceptions of the scholarship of teaching and learning found in the literature

Nevertheless, despite its somewhat slow start, the concept, or at least the principles of the scholarship of teaching and learning appear to be gaining ground as witnessed by the establishment of the International Society for the Scholarship of Teaching and Learning (ISSOTL) and the newly established *Journal of the Scholarship of Teaching and Learning*. In view of its development with different emphases in different countries, it is perhaps not surprising to find that in the literature there are also different views of what the term means and how it can be realised in our everyday academic work. For example, Kreber (2002a) has described four differing conceptions of the scholarship of teaching based on earlier work she did with Cranton (Kreber and Cranton, 2000).

1. The process by which teachers conduct and publish research on how to teach their discipline.
   (This relates closely to pedagogical action research, which will be discussed in more detail later in this chapter.)
2. The scholarship of teaching as teaching excellence.

(In her later work Kreber (2005) downplays the importance of this conception, but she originally wrote about the distinction between excellent teachers, expert teachers and teachers engaged with the scholarship of teaching and learning (Kreber, 2002b). She argued that excellent teachers are characterised by knowing how to motivate their students and help them when they experience difficulties in learning. Their excellence is borne out of their own experience and practice. Excellent teachers do not necessarily have to be expert teachers, but experts do have to be excellent, because they go beyond their own experience and personal reflections to considering educational theory and the literature reporting on educational practice. Teachers who engage with the scholarship of teaching and learning, go one step further by making their knowledge, practice and understanding public. This can be through research or through other methods of dissemination. It might be helpful to think of this third category as 'academic scholars' who take on a leadership role, though Kreber does not use this term in her own writings.)

3. Scholarly processes in which teachers make use of the literature of teaching and learning to inform their own practice.
   (This would include the experts and the academic scholars, described above. Using the literature is an essential part of pedagogical action research and of reflection, and is, to my mind, the essential criterion for advancing a scholarship of teaching and learning in its call for more than untheorised practice.)

4. A combination of the first three elements, which also includes essential scholarly elements of reflection and communication.
   (In their paper, Kreber and Cranton suggest that academics need to conduct research on teaching and learning in their own discipline. This, of course, may not be the only way of reflecting and communicating, but it remains unclear from the literature generally whether or not this is considered as an essential element. Readers of this book will not be surprised that I believe conducting your own research is essential and is a point which I will return to in Chapter 4.)

How do experienced and expert academics see the scholarship of teaching and learning?

Trigwell *et al.* (2000) interviewed 20 university teachers about their understandings of the scholarship of university teaching and concluded that there were distinct differences between teachers who were more likely to engage with the scholarship of teaching and learning and those who were less likely to do so. The former group were characterised by a readiness to understand teaching by consulting and using the literature on teaching and learning, investigating their own teaching, reflecting on their own teaching (from the perspective of their intentions in teaching) and by communicating their ideas and practices to their peers. The latter group tended to be more teacher centred than student centred, were less likely to engage in reflection on what they do in teaching and, if they did reflect, they focused on their own actions not on what their students experienced. They were also more likely to see teaching as a private activity and to keep their ideas on teaching and learning to themselves. In a later paper, Trigwell and Shale (2004) in acknowledging the ambiguity over the precise meaning of the term, said it nevertheless has some generally accepted core values. These are reflection, communication, pedagogic content knowledge, scholarly activity and pedagogic research.

Kreber (2002a) was interested in finding out what expert educationalists thought of the scholarship of teaching and learning. She used the Delphi method with 11 experts and found six factors on which there was high expert consensus that characterised the scholarship of teaching. These she labelled as follows.

1. Exploring relationships between teaching and learning, research, and integrating and applying knowledge.
   (This means a view of the scholarship of teaching that involves an academic in being curious, ready to explore, innovate and share. In addition, academics who were versed in the scholarship of teaching would have knowledge about how to conduct research as well as how to integrate and apply knowledge.)
2. Effective teaching through the wisdom of practice and standards of disciplinary scholarship.
   (By this, Kreber's experts mean that the scholarship of teaching is informed by the same standards as disciplinary scholarship, and effective teaching is linked to learning about the discipline, learning about how students learn and learning about the wisdom of practice.)
3. Knowledge about teaching and learning through reflection on practice.
   (Essentially this factor is concerned with a view that the scholarship of teaching is based on a knowledge about teaching and learning through reflection, preparation and inquiry, and is concerned with the enhancement of student learning.)
4. Specific research skills, attitudes and products.
   (Kreber found that the experts' view on this was unequivocal in stating that the scholarship of teaching requires academics who have research skills which enable them to analyse and interpret observations, an enquiring attitude and the willingness to publish the outcomes of their research.)
5. Development of pedagogical content knowledge through reflection.
   (This means a concern with the development of context-specific pedagogical content knowledge attained through constant reflection.)
6. Sharing of peer review of information and insight.
   (This factor is self-explanatory.)

   (Kreber, 2002a: 160)

Kreber also reported on a number of unresolved issues for which there was a high consensus from the experts including:

- the recognition, assessment and evaluation of the scholarship of teaching;
- the difference between scholarly teaching and the scholarship of teaching;
- the role of expertise;
- how to build on and document the wisdom of practice;
- the role of graduate education and faculty development in educating academics in the scholarship of teaching;
- how to promote the concept within the disciplines;
- the relationship between research and the scholarship of teaching.

With this last point, we turn full circle back to Boyer's arguments that both research and teaching should be equally valued. Interestingly, Kreber notes that the experts who took part in her study said that not everyone has to be a scholar of teaching. In other words, their view was that not all academic staff should be required to make the scholarship of teaching the focus of their career, and that the rewards for teaching excellence and the scholarship of teaching should be differentiated accordingly. Importantly, however, they also said that academics and graduate students need to be educated in the scholarship of teaching, that they need to develop the language to address teaching and learning in their respective disciplines, and that this requires institutional support.

These views of Kreber's experts resonate very closely with Shulman (1986) who writes about pedagogical content knowledge, which he describes as:

> a linking of subject matter knowledge with pedagogical knowledge which goes beyond the knowledge of subject matter per se to the dimension of subject matter knowledge for teaching.
>
> (Shulman, 1986: 9)

He goes on to argue that pedagogical content knowledge is developed not only through experience and practice, but also by sharing, reflecting and collaborating with other teachers. It has to be applied, which means it has to be transformed in some way, perhaps by questioning one's dearly held beliefs about students, as well as about the subject and the nature of teaching. Finally, Shulman says, like Kreber's experts, that pedagogical content knowledge must be communicated.

How do new academics see the scholarship of teaching and learning?

Looking at research on how relatively new academics see teaching as opposed to research, there is some evidence from Nicholls (2005) that the scholarship of teaching and learning is not seen to be as important as the scholarship of research. In a study with 20 new lecturers from a range of disciplines at the University of London, she explored their constructs of teaching, learning and research using a form of Kelly's (1955) repertory grid methodology. Her main findings indicated that the new lecturers saw themselves as experts in their subjects but novices in teaching. They perceived teaching to be predominantly about presenting knowledge and the facilitation of learning. Her study also found that new lecturers do not equate teaching with scholarship, despite the increased attention currently being given to teaching excellence and the recognition and rewarding of teaching in human-resource promotion strategies.

To explore this anomaly further, Nicholls interviewed a subset of ten self-selected lecturers of the original 20 participants. From this she found that the reason why research was so much at the front of their minds was due to the pressure they consciously perceived about their institution's expectations that they should gain research funding, publish and raise their research profiles, even if this was not actually stated. Nicholls quotes one of her interviewees:

> When you are on probation you want to do well all round, yet the ever increasing pressure to perform in the RAE [Research Assessment Exercise] dominates what is expected of you. Whether this is said explicitly or not, it's what I feel needs to come first.
>
> (Nicholls, 2005: 621)

Similar pressures and competing demands were found in an interview study we carried out recently with ten new lecturers in a small university in the north-west of England (Norton and Aiyegbayo, 2005). This research study was one of a number of studies on assessment carried out for a HEFCE-funded psychology consortium project called Assessment Plus. Details of this project can be found on the Write Now CETL website (www.writenow.ac.uk/). Eight of our interviewees were on full-time, permanent contracts, one was on a one-year, fixed-term contract and the other was on a fractional but permanent contract. All of them were at various stages of completing the Postgraduate Certificate of Learning and Teaching in Higher Education. This is a requirement of our institution for all new academics who do not have a university teaching qualification.

In an in-depth interview, one of the questions we asked them was how they balanced the roles of teaching, administration and research. Five of them said they prioritised teaching and five said their research suffered; four felt that they were coping and three felt they were not able to balance the competing demands on their time. Interestingly, the illustrative excerpts presented here show that there was an underlying conflict and ambivalence about privileging teaching over research. This confirms Nicholls' findings.

Prioritising teaching

I don't think I have the balance right. I put too much effort into teaching. I don't particularly like the administration side of lecturing. I find the small things irritating ... I prefer teaching to research and I will rather write a lecture than I would write something for my PhD.

(Lecturer D)

Research has suffered

I am new to HE and I am very eager to learn and to research but as of yet I have done no research. In terms of managing, that is my background in school. I was a deputy head teacher in my last job so I was used to organising things and making things happen but I have no time right now to do any research. I need to address [this] as I am not balanced.

(Lecturer F)

Feeling of coping

Sometimes it is hard to prioritise ... It does not feel as if I am so busy. I do my research in the evening and the teaching during the day while in the office. It might be different if I was a full-time lecturer and was not doing a PhD. I might try to allocate a full day to research then if that was the case.

(Lecturer G)

Feeling of not coping

I am having trouble organising my mind and day. My mind is divided between course work, my masters, a piece of research due soon, getting [student] handbooks ready for next year. There is a lot of work involved and I have not got the organisational skills to tackle all these demands and roles. I know I will be expected to do lots of research and I am in an area which provides such research opportunities but whether this will help my learning and teaching is debatable. I have struggled to get my masters written up because of my teaching commitments.

(Lecturer B)

Tellingly, the one participant who was on a one-year contract reported that he felt his prioritisation of teaching in his first year had made him unemployable when his contract came to an end. He definitely had come to believe that research was privileged over teaching certainly in the employment market within the sector:

I think being in my first year I wanted to prioritise teaching. And that has meant I have done no research or rather I did do a small article and [sic] which was rejected. I have become unemployable because of that ... I think what I should have done is ignore teaching completely and done the research because I would be able to secure another job.

(Lecturer H)

Clearly there are a lot of issues that beginning lecturers have to grapple with and what both these research studies have shown is the pressures and many competing demands that new lecturers face. There is a strong consensus, among these new lecturers, that research is privileged over teaching, and even if that is not the case in the institution they happen to be working in, they feel that this is the case in the sector overall which, as Lecturer H points out, affects employment prospects. It is also interesting to note that Lecturer B was doubtful that doing such research would benefit learning and teaching. Given the demands on their time, new lecturers are unlikely to value the scholarship of teaching and learning as they do the scholarship of research, unless there is a radical change throughout the sector.

Why is the scholarship of teaching and learning important?

Given that the scholarship of learning and teaching appears to be contested in the literature and has yet to make a big impact on higher education institutions, you may be forgiven for wondering why I am devoting a whole chapter to it. I am doing so because I believe that the importance of helping students learn cannot be overemphasised and I see this as only happening when all who are involved in universities acknowledge that there is a literature (theoretical and empirical) and a wisdom about the practice of teaching. While not insisting that everyone who works in universities needs to become expert in the field, I do believe that the systematic study of the nature of student learning and teaching must become part of every academic's knowledge base.

To be an expert in your own subject discipline and even the world-leading researcher in an area is, on its own, not enough if you teach and facilitate student learning. The scholarship of teaching and learning is important because it includes both ongoing learning about teaching and the demonstration of teaching knowledge (Kreber and Cranton, 2000). It is also important because it can help raise the status of teaching, it can enable teachers to teach more knowledgeably and it can provide a framework in which teaching quality can be assessed (Trigwell and Shale, 2004).

The scholarship of teaching and learning movement has a further influence to exert. In commenting on her earlier work, Kreber (2005) says progress has been made but in terms of its potential to bring about change there is still much to be done. By 'change' Kreber is using Elton's (2001) terms of changing the system rather than fitting people into it. She argues that, so far, little has come from the scholarship of teaching and learning movement in terms of critically engaging with the purposes and goals of higher education and by extension the curriculum. She confines the curriculum to that of undergraduates, but I would add the postgraduate curriculum as being equally important when considering the nature of higher education.

What Kreber is saying is that within the scholarship of teaching and learning discourse, there is much about how to teach certain concepts better and about how students learn but there is relatively little about the kinds of learning experiences we hope students will have during their university years. She asks us to think about why we believe certain experiences are more valuable than others. In other words, Kreber is putting forward the view that the scholarship of teaching and learning movement could, and should, become a catalyst for curricula changes in higher education.

In developing her argument, Kreber writes about three significant educational goals of higher education, which she explicitly links to the concept of lifelong learning:

1. self-management (the capacity to engage in continuous adaptive learning);
2. personal autonomy (critical thinking and intellectual development);
3. social responsibility (moral development).

Other significant goals that she does not concentrate on include:

4. cultivating in students an appreciation for the field they are studying;
5. developing their capacity to solve problems within the discipline;
6. preparing people for the workforce.

(Kreber, 2005: 392)

Kreber is arguing that a critical postmodern framework applied to the scholarship of teaching and learning would raise issues about how it is defined and how inclusive are the definitions, about the purpose of the movement, and to what extent our teaching practices are aimed at the empowerment and emancipation of students. In this article, she appears to be rethinking what she said in her earlier (2002a) paper where she recommended a more discipline-focused scholarship of teaching and learning. Here she is saying that in the traditional conventions of publishing research in peer reviewed scholarly journals there is a danger that the focus is more on instrumental knowledge about teaching and learning rather than on emancipatory knowledge.

When we apply a critical paradigm to the scholarship of teaching and learning, Kreber argues, we should begin to question the goals of higher education, and ask why we have these goals and not different ones. Such research would also question why we promote certain forms of knowledge, skills and attitudes through our curricula, rather than others. This line of reasoning excites me for it seems to resonate with the notion of critical reflection, and what Barnett (1997) has described as 'critical being', and it certainly would be consonant with Ledwith's (2007) call for more action research to be emancipatory. Going beyond the narrow confines of the discipline may even serve to challenge disciplinary epistemologies. The critical purpose of education is seen by some as occurring when students are able to see beyond their disciplinary boundaries. Currently, critical abilities seem to be being replaced by more superficial generic type of skills, which can more easily be written into learning objectives (Rowland, 2003).

While recognising that I may be going beyond the confines of what is essentially a practical guide, it does no harm to realise that pedagogical action research has the potential to reach further than the bounds of improving teaching and learning in a specific context, to actually challenging that context, particularly in thinking about the purpose of a university education. This is not a new activity, as the following extracts from Cardinal John Newman's *The Idea of a University* (first published in 1873, edited by Ker, 1976) illustrate.

> There is a knowledge which is desirable, though nothing come of it, as being of itself a treasure, and a sufficient remuneration of years of labor.
> (Discourse V, pt. 6)

> Knowledge is one thing, virtue is another.
> (Discourse V, pt. 9)

> The world is content with setting right the surface of things.
> (Discourse VIII, pt. 8)

> A great memory does not make a philosopher, any more than a dictionary can be called grammar.
> (Discourse VIII, pt. 10)

How does pedagogical action research fit into the scholarship of teaching and learning?

In the abstract discussions that are made in the literature about the need for a scholarship of teaching and learning, there is also an imperative to turn these abstractions into practical realities in order that those of us who are working as academics 'on the ground', can move towards making our students' learning better than it was before. Many of the proponents of the scholarship of teaching and learning agree that researching one's own teaching should be an essential element, often referred to as pedagogic or pedagogical research.

Pedagogical action research is a specific form of pedagogical research because it has certain defining characteristics, which will be described more fully in Chapter 4. What it does have in common with other types of pedagogical research is a dual focus on practice and theory and, because it is carried out by practitioners rather than by researchers, pedagogical action research is a compelling way of enabling us to actively engage with the theoretical knowledge that underpins the scholarship of teaching and learning.

Such enquiry-based learning is much more likely to appeal to our intellectual curiosity as academics than more 'compulsory' methods of becoming more knowledgeable about the learning and teaching literature (Breslow *et al.* 2004). It puts us in charge of our own learning about learning. It addresses very practical needs and, much like problem-based learning, it is done in order to address a real issue that is of relevance to us when we are undertaking the investigation. Pedagogical action research is a systematic process, which ensures that in following the conventions of doing research we will seek out the relevant literature in our topic. This is a natural way of engaging with relevant pedagogical theory as it is determined by our need to know and, as such, it means we are in control of what and how much we read.

In writing about the development of primary-school teachers, Ginns *et al.* (2001) say that, as part of their professional growth, they should develop a framework for making decisions about what is, or is not, useful or effective in their own practice. Like many others writing in the field, they say that knowledge gained through experience is important but on its own is insufficient, because it tends to be about the development of recipe-type or even craft knowledge.

> The teacher has to draw on a body of systematic knowledge requiring personal professional development initiatives in order to acquire a more comprehensive and reflective understanding of practice. Because knowledge-based skills are exercised in uncontrolled situations, it is essential for the professional to have the freedom to make his or her own judgements with regard to appropriate practice.
>
> (Ginns *et al.*, 2002: 113)

In their paper Ginns *et al.* looked at the feasibility of using action research as a way of immersing beginning teachers into the profession and enhancing their professional growth. Much of what they say about primary-school teachers and the lack of induction and support holds true of new university teachers. They found that new teachers did not always know clearly what they wanted to investigate at classroom level and what part they were supposed to play in the study, but they did gradually change in the later stages. Pedagogical action research is not a 'quick fix' solution for professional development but it does give us, as practitioners, the freedom and the responsibility to engage with theoretical knowledge in a way that meets our own perceived needs and concerns.

Winkler (2001) writes about similar issues when considering the role of theoretical knowledge in teacher development. She argues that teachers' experiences and the practical knowledge they gain from it are not sufficient to produce teacher expertise. Theoretical reflection is needed to produce qualitatively different insights about teaching and learning which can provide teachers with conceptual tools to establish new links between what they know and what they do. This is very close to Kember's (2000) use of the term 'perspective transformation' (see Chapter 2).

Can the scholarship of teaching and learning rescue David's pedagogical action research?

To see how perspective transformation might work hypothetically, I want to 'rescue' David whose case study I described in Chapter 2.

David is a biology lecturer who was keen to introduce problem-based learning but the findings from his first attempt at action research were disappointing in that they did not produce the increase in motivation he was expecting. Rather than give up and go back to the traditional way of teaching his first-year module, let us suppose he did seek the advice of an academic developer. This person encouraged David to read some classic texts on problem-based learning, and gave him some modest funding to travel to a PBL workshop that the HEA Biosciences Subject Centre had organised.

This gave David the opportunity to hear a presentation from a leading PBL practitioner about the theory of learning which underpinned this way of teaching. Let us imagine that, even more importantly, he was also able to explore with a couple of colleagues from other universities similar barriers that they were experiencing in their own departments to introducing this method. They were intrigued to hear about David's action research study and together they resolved that they would undertake a second cycle of action research, but this time it would be collaborative and they would support each other, sharing theoretical resources, meeting occasionally to reflect not only on the actual research but the wider context in which they were all working.

I develop this scenario a little more as follows.

> Being relatively young with much energy and enthusiasm, these three biology lecturers decide that they want to mount a challenge in each of their respective departments about how biology should be taught and what is expected of a biology graduate. They decide that the only way to begin to get their colleagues to take them seriously is to conduct a careful and rigorous pedagogical action research study, which they will present firstly at a conference but they will then aim to produce a journal article. Together, they encourage each other to build up a convincing theoretical argument based on their own data as well as on theory derived from the scholarship of teaching and learning literature.

This extended scenario illustrates what Stead *et al.* (2001) mean when they say that data can be used both as a starting point for questioning and as a method of theory creation. They cite grounded theory as proposed by Strauss and Corbin (1990), which seeks to generate theory that is grounded in the data rather than prove theory through data collection. Stead, Mort and

Davies (2001) argue that using an action research methodology serves the twin aims of theory generation by:

- theory generation in that they seek to reconstruct the theory or theories of action that are operative in the problem situation;
- practice improvement in that they seek to offer alternative or changed ways of doing or understanding.

(Stead, Mort and Davies, 2001: 62)

David and his two colleagues might not necessarily be successful in introducing a PBL approach wholesale into their departments. They would, however, learn a great deal about how students learn and how to challenge the whole purpose of higher education, as Kreber (2005) has suggested. Hopefully, there would be a long-term benefit to each of these three young academics because, regardless of whether or not they wished to make the scholarship of teaching and learning a major focus of their academic careers, they would inevitably have become reflective practitioners who were informed by a pedagogical content knowledge. It would be hard to see how their students could not help but benefit from their concerted efforts, whatever the ultimate outcome of the PBL initiative.

Conclusions

It is clear from the literature that I have discussed in this chapter that the scholarship of teaching and learning has not yet been fully embraced across the sector in the UK. This may be because the ambiguity of the term means it has not been accepted into the discourse in the same way as 'reflection' and 'the reflective practitioner' (although these terms too are not without their critics). Even if the actual terminology of the scholarship of teaching and learning does not survive, the core elements of it surely will.

Trigwell *et al.* (2000) encapsulate this point by saying that the aim of scholarly teaching is to make transparent how we have made learning possible. To do this, they argue that, as academics, we have to become familiar with the theoretical perspectives and the literature of teaching and learning in our own disciplines. We also need to be willing to collect and present evidence for the effectiveness of our different initiatives and approaches. This, in essence, is the aim of doing pedagogical action research.

Synopsis

- In this chapter I have reflected on why those of us who have an interest in pedagogical research should engage with the scholarship of teaching and learning. I have argued, using views that have been expressed in the literature, that as academics we need to do more than reflect on our own practice. We need to become aware of the significant pedagogical content knowledge that exists in the theoretical literature and in the empirical research.

- Since the scholarship of teaching and learning is still not widely recognised in the UK, I have attempted to show why this is the case by recounting a brief history of the movement's development. At the same time, whatever the terminology, I believe that the essential core elements of the scholarship of teaching and learning are valuable and will continue to raise the profile of teaching in universities.

- A particular focus of interest throughout the chapter has been new or relatively inexperienced academics, as I believe they are in the best position to embrace new ways of thinking about and doing practice. I am hoping that many readers of this book might be exactly in this situation.

- I have, therefore, not only reported some of my own research with new lecturers but also referred back to the scenario of David described in Chapter 2, in which I suggest an alternative outcome based on the scholarship of teaching and learning.

- Throughout the chapter I have argued that whatever stage we are at in our academic careers, we should all engage with the scholarship of teaching and learning, and one of the most effective ways to do this is through the medium of carrying out pedagogical action research.

Chapter 4

What is the case for pedagogical action research?

Introduction

Having discussed the demands and the pressures that academics have to deal with, as well as the need to be reflective and engage with the scholarship of teaching and learning, I attempt to bring all the arguments together in putting forward a case for pedagogical action research. In so doing, I want to consider briefly the history of the action research movement and show how being a practitioner doing action research in higher education is distinct from being a practitioner doing action research in other educational contexts. This is why I have coined the term 'pedagogical action research'.

In this chapter, I will look at the criticisms that have been raised against action research and my responses to those criticisms. I will end by discussing the potential of pedagogical action research not just to change student learning and individual teaching, important though that is, but to bring about more radical change in which the very nature of higher education should be open to critique and fresh perspectives.

History of action research

Before making the case for pedagogical action research, I want to spend some time describing the action research movement. This, I think, will help provide the context for enabling us to understand where some of the criticisms come from and how we can rebut them. I think this is very important in a book of this kind; it is my contention that I want to portray a realistic picture of what pedagogical action research can and cannot do rather than present an idealistic view of it.

The whole intention behind the theoretical section of this book is to introduce you to some of the arguments and background knowledge if colleagues who do not think pedagogical action research is as valuable as subject research challenge you. It is! Having the theoretical underpinning together with a basic critique of research approaches should help you to mount a robust defence, if you need to.

'Action research' is a broad umbrella term for what is actually a wide range of research paradigms and processes, each with its own philosophies and rationales. In this section I want to explore some of these philosophical perspectives concentrating in particular on the place of action research in a world where research is often conceived of as following the 'big science' positivist model.

A brief history of the main movements in action research

Most books and many journals that are written about action research in education will begin with an account of its history. One of the most accessible for me has been the online article by Masters (1995), which helped me to understand how a research movement like this can gain favour, fall out of favour, and then come back with renewed vigour, and why this should be. Masters writes that while it is generally accepted that action research originated with the work of Kurt Lewin, the American psychologist of the 1940s, it has evolved over a number of decades and there have been different emphases put on it according to the purposes of the researchers.

Broadly speaking there have been two distinct traditions:

1. A British tradition that links research to improvement of practice and is education orientated.
2. An American tradition which links research to bringing about social change.

In her account, Masters draws on the work of McKernan (1991) who outlined five movements that have had an influence on how action research has developed in education.

1. The Science in Education movement (nineteenth and twentieth centuries)
   In this movement, the scientific method was applied to education, where science was seen as producing knowledge that could provide universal truths about the world.
2. The experimentalist and progressive educational work especially influenced by John Dewey (1859–1952)
   Dewey was an American philosopher and educationalist whose philosophy of pragmatism and whose view that education should be experiential, led to the progressive education movement in the USA. Dewey also has had a profound influence on our notions of reflective practice by saying that reflective activity should include some form of 'testing out' ideas derived from reflective thinking.
3. Kurt Lewin's group dynamics movement (1940s)
   Lewin taught people to analyse and become leaders of change by being aware of the social forces that were operating on them. The consistent theme in all Kurt Lewin's work was his concern for the integration of

theory and practice. This was symbolised in one of his best-known quotations:

There is nothing so practical as a good theory.

(Lewin, 1951: 169)

4. Post-war reconstructionist curriculum development in education (1950s)
   Action research was used at this time to bring in educational researchers to tackle perceived post war problems with the curriculum. (Examples of post war issues included dealing with prejudice and difficulties in relations between different groups.) Bringing in 'outside' researchers rather than allowing teachers to do the research themselves led to a bigger split between theory and practice ('them and us'), rather than the integration that Lewin had been arguing for, and as a consequence action research fell into a decline.
5. The teacher-researcher movement (1970s)
   This originated in the UK with the work of Stenhouse (1971; 1975) who believed that all teaching should be based on research and that such research was the preserve of teachers not researchers. Stenhouse was to influence the work of Carr and Kemmis (1986) who wrote a seminal book in educational action research called *Becoming critical*; knowing through action. In it, they gave a detailed critique of educational research by analysing the failure of educational research to relate to educational practice. This, in their view, was one of the reasons why the expert educational researchers failed to influence reconstructing the curriculum.
   Carr and Kemmis proposed a way forward by offering an explanation, which would suggest a satisfactory alternative to the perceived failure of educational research. This was based on critical theory and the philosopher Habermas' idea of a critical social science. Habermas, working in the field of social theory, published three main works in the early 1970s (*Towards a Rational Society*, 1970; *Knowledge and Human Interests*, 1972; *Theory and Practice*, 1974). In his writings he was trying to incorporate theoretical and practical reasoning into a social theory that had a practical aim that was emancipation of the oppressed.
   Building on Habermas' concept of a critical social science, Carr and Kemmis put forward the concept of a critical educational science which could impact on practice through what they called emancipatory action research. Their definition of action research is commonly quoted and much beloved by action researchers.

Action research is implying a form of self-reflective enquiry undertaken by participants in social situations in order to improve the rationality and justice of their own practices, their understanding of these practices, and the situations in which the practices are carried out.

(Carr and Kemmis, 1986: 162)

Under their influence, action research has become accepted again and is readily practised by teachers, but it has yet to make the same sort of impact in the university sector. There are many reasons why this might be so, but one of them might lie in the very different types of research approach that are characterised as action research.

Types of action research

Masters also describes a useful typology of action research in which each has its own scientific epistemologies and research approaches. In describing each of these approaches, I have added a hypothetical illustration.

1. Technical/technical-collaborative/scientific-technical/positivist
   This tends to be research that is carried out to test a particular intervention. This type of research has been described as a collaboration between the expert researcher who provides the technical research expertise and the practitioners whose focus is on the improvement of practice.
   (Imagine a group of history lecturers who want to see if incorporating museum trips into the third-year curriculum will bring more creativity into their final-year dissertations. Not having the social science research background to know how they might begin to evaluate the effectiveness of this innovation, they employ a researcher to work with them. Instead of employing a researcher, however, they might prefer to seek advice and learn the appropriate research skills themselves. Highly trained researchers might be affronted by my view, but I would argue that we all have to start somewhere and there is absolutely no reason why a historian or a musician or a fine arts specialist cannot learn the same research skills as a scientist or a social scientist, if they want to.)

2. Mutual-collaborative/practical-deliberative-interpretivist perspective
   In this type of research, again there is an assumption that there will be a researcher and practitioners but the approach is much more fluid and the aim is to enable practitioners to interpret (and thereby change) their practice. Action research that falls into this category foregrounds the practitioner and her or his way of knowing and understanding, as opposed to the technical type of action research where the problem is delineated using an established theoretical framework.
   (If we take the same group of history lecturers, the researcher may be more of a facilitator, perhaps a member of staff from the learning and teaching unit who would be able to facilitate group discussions. The same individual could perhaps set up an action learning set, as described in Chapter 2, and encourage reflection and practitioner insights which would lead the lecturers to think beyond the simple issue of museum

visits, to thinking of other ways of encouraging creativity in their students' work.)

3. Enhancement approach/critical-emancipatory action research/critical science perspective

(In this approach, the emphasis is not so much on the individual practitioner/s themselves, but on understanding the social and political context in which their practice occurs. Rather than beginning with theory, we begin with a critique of theory in the light of our experience of practice. Reflection, enlightenment and insight provide the impetus to change not only practice but theory as well.

Here our history lecturers, again with some facilitator from learning and teaching, might actually begin to look at the whole way that history is taught and question to what extent originality should be something that a history graduate is expected to practice. This wider critical potential of action research has been mentioned in Chapters 2 and 3, but will be returned to later in this chapter.)

This typology is useful for us to get an understanding of action research and how it has many different strands all coming under the same broad umbrella term, but it should not be seen as a framework to confine those of us who are academics and who want to research our own practice. It is for this reason that I have written this book.

The next section deals with the commonly accepted elements that characterise action research. In the literature, I have found Kember's (2000) descriptions to be particularly clear and helpful.

Characteristics of action research

Kember (2000) has distilled seven major characteristics of action research from Carr and Kemmis' (1986) original description as follows.

I. Social practice

Since education is a social practice then positivism is inappropriate because its methodology is derived from the physical sciences, and educational issues are inevitably messy and ill defined and take place in complex contexts.

> University departments are hives of intrigue and conspiracy. Trying to reach an understanding of issues concerned with teaching and learning, therefore, implies getting to grips with a whole range of human issues such as the attitude of students, the politics within departments and the ethos and environment of the institution.
>
> (Kember, 2000: 25)

2. Aimed towards improvement

This, in my view, is an essential element in action research and is basically what distinguishes it from other research approaches. Action research has the avowed intention of making things better than they were before. In higher education, this can be done at many levels:

- the individual students
- the curriculum
- the department
- the institution
- changing or informing policy making and strategy across the sector.

3. Cyclical

Often this characteristic is described as carrying out simple spirals of reflection, planning, acting, observing, reflecting and so on, but of course it does not work as simply as this. Issues that were unforeseen when the research was planned are very likely to come up during the course of the research study. Kember suggests that while we should progress in a logical way, it is a good strategy to accept that there will be diversions, which might need parallel cycles of research overlaid on our original research course.

Smith (1996; 2001; 2007) cautions against taking the concept of an action research spiral as simply a procedure that must be used as a template for all action research studies. What we have to be aware of is that action research is interpretive and needs to be thought of in terms of further refinements in following studies. I think this is an important point, as it is by carrying out further cycles of research that we begin to form a holistic view of our practice and the elements that need progressive refinement.

4. Systematic enquiry

Action research appears to be a very flexible way of doing research and so is attractive to those who might not have complex or advanced research skills but Kember warns that it is not a soft option. My belief is that because action research is based on a different approach to that of 'big science' this does not mean that we can be any less rigorous. In fact, I would argue that, as pedagogical action researchers working within the university context, we have to be even more careful about our research designs and analyses of our findings. This is because of the likelihood that action research may not be viewed as mainstream research.

5. Reflective

Chapter 2 was devoted to a full discussion of what it means to be a reflective practitioner. It is worth stating again, though, that because of its interpretivist stance, action researchers must be transparently reflective about their own practice and the implications for that practice that their research has shown.

6. Participative

Sometimes action research is called participative action research, which is slightly irritating for me as it uses the same acronym that I use for pedagogical action research (PAR). This aside, there is a strong emphasis on action research being a group activity because it protects against the danger that, as a solitary researcher, I might make false assumptions about my practice. Similarly, I might make equally mistaken assumptions that my findings are confirming my way of teaching. This was also explored in some detail in Chapter 2.

My own view is that action research should not attempt to be too prescriptive, as so much depends on the context and on the particular interests, skills and values of the practitioner who is doing it. What determines it as research rather than curriculum development is that it must be made open to peer scrutiny and review. Typically, this would take the form of conference papers and journal articles, but other ways of seeking peer comment can be used, such as:

- electronic discussion fora;
- posting on the many mail base lists that exist in higher education;
- seeking comment through the Higher Eduction Academy (HEA) Subject Centres;
- running workshops and research seminars within your own institution.

7. Determined by the practitioners

Those of us who are actively involved in the practice must decide on the topic of the research (sometimes in collaboration with outside researchers who might be able to advise us on how to turn a topic into a research study). Kember's last characteristic is fundamental to pedagogical action research. It is driven from your own need to know why there is a problem or an issue in your students' learning and what you might be able to do to improve matters.

Making the case for pedagogical action research

Having briefly considered educational action research in its generic form, I now want to focus even more and make a distinction between being a practitioner doing action research in higher education and being a practitioner doing action research elsewhere in educational contexts. I am indebted to one of my book proposal reviewers for urging me to make this point.

There are several reasons for making such a distinction. The higher education context, as we all know, is one that is constantly changing and it does so quite rapidly. I believe that pedagogical action research is a sustainable form of educational research, which can have social as well as pedagogical implications, as I have argued in Chapters 2 and 3. It can also help the academic world focus on which kinds of new epistemology and methodology are going to endure in higher education.

Reading through many issues of the journal *Educational Action Research*, I have been encouraged by the evidence that pedagogical action research is an approach that is growing in confidence and establishing itself in its own right. Universities produce practitioners who are already versed in research skills and understandings, so pedagogical action research can benefit and grow from the involvement of people with this type of experience and expertise. Institutional pressures to 'publish or perish' can be addressed by academics choosing to do pedagogical action research, rather than (or possibly in addition to) traditional discipline-based research.

Cook and McCallum (2007) write about making their own research space in the context of higher education in the UK where research capacity and competition across the sector have been underpinned by the national research assessment exercise which has had the effect of further intensifying the competition for research income. All this has had the effect of intensifying pressure on academics to find new ways of supporting research. For Cook and McCallum, the answer has been to combine the roles of action researcher, tutor and lifelong learner. They argue that one of the strengths of action research is that it can offer its participants a common ground and common language to develop collaborative ambitions by

> providing a steady anchor in the choppy seas of change in the UK's higher education system.
>
> (Cook and McCallum, 2007: 67)

Other advantages include:

- strengthening an existing interest in teaching and learning;
- engaging actively with continuing professional development and quality enhancement of teaching;
- establishing a research track record to enable bids for external funding for pedagogical research projects as well as learning and teaching projects.

The establishment of the Centres for Excellence in Teaching and Learning (CETLs) is a good illustration of how important pedagogical research is in the need to evaluate their effectiveness. There are increasing opportunities in the UK and worldwide to develop careers in learning and teaching, so a track record as a practitioner researching one's own practice is a double advantage when applying for such posts.

Perhaps, though, the strongest argument in my mind is the need for university academics who are keen to improve the student learning experience to research the many initiatives, trends and policies related to teaching and learning that are so often imposed from a managerial top-down perspective. Lindsay, Breen and Jenkins (2002) and Lindsay, Breen and Paton-Saltzberg (2002) have written two linked articles examining the potential and power of pedagogical action research in influencing policy within universities. They argue that in higher education today, policy making tends to be influenced by the managers, who rarely use pedagogical evidence, rather than by the academics. They go on to point out that although academic staff can, and do, make changes within their own courses, they have little influence at the macro level. I would add that this might well extend to the meso level as well (see Chapter 1).

Lindsay and his colleagues put forward a convincing case for suggesting how generating evidence through research can

> both intervene in debates outside conventional control, and assist management decision-making processes to move towards becoming evidence-based.
>
> (Lindsay, Breen and Jenkins, 2002: 5)

Realistically, they point out the potential weakness in standard models of action research where the researchers only have powers of intervention and control of the system they are studying. This means that pedagogical action research is repeated on relatively small system issues over which the practitioner-researcher actually has some control. This, they say, is a 'methodological-cum-organisational' problem, which has no easy solution. They do, however, suggest a series of general principles that may help. They say that although this strategy does not guarantee that university senior managers will necessarily base their policy on the research evidence, it does at least mean that evidence will be considered in any debate.

Here are their principles.

- Ensure that research projects are directly relevant to specific policy issues.
- Try to enlist the support of a management 'champion' (without losing control of the data).
- Try to design studies that produce compelling (often quantitative) evidence and support definite conclusions.
- Produce research reports of research outcomes and policy implications that are widely disseminated within the university (and outside).
- Present research findings and their policy implications to as many committees as possible.

> (Lindsay, Breen and Jenkins, 2002: 8)

I would like to add to their well thought out argument, that critical mass in pedagogical action research may also be a power for change. By this I mean a whole subject department or several practitioner-researchers from different disciplines involved in collaborative action research may well provide more weighty evidence that would not necessarily have to be quantitative in nature. Like correlation studies, a single finding on its own may not be very convincing but when you get strong results done in a number of studies in different contexts, the cumulative power is persuasive. In a way, it is like a prosecution or defence lawyer might bring together evidence from many different sources in order to make a case that will convince the jury.

Purposes of pedagogical action research

Pedagogical action research can take many different forms and can be carried out for many different purposes. As I proposed in the Preface to this book:

> The fundamental purpose of pedagogical action research is to systematically investigate one's own teaching/learning facilitation practice, with the dual aim of improving that practice and contributing to theoretical knowledge in order to benefit student learning.

Exploring this in a little more detail, I am using the word 'pedagogical' to refer to the principles of learning and teaching that occur at tertiary level. I recognise that I am attributing a special value to the word that does not exist in dictionary definitions, but I want to make the distinction between educational action research that is done at primary and secondary-school levels to the tertiary sector, which includes further as well as higher education.

As in many other definitions, by the word 'action' I mean that there must be some sort of change resulting from the research. This can be interpreted very differently and can range, for example, from a personal reflective insight as a teacher, to making small changes to the courses you are responsible for, through to challenging discipline conventions and/or influencing policy making by management.

Finally 'research' is the term I take to mean not just systematic collection, interpretation and dissemination of one's findings, but also systematically studying action research principles so that educational theory continues to grow as advocated by McNiff (1993), among others.

Some of the mainstream purposes of pedagogical action research, that emerge from the literature, include:

- a training for university academics in systematically analysing their own practice;
- a training for university academics in systematically analysing their research methods and expertise (Rees *et al.*, 2007);

- an aid to reflective thinking which results in action (Ponte, 2002);
- a support for professional efficacy;
- a way of challenging existing beliefs, concepts and theories in the scholarship of teaching and learning (Wahlstrom and Ponte, 2005);
- a method of improving the student learning experience and their academic performance;
- a process that enables university academics to articulate their knowledge about learning and teaching;
- an approach that enables university academics to understand better the process of teaching and learning (Freeman 1998);
- a method of continuing professional development for university academics (Kember and Gow, 1992);
- a method of enhancing the quality of teaching and learning in universities (Kember, 2000);
- a method of inducting new professionals (Seider and Lemma, 2004; Staniforth and Harland, 2003);
- an approach that helps university academics understand how practice is socially constructed and mediated (Goodnough, 2003);
- a process which can ameliorate the theory–practice gap in university learning and teaching, referred to by Carr and Kemmis (1986) as 'praxis' (Goodnough, 2003).

Of course the above list is by no means exhaustive but it does, I hope, give you some idea of the potential that pedagogical action research has to offer. Armed with this knowledge, the next issue I want to explore is what the critics of action research have to say.

Criticisms of action resarch and its methodology

Whenever I give presentations or workshops about pedagogical action research I always mention two of the most commonly voiced objections as being:

1. Action research is not 'proper' research as seen in the positivist, scientific tradition.
2. Action research is largely untheorised descriptions of practice.

In this section, I will draw on the literature, much of which is based on teacher action research rather than university academics' action research (because there is more of it) to mount my defence against such criticisms. In so doing, I am not offering a critique of other established research approaches, but simply attempting to show that there is a justification for pedagogical action research to be equally valued as all other research paradigms.

Action research is not 'proper' research

Roulston *et al.* (2005) make a telling point in a paper they wrote discussing the role of research for teacher-researchers. In it, they pointed out that although the teacher-research movement has long advocated teachers being involved in educational research, academia tends to critique such work and it is frequently left uncited in the academic literature.

> It is not only that teachers are thought to be inadequate to the task of conducting quality research … also, some consider the kind of knowledge that teacher research produces to be inferior to and less valuable than other kinds of academic work.
>
> (Roulston *et al.*, 2005: 182)

This is a narrow view of research, which privileges knowledge and experimental methods where causal explanations are sought, over others. Seider and Lemma (2004) address the same point, in a study looking at the effect of action research on those teachers who carry it out. One of their findings was that there were questions raised about the 'rigour' of an action research approach, which by its very nature is immediate and contextually centred.

In a timely exposition on educational research, professional learning and capacity building by Rees *et al.* (2007), the authors discuss how educational research has developed in the last ten years or so, following a number of critiques in the late 1990s (such as Hargreaves, 1996). These critiques of educational research mainly centred round the argument that such research has not resulted in a robust body of systematic evidence and conclusions to provide an adequate basis for the improvement of educational policy and professional practice.

This has led, Rees *et al.* argue, to the UK government seeing a need to develop appropriate evidence in order to initiate policies and forms of professional practice, which would then contribute to the raising of educational standards. 'Evidence' is seen as large-scale quantitative studies, inter-disciplinary approaches and randomised controlled trials. Rees *et al.* go on to say that the government has also taken a much more proactive role in organisation funding and directing educational research, including setting up government-funded research centres such as the Evidence for Policy and Practice Information and Coordinating (EPPI) Centre and Teaching and Learning Research Programme (TLRP).

The government has also been concerned to introduce research capacity building initiatives, which are meant to address perceived shortcomings by changing the everyday practices of individual educational researchers. A key element of this drive has been to promote professional learning that is intended to improve the technical competencies of researchers especially with respect to research methodologies, data collection and analysis.

The way this has been done has largely been through formal means such as PhD requirements, training through workshops and so on, but, as Rees *et al.* point out, this has meant that other ways of learning about research methods have been neglected. They mention, as an example, learning by participation in research studies, the development of experience through critical reflection and, most significantly, interaction with more experienced researchers and peers. This, of course, includes action research, although the authors do not specifically mention this type of research.

Clough and Nutbrown (2002) make the point that all social research is persuasive, purposive, positional and political and these are the very reasons why it is conducted. Such an argument firmly situates a positivist educational research paradigm in the same framework as a practitioner research paradigm, in terms of their ultimate purpose. The only difference is in the research methodologies that are favoured, but this should not necessarily mean that one is somehow 'better' than the other.

Kivinen and Ristelä (2002) make a similar case when they use some of John Dewey's arguments that scientific research and everyday inquiry are both aimed at acquiring and controlling new kinds of connection. By this they mean that although scientific research is more disciplined and more goal orientated than everyday inquiry, both have essentially the same outcome: we gain experience and new understanding, and so we learn.

Kivinen and Ristelä go on to discuss the reality shock that PhD students face when doing their research 'absolutely by the book' only to find that despite using 'correct' research methods their findings often turn out to be of little practical use. I can remember this same shock from my own PhD and, more recently, from supervising others who are occasionally disappointed that their positivist research findings did not produce more that was of practical significance. This is the same fate that befalls many articles that appear in peer-reviewed journals where it is well known that the number of people who actually read your research is typically only about half a dozen or so. Viewed in this light, does it not make sense that action research with its emphasis on collaborative ways of working and engaging professionals is an equally effective way of changing both knowledge and practice?

Kreber (2005) also questions the exclusivity of peer-reviewed conference and journal papers as the criteria we use, for those outlets are about assessing the validity of conclusions or claims made. Taking a critical perspective means that the question of whether the research makes sense can be answered fully only by those directly involved in the research. Kreber, cites Lather's (1991) concept of 'catalytic validity' in which insights gained through critical reflection are used to effect change or improve practice.

In pedagogical action research we should be more creative and flexible about where we publish our findings, depending on the purpose for which our research was carried out. The HEA Subject Centres Network is an excellent place to start, as many of them offer a variety of ways to disseminate research outcomes.

There are also more inclusive and flexible ways of considering what data can be collected. For example, Clarke *et al.* (2006), in writing about a collaborative CPD project on science teaching in schools, mentioned the following as potential data for a case study approach:

- journals written by the participants;
- email correspondence;
- case study drafts and final versions;
- copies of children's work;
- photos, drawings and recordings of children at work;
- notes for the meetings;
- conference presentations;
- feedback from local authority advisers and inspectors;
- feedback from an external assessor;
- interviews with a third of head teachers and participants;
- Delphi technique questionnaires from heads and colleagues in school.

It can be seen from this list, that we could, in freeing ourselves from positivist interpretations of what counts as data, use a number of types of evidence in building a case to convince a reasonably minded person to effect change.

Pedagogical action research, then, does not have to follow traditional models of experimental design; indeed there is quite a strong case for why it should not. Since the aim of action research is to implement change, such experimental methods are not so useful because they are based on tightly defining and controlling variables that do not allow you to fine tune or change the experimental design. Action research, however, because of its cyclical nature aims to introduce change and refine the next cycle of research based on experience and reflection. As Kember (2000) argues:

> The intention is to produce a body of evidence that would convince a reasonable person to make a judgement that the project or approach had been effective. In practice this position differs little from the level of proof normally presented in positivist research. Particularly in human or social sciences, the claim that hypotheses are irrefutably proved by experiment is often illusory....
>
> (Kember, 2000: 41)

The lack of generalisability is a common accusation levelled against action research but this is a principle associated with a largely quantitative method of data collection. I agree with Kember when he says that if our action research study finds that an innovation works well, it is only sensible to recommend to our colleagues that they try something similar, if they are facing a similar type of issue. This is an approach where the research findings from one situation are adapted to suit the context and the circumstances in another, rather than aiming for the type of universal law the positivists strive for. An action research cycle is admirably fitted for this type of 'sensible adaptation' approach where during the subsequent implementations or cycles, feedback can be gathered, and further adaptation made if necessary, in a process of what Kember calls 'fine-tuning'.

Bartlett and Burton (2006) make the point that because action research is carried out by professionals, it starts from practical questions that are embedded within their working context, so each research project is necessarily unique as it has been designed for a specific set of circumstances with methodology tailored to suit those circumstances. They go on to argue that while it is not possible to generalise from the findings of such small-scale research, its strength lies in its 'relatability' to similar situations. Validity, they say, can be significantly strengthened if communities of action researchers come together to discuss each other's findings.

Action research is largely untheorised

The emphasis on large-scale quantitative and randomised control studies is an extreme stance of the positivist approach. At the other end of the positivism–interpretivism dimension is the position held by Whitehead (2000) who writes about living educational theory by grounding the epistemology in the experience of 'I', which he calls a 'living contradiction'. What he means here is that in foregrounding the experience of the practitioner-researcher, educational research methods cannot be reduced to social science research methods, as they need to include the improvement of practice, the individual's professional learning, educative responsibility and educative values.

Such extreme positions do not reflect the capacity of educational action research to embrace the rich middle ground. For example, Bartlett and Burton (2006) have argued that descriptions of practice should not be critiqued as untheorised research, as frequently happens. They report on a study of seven primary-school teachers who formed an action research network for a year to investigate issues that were of interest to them. Over the course of the year in which the project ran, the teachers met four times to share their progress and findings. What the authors found was that the very descriptions of classroom practice actually constituted the research data. Bartlett and Burton concluded that it is not possible to conduct practitioner research without descriptions of practice. It is the critical questioning and appraisal that makes such description evolve into research. In their paper, they use the term 'discursive consciousness', first coined by Elliott (1998), to argue that it is the process itself, which helps teachers to construct new knowledge and gain a richer understanding of classroom issues that they work with. This, in effect, is what Whitehead is arguing for.

Cotton and Griffiths (2007), who are both philosophers and action researchers, make a similar point. They argue that the collaborative production and articulation of 'little stories' engages the teacher and the learner in a rigorous exploration of what it is like to be them in a particular situation at a particular time. They argue that the framing of these stories is a critical and creative act that is measured using their colleagues as a critical audience. The very creation and telling of the stories improves the quality of their work. In describing their world, they change it, because rigorous theoretical work is needed to describe their practices in a way that has an impact on those who listen to their stories. Also they argue that we must acknowledge that the interpretivist paradigm has had a long tradition, which has not only given rise to rich descriptive accounts but also given teachers a voice in which their professionalism has been acknowledged

Conclusions

In this section I have argued that if we do engage with pedagogical action research, we need to be aware of the major criticisms and have confidence in a research approach which has a different epistemological and philosophical stance. Having said that, my own research approach tends to be more positivist than interpretivist as you will see in Chapter 5 where I describe a pedagogical action research study from both perspectives.

Teachers have been carrying out action research for years but sometimes have been criticised for not being equipped with the basic knowledge, skills or research methodology in order to do research of any value. The same criticism could well be levelled at academics doing pedagogical action research, but equally the same counter arguments apply. It all depends on what we mean by the critical word 'value'. I would argue that if our research is of value to ourselves as academic practitioners or of value to our students or of value to our colleagues, then it is 'of value'.

Conditions for pedagogical action research to flourish

Having put forward some arguments for why we can, and should, feel confident in carrying out pedagogical action research, I also want to be honest and point out that nevertheless, in spite of these arguments, it can still be difficult in some university contexts to get this type of research to be seen seriously and supported.

Kember and Gow (1992) looked at action research as a form of staff development and concluded that it would not work if it was pushed from a central staff development unit but was much more likely to be successful if action research projects came out of other developmental activities, or were part of an implementation of some element of a new or revised curriculum. In short, it will work best when academics perceive the need for some form of enquiry into what they are already doing.

In my own university, a thriving pedagogical action research network has emerged over a number of years, from the grass roots up, in which individual academics are encouraged and supported to carry out their own action research. Colleagues join a 'loosely formed' network, in which they can choose to attend the monthly meetings, contribute to an annual pedagogical action research symposium day and bid for modest funds to support action research projects that relate to an annual university teaching and learning theme. This is more fully described in Breslow *et al.* (2004).

In the literature, Peters (2004) writes about her growing awareness of the extent to which teachers struggle to implement action research within contextual conditions that are inconsistent with the process of teacher inquiry. She found that the technicalities of doing action research such as defining the questions, deciding on the methodologies and so on were dominating to such an extent that there was little time to reflect on what was going well in their teaching and what was not. This is a common difficulty and in the literature there are numerous examples of other constraints to doing successful action research. This, in a curious way, is also a strength of action research as it can simultaneously serve many functions, such as:

- testing the quality of curriculum redesign;
- engaging with continuing professional development;
- producing research output;
- impacting on student learning.

In the final section I elaborate on these points by turning to the 'external' potential of pedagogical action research.

Disseminating pedagogical action research findings

If pedagogical action research is ever to have a substantial influence within the university sector, it must be disseminated as widely as possible in committees, in staff meetings and even over a coffee break. Since it is also cyclical and collaborative, it is in a strong position to build bridges between theory and practice, and this is where it has the potential to make the greatest impact. But this is no easy task. Winkler (2001) has written a very honest paper about the difficulties of incorporating theoretical knowledge into teacher development. In a South African study looking at the effects of a residential week's training course for 15 primary-school teachers in the Northern Cape province of South Africa, she noted teachers' reactions to her sessions and compared them with her intended learning outcomes. She then used her observations as the basis of developing a largely conceptual argument about the role of theoretical knowledge in teacher development.

Her basic argument was that teachers' experiences and the practical knowledge they gain from it were not, on their own, sufficient to produce teacher expertise. Theoretical reflection is needed to produce qualitatively different insights about teaching and learning, which can provide teachers with conceptual tools to establish new links between what they know and what they do.

What Winkler found, however, was that the practical orientation of the course had a limiting effect on her teachers because their engagement and interest in it was dominated by the practical concerns that had motivated them to attend in the first place. They were not interested in discussions about theory unless they had explicit links to workable strategies. Her teachers were looking for practical solutions that would enable them to increase their sense of familiarity and predictability of the learning process. They did not seem keen to explore alternative ways of thinking about learning, and stayed on a 'how to' level of reflection, which relied on their existing theories about learning and allowed them to add a few more strategies to their tool kit. Winkler concluded:

> It is a struggle not to equate theory, expertise and truth, nor to give in to the tempting illusion that there is an ultimate theory about teaching and learning, and that this truth has transformative powers which can change experience into expertise. Yet I do believe that we need the act of theory to develop expertise. If no truth can transform us, perhaps the search for it can.
>
> (Winkler, 2001: 443)

Winkler's dilemma is at the heart of a pedagogical action research approach, which begins with a practical problem. Because practical experience offers only limited solutions, we soon find that we need to engage with theory, and this is usually at the inquiry stage. Sometimes we proceed without much theoretical underpinning, but then find when it comes to interpreting our findings that our small-scale study has been influenced by the larger context, so we must turn to theory if our research is to have any influence or applicability.

The final paper I want to look at in this chapter is one by Titchen and Manley (2006) who write about the concept of transformational action research. They use this term to mean critiquing practice in order to problematise the status quo and predominant ideologies, and to create new critical practice about the particular issue that is being investigated.

Titchen and Manley both work in the field of nursing education and have been doing action research for a number of years during which time, like many others, they have been influenced by Carr and Kemmis' book, and by Habermas' philosophy. In so doing, they write about how principles for action and other findings from their action research studies can be used to develop critical practice theories. They have been working with the idea of widening critical communities of practice and promoting critique, contestation, and debate of principles for action and knowledges created in and from practice for the refinement of theory and increasing its transferability potential.

Titchen and Manley conceptualise this work as occurring in ever-widening spirals. Initial critique by the practitioner-researchers, who created the theory, is followed by local, national and then international critique on a variety of platforms and workshops. I think their paper is important for they are demonstrating how action research, and I would add pedagogical action research, has the potential to have influence at Fanghanel's (2007) three levels of academic practice: the micro, the meso and the macro.

Summary

It will be clear to you, having read this chapter, that choosing to do pedagogical action research is not an easy or a safe option. There are many challenges along the way, but you can rebut, or at least robustly defend, many of the criticisms. The potential and the practical advantages of pedagogical action research as outlined here are serious and significant. You will also find that carrying out a pedagogical action research study is immensely rewarding.

Synopsis

- This chapter has been the longest of the theoretical part of the book in order to present you with an honest appraisal of some of the hurdles that you might face in carrying out pedagogical action research in a university context.
- In the first part of the chapter I have concentrated on presenting a brief history of the action research movement, its characteristics and the special place it has played in education, although not necessarily higher education.
- In the latter part of the chapter, I have made the case for defining pedagogical action research as a specific form of action research which can stand up to criticisms and, more importantly, improve teaching and learning as well as contribute to theory, and critique the status quo of university practices and conventions.
- In this way it can have a sustainable and long lasting influence in a volatile sector where both change and resistance to change can equally be manifest without any apparent evidence base.

Chapter 5

Where do you start a pedagogical action research study?

Introduction

Having hopefully now persuaded you that there are sound reasons for undertaking a pedagogical action research project, how do you actually go about it? In this chapter I will describe the stages that you will need to take, by illustrating them with an example from a study I did a few years ago and using a hypothetical example. This is to show you how a single research question can be investigated in very different ways, depending on the research paradigm you are using and the approach you feel most comfortable with. This issue will be taken up in more detail in Chapters 6 to 8, when I describe research methods and analysing your data but, for now, I want to show you how to make a start.

The spiral of action research

There is no secret or magic formula for carrying out an action research study; much of it depends on your own teaching/learning-support context and your familiarity with different types of research methodology. The classic advice is to think of action research as a spiral where you plan, act, observe and reflect (Kember, 2000). This was originally based on Kurt Lewin's work who, as discussed in Chapter 4, is generally credited as being the founder of action research (Lewin and Lewin, 1948). Lewin's approach can be summarised as a series of steps composed of planning, action and then fact finding about the result of the action taken.

My own view of the action research cycle is that you:

1. observe or notice that something is not as it should be and/or could be improved (observe);
2. plan a course of action which involves changing something in your practice (plan);
3. carry out the change (act);
4. see what effect your change has made (reflect).

Of course, this is an oversimplification of what actually happens and tends to be reified and 'neatened up' when you write it up for presentation at a conference or as a journal article. Researching in higher education is a messy process, where the environment is a complex and social one, and where the problems are ill-defined and ill-structured. Typically, the researcher goes back and forth in a number of spirals of the action research project, reflecting, reformulating and retesting. Kember's (2000) term of 'fine-tuning' mentioned in Chapter 4 is a helpful way of describing what happens.

A simple process for carrying out action research

Thinking about this in the abstract is likely to put off even the most enthusiastic academic who is keen to carry out a small research project, but a simple five-step process remembered by the acronym ITDEM will help you to get started. Once you have begun you will quickly find you become your own expert, as you find out for yourself more about the benefits (and the drawbacks, of course) of researching your own teaching or learner-support practice and the effects that this has on your students' learning.

Step 1 Identifying a problem/paradox/ issue/difficulty
Step 2 Thinking of ways to tackle the problem
Step 3 Doing it
Step 4 Evaluating it (actual research findings)
Step 5 Modifying future practice

This ITDEM acronym was first published in a paper I wrote for psychology lecturers (Norton, 2001b) but since then I have run a number of workshops using it with colleagues from many different disciplines, where it seems to have been acknowledged as a useful way of thinking about the process of doing a feasible pedagogical action research study.

To illustrate how it actually works in practice, I will now describe the ITDEM process with some of my own work. The extract I am taking is one cycle of a long series of action research projects in the area of helping psychology students to write better essays. Interestingly, what sparked this off was an experience that, at the time, I found distressing and one which seemed to threaten my self concept as a lecturer who had a particular interest and commitment to helping students with their writing skills.

Having always taken pride in the care with which I marked essays and the amount of detailed written feedback I gave to each student, I was discomfited when students reported in their evaluation forms that my feedback was confusing and unhelpful. I recount this brief anecdote because it has been a real lesson personally in that what might seem like a 'teaching failure' can actually be the impetus to modify your practice. For me, this was through the process of pedagogical action research, which has produced numerous conference papers, journal articles and a feedback tool as well as hopefully improving my students' essay-writing skills. 'Failures' of teaching or assessment such as this are, therefore, very helpful to the action researcher/ reflective practitioner who is always looking to improve practice.

Bass (1999) makes the telling point that one of the differences between the scholarship of teaching and learning and discipline-based research is the way we think about the 'problem'. In discipline-based research, the problem is at the heart of the enquiry and we are proud to have identified it. In the scholarship of teaching and learning, the problem is something we do not want to have and we are ashamed of it. In pedagogical research, however, we change the status of the problem to reflect that of discipline research, where it becomes the heart of our enquiry. The cycle reported below is derived from many previous cycles (six in all) in this particular strand of action research. In so doing, I have given you related references, not to be self-referential but to demonstrate how possible it is to actually carry out a number of publishable research studies from one initial observation.

Identifying the issue

Psychology is a discipline that expects that students will back up their arguments in essays by referring to up-to-date research (most often to be found in journals) and by evaluating that evidence to support their arguments. Many university teachers everywhere will no doubt recognise the issue I identified:

Students simply were not using many journals in their essays.

Earlier research had shown that this was not because they did not recognise that such a strategy was an important assessment criterion (Norton, Brunas-Wagstaff and Lockley, 1999), nor was it because they lacked confidence in information seeking and using the library (Norton et al., 2003).

Context

The context of the issue was a third-year module on counselling psychology, which I have taught for a number of years. The module was 12 weeks long and was designed to introduce students to the application of psychology theory in the field of counselling. The assessment was constructed to encourage students to consider the strengths and weaknesses of individual therapies applied to real-life situations through the use of carefully written case studies, which I called psychology applied learning scenarios (PALS).

These are hypothetical case studies that represent situations which professional psychologists typically face. The essential feature of PALS is that they are ambiguously phrased to allow students scope to develop their own thinking to the given problem. By applying different theories to a PALS case study, students realise for themselves how different approaches to the issues raised are derived from the different theoretical perspective they adopt. This aids them in developing a critical approach to theory and a better understanding of the contingent nature of knowledge. PALS are also designed to give students the opportunity to develop and practice skills such as critical thinking, evidence-based reasoning and decision making.

(Norton, 2004: 2)

Since assessment was crucial to my overall aim of enabling students to apply their psychological understandings of research to evaluate an appropriate counselling therapy, I set three assignments, which built on each other and helped students to develop the necessary skills and understanding.

1. A team presentation applying a theoretical therapy to a given PALS study (group mark worth 15 per cent).
2. An individual critique of a relevant journal paper applied to the team's PALS study (individual mark worth 15 per cent).
3. An essay applying a theoretical therapy to a second much more detailed PALS case study (individual mark worth 70 per cent).

In this way it was intended to give students practice and feedback in the essential elements of the main assignment task, which was the essay. One of these elements was demonstrating an in-depth critical understanding of a relevant therapy through applying it to a given PALS case study. The other essential element was developing a critical evaluation of the weight and robustness of the research that underpinned their chosen therapy.

In order to do this successfully, students had to engage with journal articles because secondary sources, such as books, would not give them the detail of research methodology that was needed to make such judgements. Despite this careful design, scaffolding of assessment tasks and feedback in their assignments, students in general were still using very few journal articles. Worse still, of those journal articles that were being used, many were more than five years out of date. This then was the identified issue, which needed attention: the I part of the ITDEM process.

There could be many approaches to this 'issue', depending on the practitioner's familiarity and experience with different types of research methodology. To give you an idea of possible research designs, together with their consequences, here are two possible approaches to take.

1. Asking the students (a qualitative, interpretivist approach).
2. Designing an intervention (an experimental, positivist approach).

I shall now explore the TDEM part of the ITDEM process, using each of these different designs so that you can get an idea of how the same issue can be tackled in two very different ways. The first example of an interpretivist approach is a hypothetical description of what might be done. The second example of an experimental approach is the one I actually took and is a description of a real piece of action research.

Asking the students (a qualitative, interpretivist approach)

Identifying the issue (recap)

Third year psychology students were using too few up-to-date journal articles in their essays.

Thinking of ways to tackle it

There are many ways I might have investigated this issue from an interpretivist perspective. One of the most straightforward inquiries could have been to carry out an interview study with psychology students at all levels to find out why they were not using journals, instead of making my own assumptions about their reasons. I referred earlier to my own previous attempts to tease out why students were not using journals. I had firstly hypothesised with my psychology lecturer colleagues that our students were not aware of the assessment criterion related to use of evidence and the part that journals played in that criterion. We investigated this with a questionnaire study for third-year psychology students and found that not only were they keenly conscious of the importance of using journals, but that they still did not do so. This led us a few years later to consider the possibility that they were not confident in information seeking, particularly in using the university library, but again the research we carried out showed us that this was not the case. Reflecting on these earlier studies, I can see that both of them were driven by our assumptions, derived from my colleagues' and my experiences as university teachers.

Researchers in the social sciences and in education often make similar assumptions about the human beings they are working with. This is a consequence of carrying out research following a positivist model, and leads to what is called the first-order perspective where the field of enquiry (i.e. your human participants' behaviour) is treated as an objective act influenced only by the experimental conditions and carried out by people who are not trying to outguess you or find out what it is you actually want them to do. I still remember my surprise as a student of psychology many years ago when reading the works of Orne (1962) on demand characteristics, to find out the extraordinary lengths people will go to in order to behave in a way that they think you, as the researcher, want them to behave. Human beings are sentient and intelligent, and do not behave as objects in the material world, so first-order research can only partially explain their behaviour.

The second-order perspective is one that acknowledges that how humans perceive the demands of the experiment or research will inevitably affect how they react to any given research situation. Hence the important rise of the phenomenographical approach in research in teaching and learning in higher education (i.e. 'getting inside' your participants' heads and seeing the world as they see it) led by Swedish researchers in the 1970s.

This valuing of the subjective experience has had a profound effect on the way we think about student learning in higher education, such as deep and surface approaches to studying (Marton and Säljö, 1976), conceptions of learning (Säljö, 1979) and epistemological beliefs (Hofer, 2004), to name but a few. To carry out an interview would be to take a second-order approach, which aims to understand the issue from the perspective of the student and not mine as the teacher-researcher. This type of methodology also sits very comfortably within the action research framework, which often favours an interpretivist stance (see Chapter 4).

Doing it

Asking students to take part in interviews in itself raises many different methodological issues which all have to be examined when designing my study. I would have to decide, for example, what sort of interview I would carry out. Is it to be structured (where all the questions are predetermined) or semi-structured (where an interview schedule determines the main questions but there is scope for probes to elicit more information at certain points)? Both these types of interview lean more to the first-order perspective of research. Carrying out an in-depth unstructured interview is much more likely to establish a richer picture of the student perspective and might take the form of an opening question such as:

Are there any problems about using journals for your psychology essays?

This gives the interviewees scope to raise their own concerns and issues.

Other design decisions revolve around which students would I ask – all years, or just one? How big a sample should I take? What age range, gender etc. should I use? I might also want to consider whether I should concentrate just on psychology students or broaden it out to students studying other subjects. Thought also has to be given as to who should do the interviewing. If I do it myself there are ethical issues about power; if I ask a research assistant, I lose some of the immediacy in asking the things that I, as the lecturer, want to know about.

The above are just a small selection of the types of thing I need to consider when designing an interview study. For more details about the interview as a research method, see Chapter 6. For the sake of argument, let us imagine, however, I have decided to carry out an unstructured interview.

Evaluating it

Having decided on the type of interview, I now have a number of choices about how I will evaluate the research findings. This stage is the crucial one when thinking about the 'research part' of my pedagogical action research study. Disseminating my findings and allowing them to be peer reviewed is what distinguishes pedagogical action research from curriculum development or reflective practice. So many innovations in higher education are enthusiastically promoted at conferences and on websites but lack this essential element of research evaluation. By this I mean much more than student evaluation, which undeniably is an important part of evaluating an innovation, but is not, and should not be, the only evidence you seek to collect.

There are many reasons why student evaluations should be treated with caution. Their own expectations might be at odds with the pedagogical aims of the teacher (Entwistle and Tait, 1990), or they may be influenced by the 'Dr Fox effect' (reported in Heywood, 2000) such as lecturer charisma (Shevlin *et al.*, 2000). Simply saying students really enjoyed the new delivery and were motivated by it is part of the story but not the whole story. How did it affect their actual learning performance, for example? Reporting research findings is, therefore, a very important part of the whole research study. In terms of an interview study, this will determine some of the answers to the questions I asked earlier but also will determine how I would analyse my data.

Unstructured interviews lend themselves to qualitative analysis. There are many useful books written on the subject for those who wish to pursue this in depth (some suggestions to get you started are made at the end of Chapter 6). However, the aim of this book is to suggest easy and practical ways for you to carry out your own pedagogical action research project, so I will tell you what I would have done.

Had I carried out this study, I would have chosen a content analysis, which is my personal preferred type of qualitative analysis. The reason why I like this method is because it combines both qualitative and quantitative analyses in the one method. Put very simply, I would have recorded the interviews and then transcribed them. Another step involves iterative readings in order to construct a number of themes or categories following basic principles of thematic analysis. From my own experience 10–12 categories is ideal, any fewer and you lose much of the sense as the categories are too broad, many more and you lose the ability to make meaningful sense out of your analysis. Having constructed my categories, I would then return to each transcript and divide it into information units (these are phrases, sentences, or sometimes even paragraphs, which carry a single idea or meaning).

The next stage would be to assign every information unit to one (and only one) of the categories. Carrying out a content analysis like this would make it possible for me to have simple quantitative as well as qualitative data. For example, I could calculate the percentage of information units which fall into each category. This would then enable me to assign some sort of simple weighting to which issues or themes were most often mentioned overall, as well as to which issues or themes were mentioned by individual students. Content analysis is such a useful technique that I return to it in some detail in Chapter 7.

Modifying future practice

Since this example is a hypothetical one, I now have to imagine some major findings to illustrate the final step of this action research cycle. I am going to imagine that the most important issue to come out of the interviews was a difference in confidence between first, second and third-year students where, unexpectedly, the third-year students were less confident than the second-year students. The reasons for this might be that third-year students were very aware that the end of their degree was in sight and they needed to get good results. They were also realising how little they actually knew, as opposed to second-year students who thought they knew more than they actually did. In other words, third-year students were now keenly aware of how little they had used journals in their previous two years and felt that they could not either admit it or ask for help. This would give me the impetus to try and address this situation.

I now have a new issue that I have identified, which can lead to another cycle of action research. More importantly, I need to modify my practice to build in extra support with journal use for my third-year counselling psychology students. I could, for example, devote a class session to literature searching led by one of the librarians, I could set up self-help peer study groups, or I could run one-to-one individual consultations for those who felt they needed them. The range of possibilities is considerable, and which one I choose would depend on pragmatic considerations. Perhaps the 'best way' to go, and one which fits in with the true spirit of action research where all who take part are equal participants rather than researcher and the researched, would be to ask the students themselves what would be the most helpful way of boosting their confidence with finding and using journals.

This then has been a description of a hypothetical approach to a pedagogical action research study, but what did I actually do? What follows is a true 'warts and all' account which, I hope, will illustrate how achievable and worthwhile doing a small-scale study can be.

Designing an intervention (an experimental, positivist approach)

There are proponents of action research who will say that carrying out positivist research where one tries to establish cause and effect is not action research, and those who say unless it is carried out collaboratively it is not action research. This, I think, is a pity. In a field of enquiry where traditionally the aim has been to break down barriers and to be encompassing and inclusive, it surely behoves us to incorporate all types of enquiry where the aim is to research and to modify practice. My view, as expressed in Chapter 4, is that action research is a broad umbrella term and practitioners should be encouraged to build on their own subject expertise and methods of enquiry when venturing into the area of pedagogical research where they may well not feel so comfortable. I am a psychologist, so years of training in positivist methods have left me with a tool bag of approaches that I feel confident about using in my own research studies, adapted within the broader framework of an action research cycle. It is my aim in this book, to encourage you to adapt your methods of enquiry in the same way.

Identifying the issue (recap)

Third-year psychology students were using too few up to date journal articles in their essays.

Thinking of ways to tackle it

When thinking about designing an intervention, again the range of possibilities is endless and like all research studies, making the decision is probably the hardest part of the whole process. I could have designed an intervention study and compared students who had the intervention against students who did not. This is a classic research design in the positivist tradition where the aim is to test a hypothesis by determining an independent variable (the intervention) and dependent variable/s (students' use of journal articles in their assignments), while controlling for extraneous variables as much as possible (ensuring that the students in both groups were similar in terms of ability, age, motivation, experience, etc.).

In the context of real situations (a module where the assessment under investigation actually counts as part of the overall degree classification), the more controls you put into it, the less likely it has to have any applicability to the real-life context. Added to this are further difficulties posed by ethical considerations. Since the assessments count, what happens to the disadvantaged group who have no intervention? Controlled experiments like this are not impossible to do in educational research but they often have limited applicability as they get further and further away from the real-world situation.

For me, then, there was only one way that I felt I could reasonably go. I designed an intervention as part of the counselling psychology module, which would hopefully benefit all the students in the class. Depending on what effects this had on their essays, I could then modify future advice and guidance on this aspect of essay writing to future cohorts. Finding it very hard, though, to ignore my research training as a psychologist, I was still very keen to compare the results of what I was doing with other groups of students, so the decision was taken together with a colleague who also teaches psychology to compare the outcomes of my intervention with two other psychology courses (organisational psychology, and psychology and crime) where no intervention was being offered. This study is reported in full in Norton, Norton and Thomas (2004).

Of course this meant that there was very little we could do in the way of controlling for extraneous variables but it did satisfy my colleagues and I that we were not disadvantaging any students in this design. It was also possible to compare the intervention counselling psychology cohort with the previous year where there had been no intervention. Our hypotheses were:

1. Counselling psychology students will use more journals in their assignments than organisational psychology students and psychology and crime students.
2. The 2003 counselling psychology cohort (the cohort experiencing the intervention) will use more journals in their assignments than the 2002 counselling psychology cohort (who had no intervention).

Doing it

The aim of this intervention was to address directly the identified issue that students were not using enough journal articles in their assignments in my module. Falling back on our training as psychologists, we found ourselves hypothesising two possible reasons:

1. Our students were not up to date with how to search for journal articles. This came from our actual experience of repeatedly having our students tell us that they could find 'nothing in the library'. In a way this is not as objective and researcher driven as some hypotheses might be as it comes from actual experience of being practising university teachers, instead of from the research literature. It does, however, fit very comfortably with the action research model of professionals starting from practical questions that are embedded within their working context (Bartlett and Burton, 2006), discussed in Chapter 4.
2. The second possible cause came from reflection after a presentation on an earlier cycle from this research at a learning and teaching conference (Norton *et al.*, 2003), when a number of colleagues suggested that the

problem for students was not so much in finding relevant journal articles but in knowing how to use the information in that article to weave into an essay, which actually was asking them to do something quite sophisticated and quite different from the purpose for which the article was written.

Bearing these two potential causes of the problem in mind, the 'intervention' was two-pronged. Given that the module was 12 weeks long and class sessions were only two hours, I did not have a lot of time to play with, so to call it an intervention is actually rather a grand term for what was, in all truthfulness, a fairly small-scale modification to the delivery of the module.

One of the cardinal values of action research is that by making small-scale interventions you can often bring about significant pedagogical changes. This is what I did.

1. I spent one hour in a class session on reminding my students how to find relevant journals both in the university library and electronically (I demonstrated a step-by-step guide). I gave instruction about exactly how to write a research critique and gave them an example critique relating to a PALS case study that I had written to act as a model and to help them see what I wanted.
2. I changed the individual research critique assignment from asking students to evaluate three journal articles (as in past years) to asking just for a detailed critique on one key up-to-date journal article (i.e. one that had been published in the last five years) which was relevant to their given PALS case study. I also asked them to present a list of the journal articles they had located that were relevant to their PALS case, fully cited according to the Harvard system.

Then when I marked their critiques, I gave the students detailed written feedback, partly to help them prepare for their presentation, which was related to the same PALS case study, but mainly to prepare them for the main assignment which was the essay and counted for 70 per cent. The criteria specified were:

- evidence of an up-to-date literature search;
- accurate referencing using the Harvard system;
- critical evaluation of one key journal paper for the PALS case;
- evaluation of the usefulness of the chosen key journal paper for the PALS case.

The essay assignment presented them with a new and much longer PALS case study and they were asked to do the following.

Choose one or more theoretical approaches which you think would be helpful to the client described in the following PALS case study. Using your knowledge of the appropriate research evidence justify why you think your chosen approach(es) might be effective.

Evaluating it

In order to see if the intervention had worked or not, a positivist approach was carried out by analysing the essays after they had been marked for the number of journals cited in the reference list at the end of each essay. The references to journals were subdivided into two categories:

1. recent journal articles (published in the last five years);
2. older journal articles (published six or more years ago).

This analysis was carried out by a researcher who went through each essay and from the reference lists counted the number of unique citations to give the total number of journals used, as well as books and web sources. Doing this often reduced what looked like impressively long lists of references to somewhat unimpressive lists when he actually looked at the total number of unique sources used (one example was an assignment where there appeared to be 25 separate references, which actually boiled down to two journal articles and three books). Sometimes it was difficult to decide what were primary and what were secondary sources, given the inaccurate referencing used by some of our students, but he would consult with me and together we would make a best guess, so this was not a 100 per cent accurate process but it was as accurate as we could make it.

Looking at the results of this research, we first compared the number of journals used in the assignments of the three modules from 2003 (see Figure 5.1).

As you can see from this simple bar chart, there was no difference in the number of journals used between organisational students (black bar) and crime students (white bar) who were both using five journals on average. But there was a difference with counselling psychology students (grey bar) who used, on average, seven journals and this was a statistically significant difference.

This was a step in the right direction and some evidence that the intervention was having an effect but, of course, the difference might have been something to do with differences in the nature of the three module assignments rather than anything else. Our next step was to compare this year's (2003) counselling psychology cohort with the previous (2002) counselling psychology cohort where the essay assignment was virtually the same. The results of this comparison are shown in Figure 5.2.

Here we found that there was a difference. As you can see in the bar chart, the grey bars show that the 2003 cohort used more recent journals than the 2002 cohort (black bars), though the use of older journals was the same.

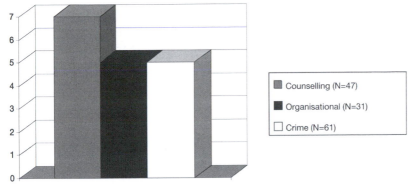

Figure 5.1 Bar chart showing average number of journals used in assignments in three psychology courses

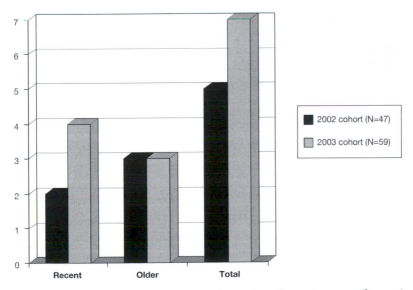

Figure 5.2 Bar chart showing average number of journals used in assignments of two cohorts of counselling psychology students

Altogether then, the 2003 cohort used more journals and, in particular, used more recent journals and this was a significant difference.

We did the same comparison with the other two modules: organisational psychology, and psychology and crime, neither of which had had any intervention. Where organisational psychology was concerned, there were no differences in the number of journals used between 2003 and 2002, but when we came to looking at the psychology and crime students' results the picture was somewhat different. See Figure 5.3.

Here we have a reversal where there was a large and significant drop in the number of journals used by the 2003 cohort of crime students (grey bars) compared to the 2002 cohort (black bars) and this applied to both categories of journals: recent and older. We really did not know why this had happened. It might have been that this particular crime cohort was not as able as last year's cohort, but we did not really think this was the case as there was not much difference in overall grades between the two years.

Speculating that it might be something to do with experience, we compared the use of journals by crime students who were also taking counselling, with crime students who were doing other modules, to see if the lessons being learned in counselling would transfer over into another module and this is what we found. See Figure 5.4.

This bar chart shows that there was no difference in the use of recent journals, which was a little disappointing, but there was a difference in the use of older journals, where students who took counselling as well as crime (grey bar) used an average of seven journals overall in their assignment as opposed to an average of only four journals overall for students who took some other module as well as crime, but this was not a statistically different difference. Nevertheless it was mildly encouraging and gave me some hope that my intervention was having a modest effect.

Modifying future practice

A simple quantitative measure like this tells us some interesting things, but what it did not do was to tell me how well students were actually applying the information in their journal articles in their essays. A few feedback comments that I had made on the essays of the 2003 cohort of counselling psychology students were picked out by my research colleague and showed that all was not well.

> You tried to do this but missed the golden opportunity of using the highly appropriate research papers that you cited.
> You used loads of research – you bombarded me with it but you did not say much about it – i.e. that's the evaluative part.
> More critical analysis needed – you cited research but you did not say what had been done; what was the basis for the claims?

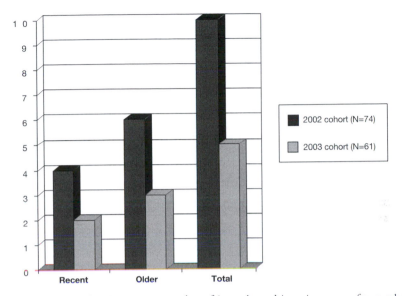

Figure 5.3 Bar chart showing average number of journals used in assignments of two cohorts of crime psychology students

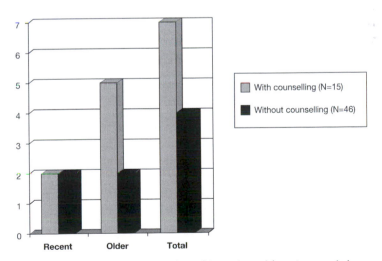

Figure 5.4 Bar chart showing average number of journals used by crime psychology students who also took counselling psychology

What was happening here? I had been successful in getting my students to use, or at least cite, more up-to-date journal articles in their essay, but in spite of the assistance on how to critically evaluate and apply a journal article to their PALS case study, they were still not doing this very satisfactorily. In terms then of modifying my practice for the next year's cohort (2004), I decided that I would need to focus more on breaking down the critical evaluation and giving clearer guidance and maybe more practice. This was a direct consequence of carrying out this study and meant that I did, in fact, modify my practice when teaching the next cohort of counselling psychology students and in so doing another issue emerged for another cycle of action research. ...

Synopsis

- In this chapter, I have described how a pedagogical action research study can be carried out with results that not only can be presented at learning and teaching conferences but which also can help improve teaching practice.
- I chose a student learning issue that will probably be recognised by many readers: the problem of students not using enough primary sources (journals) in their written assignments.
- The ITDEM process has been explained as a simple, practical step-by-step process which will get you started on thinking about designing and carrying out your own pedagogical action research study.
- ITDEM stands for: Identifying the issue, Thinking of ways to tackle it, Doing it, Evaluating the effects, Modifying practice.
- By presenting two quite different methodological approaches to the same issue (one hypothetical, the other real) I have tried to show how ITDEM can be readily adapted to a type of investigation that feels comfortable for you and best fits your own context.

Further reading and resources on practical approaches to action research

Books

There are several books on doing action research, ranging from its philosophy and history to practical 'how-to-do' guides. The two that I am suggesting here incorporate both elements and are written in a straightforward, accessible style. The third is a book that is not about action research but is useful because it is about researching higher education.

Kember, D. (ed.) (2000) *Action learning, Action Research: Improving the Quality of Teaching and Learning*, London: RoutledgeFalmer.

This book is based on experiences in an action learning project carried out in Hong Kong in eight universities covering 90 projects. It presents a framework explaining what action learning and research is, and how it compares with other schemes available for assuring quality of learning. It is particularly useful for getting a feel of how other academics have experienced doing action research and for providing basic information on how to carry out your own action learning/action research project.

McNiff, J., Whitehead, J. and Lomax, P. (2003) *You and Your Action Research Project*, London: RoutledgeFalmer.

Although this book is not specifically aimed at those who work in a higher education context, there is much practical advice, experience and wisdom that is useful to adapt to your own context. This book gives practical guidance on doing an action research project by taking you through each stage of an action research project including: 'Starting your action research project', 'Monitoring and documenting the action', 'Techniques for dealing with the data', 'Making claims to knowledge and validating them', 'Making your research public' and 'Creating your living theory'. There are a number of useful case studies to illustrate major themes.

Tight, M. (2003) *Researching Higher Education*, Maidenhead: SRHE and Open University Press.

This book is useful on a number of levels. It gives an overview of the main areas of, and approaches to, research in higher education, including some suggestions and ideas for further research. It also offers a classification and analysis of research together with some illustrative case studies.

Online resources

Articles

The number of articles available on the Internet is vast, but a good starting point is this one.

Smith, M.K. (1996, 2001, 2007) 'Action research', *The Encyclopedia of Informal Education*. Online. Available: http://www.infed.org/research/b-actres.htm (accessed 27 April 2008).

This is a straightforward article that describes the different types of action research and gives a useful introduction to some of the action research literature.

Websites

The range of resources on the Internet is considerable, and trawling through can sometimes be quite a demoralising experience as information overload rapidly overcomes you. Rather than adding to your overload at this stage, I am going to recommend just two sites that I have found over the years to be very helpful. One site is developed and maintained by the University of Sydney, and the other is a site maintained by one individual Jean McNiff (adjunct professor at the University of Limerick and a leading education action researcher).

AROW (Action and Research Open Web). Online. Available: http://www2. fhs.usyd.edu.au/arow/ (accessed 27 April 2008).

The new layout of this website is unfortunate in that the pages are now harder to read. Nevertheless, as a starting point, the Action Research Electronic Reader has many useful articles, particularly for those who want some background to the philosophy of action research and some of the debates that surround its use, as well as advice on planning and running action research projects. Since this website is related to action research in all fields, you may have to pick and choose a little.

Jean Mcniff's website. Online. Available: http://www.jeanmcniff.com/ (accessed 27 April 2008).

For someone just beginning to explore the potential of educational action research, this is an excellent website – friendly, informative and scholarly, with resources to help new action researchers. There are links to McNiff's books and papers, many of which are downloadable, as well as examples of action research theses. A useful starting point might be the action research booklet.

Journals for publishing pedagogical action research

Many subject related and generic journals in the field of higher education publish action research studies but Educational Action Research is one that is dedicated to action research in education (at all levels). It is published by Routledge four times a year. It is a fully refereed international journal concerned with exploring the dialogue between research and practice in educational settings. It is available in print and online.

Educational Action Research. Available: http://www.tandf.co.uk/journals/ journal.asp?issn=0965–0792andlinktype=5 (accessed 27 April 2008).

Chapter 6

What are the most suitable research methodologies?

Introduction

Carrying out your first action research study can be intimidating particularly if your subject expertise is not in the social sciences. So in this chapter, I intend to introduce some of the more well-known methods of enquiry. In Chapter 5 we worked through the stages of carrying out a research study using the ITDEM acronym. In this chapter we unpick the stages in more detail, particularly focusing on the identification of the issue or problem, and the thinking through of appropriate ways to research it.

In pedagogical action research, the fundamental aim is to research:

- some aspect of your teaching or assessment practice;
- some element of your students' learning experience or academic performance;
- some other appropriate variable.

Fundamentally, as with all practitioner research, the goal is to develop, evaluate and improve your practice. In deciding on the most appropriate research methodology, there are many questions to ask yourself before you make a decision. This planning stage will reap dividends as it enables you to think through the feasibility of the whole study before you actually embark on it.

One of the most common pitfalls for the inexperienced researcher is to embark on a project without thinking through the aims, methods and possible analyses, so if it is at all possible, I would recommend you to follow the process of writing a skeleton research protocol. This has two benefits:

- it helps clarify your thinking at the beginning of a research idea;
- more importantly, it acts as a written reminder of the research aims.

This might seem unnecessary at the time, but halfway through a piece of research, it is very easy to lose track of your original research aims and start spinning off in a multitude of different directions. This common pitfall can reduce what was originally a sound research study into an unformulated and incoherent set of research findings, which bear little relation to your original research questions.

Writing a research protocol might seem like an unnecessary waste of time, particularly if you are keen to make a start on the actual research study but, when it comes to writing up the outcomes of your research for dissemination at learning and teaching conferences or in journal articles, you will already have the skeleton of the paper in place and it will save a great deal of time in what is often the hardest part of doing an action research study, namely, writing it up for publication.

Drawing up a research protocol

The guidance in this section has been adapted from a version used by the Write Now CETL (www.writenow.ac.uk (accessed 27 April 2008)). An example of a completed research protocol is presented in Appendix B. All protocols differ slightly but, in general, you should aim to include the following.

1. Front page with the full title, a version number, the date and contact details of research team (names, institution/s, email addresses and telephone numbers).
2. Description of proposed research.
   This should be a succinct summary of the aim, significance, design and proposed methodology of your study. The main aims of this section are to synthesise/summarise your intentions so as to give an indication of the study's overall purpose and content.
3. Theoretical background, including a critical review of the current research literature, i.e. What is already known about the problem? What is not known? What are some of the problems or shortcomings of previous work in the area? How will your proposed study expand this body of knowledge?
4. Research methodology with justification for proposed methods to be used.
   This section normally describes the plan for accomplishing the proposed work and usually consists of several subsections. These subsections relate to the 'heart' of the study and it is important that you include sufficiently detailed information – especially since action research can sometimes be viewed as not real research in some of the more traditional universities. The more thought you could put into your research study at this stage, the greater the confidence you will have in its findings. As well as your broad research strategy, which should include a justification of methods you intend to use, it is a good idea to outline any potential methodological difficulties and plans for addressing them.
   Design
   Clearly describe the type of design to be used and the rationale for its selection. Ensure that the design is congruent with the study's main aim and specific objectives.

Materials

Describe any quantitative/qualitative data – producing instruments, questionnaires or interview/observation schedules that are being proposed. If you are going to use a published measure, as opposed to a newly constructed measure, include estimates of the instrument's reliability and validity, which may be taken from previous studies or applications. You will also need to indicate how you will obtain materials that are protected by copyright. If you are going to construct your own instrument, detail the steps to be taken in order to establish its reliability and validity. (Guidance on this is given later in the chapter.) It is also a good idea to include a copy of any measure in an appendix, or at the least give some sample items or questions. Outline any potential difficulties or limitations associated with the use of the proposed materials.

Sample

Describe the target population/sample/key informants/participants for your study and the procedure for their selection. Detail the rationale for the sample size and characteristics, and outline any inclusion or exclusion criteria that you will apply.

Procedure

Detail any procedures relating to the 'how, when and where' of data collection. (e.g. How will you gain entry to a particular setting such as lectures and seminar groups? What will participants in your study be asked to do? How will you deal with non-participation?)

5. Analysis of data justified in accordance with the research design

It is sound research practice to give detailed consideration to the proposed data analysis at the design stage of the proposed research. If you are planning to use statistical analyses, outline which statistical tests will be used with justification (e.g. parametric or non-parametric tests, level of statistical significance to be set). If you are planning to use qualitative data analysis, give as much information as possible relating to data collation, coding, classification, categorisation and/or verification. Outline the general rules or principles, which will drive the proposed analysis (e.g. grounded theory, discourse analysis).

6. Timetable and stages of completion

This is an integral part of all research proposals and should indicate a realistic time scale, including contingency plans should the research process be held up for any reason. It should indicate research end points and include a flow chart of the research schedule.

7. Dissemination plans

Give a brief outline of how the research outcomes might benefit

- students;
- policy and practice at your own university and at any other participating institution/s;

- the wider academic community at national/international level (include targeted journals, conferences, other publication opportunities).

8. Continuation plans

    This section is a key element in pedagogical action research, which is defined by its cycles of research. While it is not possible to prejudge your results, it could be helpful to think through how your findings might modify practice and what the next cycle of action research might look like.

9. References

    Include a full list of all references.

Basic principles of quantitative and qualitative research methods

For the remainder of this chapter, I will focus on describing some basic principles of survey research, experiments and observation studies, which are the more commonly used research methods in quantitative research. I will then describe some basic principles of thematic analysis and content analysis, which are frequently used in qualitative research. In order to make this as interesting and relevant as possible, I present a hypothetical vignette, but one which readers will realise have many common elements of their own experience.

The case of Dr Jones

Dr Jones is a recently appointed lecturer in sport psychology at the University of North West England (a 'new' university that was originally a polytechnic). She is an authority on dyspraxia and the 'clumsy child' syndrome having obtained an outstanding PhD, written several books on the topic and given keynote addresses at international conferences, as well as having published extensively in the top journals.

Dr Jones has also brought into the department research funding and is currently working on evaluating a new coaching system for children with dyspraxia and related syndromes. As a new lecturer she has somewhat unfairly been given a full teaching load as well as her research responsibilities. One of the classes she has been asked to teach is an introductory module to second-year sports studies students on childhood disabilities.

After four weeks of this module, Dr Jones goes to see her head of department in some distress. Apparently the number of students attending have dropped from the original 80 to less than 30. The ones who are still on the course do not, according to Dr Jones, pay much attention in the weekly lectures that she so carefully prepares and which are at the cutting edge of knowledge; they clearly have not done any of the journal readings she recommends and do not participate at all when she invites them to respond to her questions. Even worse, are the weekly seminars where the same pattern is even more obvious and Dr Jones finds herself having to do all the talking to fill the silences.

Of course there might be any number of reasons for this state of affairs and, like all pedagogical problems, there are layers of complexity that preclude any simple solutions. It is likely, for example, that the lack of engagement is a combination of Dr Jones' inexperience in facilitating students' learning, combined with a lack of motivation on the part of the students who might not see the purpose of such a course in their overall studies. However, let us suppose that Dr Jones is willing to carry out a pedagogical action research study and identifies the following problem:

Students do not read for lectures or seminars.

Using the decision chart shown in Figure 6.1, you can follow the basic principles of some of the more common research methods that she might choose. Of course this can only be an outline, but what I have tried to do is to give you enough guidelines to carry out a perfectly sound research study of your own.

Scenario One: Dr Jones decides the issue is something to do with her students

Let us assume that Dr Jones decides it might be something to do with her students' motivations, behaviours or interest. She basically now has a choice of two methods: questionnaire research, or interviews sometimes referred to by the generic term 'survey research.'

I will now give you a basic introduction to both of these research approaches.

Questionnaire research

Questionnaire research covers both questionnaire and measurement or attitude scale design. A common pitfall here, if you have never embarked on survey research before, is that it is relatively easy to think up lots of questions, only to find out much later when you have got hundreds of completed questionnaires that the information they provide is not analysable.

Advantages and disadvantages

The advantages of a survey are that respondents are more likely to complete it honestly than they might respond to questions in an interview, particularly if they can complete the survey anonymously. Paper-based or electronic surveys can be completed in the respondents' own time and at their own convenience, although this advantage has the flip side of surveys often getting only about 30–40 per cent response rate, which creates issues around the generalisability of your findings. Survey research is very useful when you are interested in getting a quantitative data from a large number of people.

There are two main types of instrument to distinguish when considering survey research:

- the questionnaire which is to find out information about peoples' habits, behaviours and demographics;
- the attitude or inventory which is to measure peoples' attitudes, beliefs or behaviours.

A well-known example of the latter in the field of higher-education research is the Approaches to Studying Inventory, which has gone through many iterations and is currently known as the ASSIST. This inventory has been designed to measure students' approaches to studying, conceptions of learning, studying practice, etc. (Tait, Entwistle and McCune, 1998).

The ASSIST could be a useful tool to use for the Dr Jones case study, as it would provide her with data that would help her to understand her students' habits, perceptions and practices. If she found, for example, that the majority of her class scored highly on the surface, apathetic dimension, she could think about using assessment as a 'carrot' to engage them more.

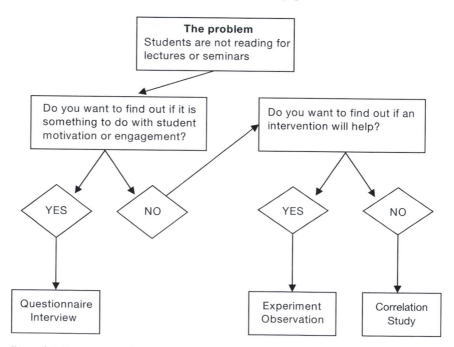

Figure 6.1 Devison chart for deciding on appropriate research method

There are three main types of question used in questionnaires.

a. Open-ended questions are used when we want to find out how the respondent thinks or feels about a topic rather than some sort of measurement.
Question: What do you think about the module on childhood disabilities?
Response: In this type of question, the respondent writes an unstructured answer, which may or may not be word limited. For example:

> I think it's basically a waste of time. I came to this university to study sports and in this module all you hear about is a whole lot of advanced research, which I can't understand. The lecturer goes too fast and refuses to give us copies of her notes and the reading she gives us each week is just too hard. I don't think it's fair.

Analysis: Like all unstructured material, the choice of analysis is considerable, but the most common methods would be thematic or content analysis.

b. Closed questions are used when we want to have some measurable count of a respondent's behaviours.
Question: How many hours a week do you read the given readings for childhood disabilities?
Response: This can be in the form of an open-ended response, which has the advantage of being an accurate measure (for example, 12 hours), but we lose the ability to easily categorise a large range of answers.
An alternative can be to present a series of options which the respondent has to circle or tick, for example:

Less than 1 hr   2–3 hrs   4–5 hrs   6+ hrs

This has the advantage of being easier to categorise but it loses precision. It might be that a respondent might spend 20 hours a week reading (unlikely but possible) and this would be captured in the 6+ hours category. A hybrid response set is one which sets out categories and also provides an 'other' category for respondents whose answers do not readily fit those predetermined categories. In this way, we preserve the advantages of both methods:

'Other? Please state the number of hours:'

Analysis: Descriptive statistics such as frequency counts, or visual representations such as pie charts and histograms or bar charts are all relatively easy ways to analyse these types of responses. This information would be helpful to Dr Jones by giving her some empirical evidence of what she suspects to be true.

c. Attitude scales or measurement scales look like questionnaires but are designed to produce a measurement of something. In this respect they are more like standardised tests, which means to be of any value, they need to go through a process of rigorous testing for validity and reliability. They are designed as a series of statements (known as items) to which the respondent has to tick or circle a predetermined response. In Dr Jones' case, if she wished to ascertain her students' attitudes to learning, she could use the ASSIST as described above, or she might prefer to construct her own scale, which could be tailored to her context.

Statement: 'In the childhood disabilities module, we are:

'Expected to learn the topics ourselves'
'Given too much reading to do'
'Given help when we don't understand'.

Response: There are many forms of response set but the three most widely used are described here.

i.   The Thurstone scale which has two response sets, for example:

'We are given too much reading to do.'
   True/False
   Yes/No
   Agree/Disagree

ii. The Likert scale produces a differentiated scale of responses (usually five or six) which allows for an overall score where a high score would indicate a strong positive attitude and a low score would indicate a strong negative attitude, for example:

'We are expected to learn the topics ourselves.'

Strongly agree	Agree	Unsure	Disagree	Strongly disagree
5	4	3	2	1

It can also be used to measure the frequency of a behaviour, for example:

'I attend the childhood disability seminars.'

All the time	Very frequently	Frequently	Sometimes	Infrequently	Never
5	4	3	2	1	0

Here the scale has been adapted to include a score of zero, since it seems intuitively wrong for 'never' to count for anything.

iii. The Osgood semantic differential scale is similar to the Likert scale in that there are differentiated response options (five or six), but its advantage is that it describes the other end of the scale where Likert describes only one end, for example:

We are expected to learn the topics ourselves	☐ ☐ ☐ ☐ ☐	The lecturer gives us all the information we need for the topics

However, as this example shows, it is often difficult to describe the other end of the scale without getting impossibly wordy.

Stages in constructing an attitude scale

1. Generate items from the relevant literature, from your practice and from experience. Aim to get as many items as possible in this first stage, as ultimately you should have between 20 and 30 items, any more and your respondents may tire of answering questions, any less and you may not validly capture what it is you are trying to measure. An excess of items at this stage allows you to retain only the best. In devising your items there are several pitfalls to be aware of:

a. Socially desirable responses
    Be careful to avoid items that are likely to encourage a socially desirable response rather than a truthful one. It is preferable, for example, for Dr Jones to construct an item about students' attitudes to her teaching that says:

    'It is difficult for the lecturer to make the subject easy to understand.'

    than

    'Dr Jones does not make the subject easy to understand.'

    The problem with constructing a scale that has a high number of items that engender socially desirable responses, means that there will be a ceiling effect where nearly everyone scores highly and there is little differentiation. A floor effect is the opposite where nearly everyone scores very low, again providing little differentiation between your respondents.

b. Response set
    If you word all your items in the same way, respondents might easily fall into an unthinking automatic pattern of just tick the same response for every item. This is known as a response set. The usual way of getting round this particular problem is to word some of the items negatively, for example:

'It is not difficult for the lecturer to make the subject easy to understand.'

As you can see, this sometimes results in wording that make items hard to comprehend. We also have to be very careful when wording some of our items negatively that we remember to reverse the scoring for these items. Even very experienced researchers have been known to have been caught out by this one.

c. Double-barrelled items
Devising items that have more than one element means that the respondent might agree with one part of the item but not with the other, for example:

'It is difficult for the lecturer to make the subject easy to understand and interesting.'

Always make sure that each item only asks about one thing.

d. Leading items
It is very easy to produce an attitude scale where the items are leading the respondent to answer in a particular way, for example:

'Making the subject easy to understand is an essential part of a lecturer's professional responsibility.'

Care needs to be taken to present your items as neutrally as possible so it is equally likely to get a 'strongly disagree' response as a 'strongly agree' response.

e. Order of items
Care has to be taken in ordering the items as sometimes the earlier ones may influence the responses of the later ones. This is an aspect of the design that you leave until the end.

2. Test for clarity of instructions. Try to keep the instructions as simple and as precise as possible. 'Rank order the following items' does not explain how or what the scale is. If there are ten items, is 1 to be given to the most important or is 10? Is it 'importance' you want the respondent to rank or is it some other measure such as relevance to them personally?

It is also important to make the instructions match the response categories. If you have a mix of behaviours and attitudes you need to signal this in the instructions, otherwise 'to what extent do you agree with the following', does not fit the frequency responses.

If the scale goes over more than one page, it is a good idea to signal at the end of the first page that there are others to follow, and a reminder at the end to make sure that all responses have been completed is also helpful, as it can be very frustrating to find that many of your respondents have completed only half the questionnaire or attitude measure. If you are using an electronic method of questionnaire design such as the software tool SurveyMonkey (http://www.surveymonkey.com), it will automatically remind the respondent if they have not done everything.

3. Test for face validity. This means checking to see that the items and the instructions make sense to the respondent. You can test this by first completing the questionnaire yourself and then piloting it on approximately 20–30 people, preferably those who do not form part of your main study. They will be able to tell you if your items are ambiguous, instructions are not clear or response sets do not make sense.

4. Test for internal validity and consistency using the data collected from your pilot study. One method of doing this is to carry out an item–whole test where what you are looking for is an indication that each item is a good predictor of the whole score, i.e. a high score on the item correlates positively with the total score. The commonest method of doing this is to use a statistical package such as SPSS to establish Cronbach's alpha, which is a measure of internal consistency based on the average inter-item correlation.

   If this is acceptable (usually regarded as 0.7 and above) it means that all your items are fine, if it is less than this it will also allow you to delete items from the scale until Cronbach's alpha is acceptable. You may find at this stage that items not only have to be deleted but may have to be rewritten and then you must go through the whole process of piloting the newly written items again with another sample of 20–30 respondents.

   A simpler method, but not so rigorous, is to carry out a split-half reliability test where you correlate the total score of items in the first half of your scale with the total score for items in the second half of your scale. Provided you have not banded together all similar items in each half, this should show you whether or not you are measuring one thing. If the correlation is unacceptably low, i.e. below 0.7, you will need to rewrite or delete items as suggested above.

5. Test for reliability. This basically means finding out whether you will get the same results from the same person if you ask them to complete your measure on two different occasions, usually at least a week apart and better if you can manage two or three weeks.

Summary

Devising an attitude or measurement scale is no easy task and there are many much more sophisticated ways of establishing its validity and reliability such as factor analysis, but should you follow the stages outlined above, you will have a basic, reasonably robust instrument that can then be subjected to further analyses, if your research interests take you in that direction.

Interviews as a research method

Dr Jones could learn a great deal from her students by talking to them about their learning, but of course they may not tell her the truth. It may therefore be more productive to carry out an interview study, possibly using a research assistant. Research assistance can be costly, but there are many graduates particularly in social sciences subjects such as psychology who are keen to gain research experience and charge very little, sometimes doing it for free. This is not exploitative if they get their names on any publications.

Advantages and disadvantages

Interviewing is a very popular research method as it seems seductively easy and tends not to involve any statistical analyses of data. It also appeals to those researchers who are interested in the 'lived experience' of their research participants, rather than some second-order perspective where the aim is to get some sort of objective reality that is researcher driven (first-order perspective).

Interviews do, however, pose their own pitfalls, as they are extremely time consuming both to carry out and to analyse. Most research interviews would take from about 20 minutes to an hour or more. If Dr Jones was to take the minimum time of 20 minutes and wanted to get responses from all her students, it would take her over 27 hours of solid interviewing. Then there is the problem of recording interviews; the best advice is to record and transcribe so as not to miss anything important, but the usual formula for transcribing taped interviews is around eight hours for every hour of tape. Dr Jones' research workload has just risen to a further 216 hours and she has not begun to analyse the data yet. Clearly, this is not a practical piece of research, given her other research commitments, so she can either choose to interview a manageable sample of her students on a one-to-one basis or conduct focus groups which are group interviews typically consisting of between six to twelve people.

Focus groups have their own advantages and disadvantages, they are useful for capturing a whole range of opinion rather than a consensus, but they can be dominated by one or two outspoken individuals.

Types of interview

There are three basic types of interview (individual or group): structured, semi-structured and unstructured, and which one you choose depends on the purpose of your research.

1. Structured interviews are like a spoken form of questionnaire where the questions are predetermined, but their advantage over the questionnaire is that they allow you to clarify questions that the respondent does not

understand or misinterprets. The same degree of care in constructing a questionnaire has to go into a structured interview schedule, as extra questions cannot be added or others taken away in the actual interview session. Responses can be, as for questionnaires, either preset (Thurstone, Likert and Osgood) or a combination with some open-ended responses allowable, for example:

Structured question:

'Do you attend the childhood disability seminars?'

> All the time
> Very frequently
> Frequently
> Sometimes
> Never

Open-ended question:

'Any other pattern?'

2. Semi-structured interviews follow an interview schedule with pre-determined questions but are more flexible than a structured interview in that you use probes designed to elicit further information when necessary. The purpose of a semi-structured interview is to understand the respondent's point of view, so you use open-ended questions to enable the interviewee to talk more freely, for example:

Main question stem:

'Do you think you are expected to learn the topics in childhood disabilities yourselves?'

> Probes:
>   In what way?
>   Is this fair?
>   Why/Why not?

Often the probes will not be needed as the purpose is to give some freedom for the interviewees to express themselves freely, but they can be useful if the interviewees dry up or if they deviate away from the topic in question and need gently bringing back.

Semi-structured interviews are not only useful in their own right as a way of gathering data on your respondents' thoughts and perceptions of the topic in question, but they can also be used to generate items for a questionnaire study if you want to carry out a large-scale study. They can be equally useful for following up a questionnaire study where you want to get some richer data than can be gained from responses on a questionnaire or when you want to explore some of the findings that the questionnaire study has thrown up. If, for example, Dr Jones found from a questionnaire study that students were saying there was too much work and yet at the same time were studying for less than an hour a week, she might wish to explore this anomaly in interviews with those students where the discrepancy seemed particularly large.

3. Unstructured interviews are for research studies where your focus is to gain insights about the respondents' world and lived experience. Such interviews tend to be very long but require a good deal of trust on the part of the interviewee and a considerable amount of experience on the part of the researcher. If you have never carried out any interviews before, it is probably not a good idea to start with an unstructured interview. Typically though, this type of interview would begin with an explanation of what the research was about, for example:

> I am working for Dr Jones as a research assistant to explore in depth with her students what they feel about the course on childhood disabilities. What we are really interested in is what it is like for you, rather than what we might think as researchers. Of course you might feel embarrassed if you have negative things to say or you might be worried that your views will somehow be used against you, but this is categorically not so. Dr Jones will not see these transcripts, only some general themes that emerge from this interview and the others I am conducting, so you will never be identifiable to her or to anyone else in the university. Are you happy to proceed with a few general questions about the course?

>> How long have you been a student?
>> What interested you to take up sports studies?
>> Are you full time or part time?
>> Do you work as well as study?

Then when these easier general questions have been asked and the student is happy to proceed, the fundamental question to be explored can be asked. In this case, it might be:

'What do you generally feel about this course?'

In such an interview, many unexpected insights might arise, as the interviewee is free to set her or his own priorities and talk freely about whatever it is that is really important to her or him. Such freedom does, of course, make analysis and identifying commonalties more difficult. This will be discussed in more detail in the following chapter.

Summary

Whatever type of interview you decide to carry out, there is a common procedure to follow that involves:

- putting the interviewee at ease;
- explaining the nature of the research;
- outlining how the data will be used;
- gaining permission for the interview to be taped or for you to take notes.

A good practice is to offer the interviewees the opportunity to see the transcription of your notes so that they can alter anything they feel was inaccurate. This can be especially useful if you carry out an interview by telephone, as you do not have the usual cues of body language to know if you are interpreting what the interviewee says correctly.

Another good practice is always to have a dry run of the schedule beforehand with a willing participant. It is surprising how difficult it is to take on the role of researcher in an interview, as it is not like a conversation where both take part equally, so some practice before you 'go live' will pay dividends. How many participants you should interview depends very much on the purpose of your research and the type of analysis you intend to do. It has been known, for example, for articles to be published based on detailed qualitative analysis on just one interviewee.

Scenario Two: Dr Jones decides the issue is related to her teaching

Of course, Dr Jones may well decide to be more proactive and design some sort of intervention to encourage her students to engage more with the course and with the work that is required. Looking again at Figure 6.1, the most usual way of testing whether or not an intervention has worked is to design an experiment. Experimental research springs from a positivist paradigm where the aim is to establish a cause and effect. Usually the researcher starts with a hypothesis and then designs an experiment to test it. In pedagogical action research, the most likely type of situation to lend itself to an experimental design is that of some sort of pedagogical intervention.

The pedagogical problem of students not preparing for seminars and therefore not contributing is one that is familiar to many of us and there have been many ingenious interventions, but relatively rarely are the effects of these interventions actually measured. This is the essential difference between 'show and tell' accounts of practice, where often the only 'measure' of whether or not it works is that of student satisfaction, and pedagogical research where there is some measure of improvement. This scenario fits very nicely into the action research model because the results of the first experiment can lead into formulating a further hypothesis or hypotheses to be tested.

Experimental designs

Let us suppose Dr Jones decides to set up a discussion forum on a virtual learning environment in order to encourage engagement with the topic. This can then be tested in one of the following three experimental designs: independent groups, matched participants or repeated measures.

1. Independent groups design

This would be used to test Dr Jones' hypothesis that:

> Students who prepare for seminars by taking part in an electronic discussion forum will perform better in the examination than students who prepare by extra individual reading without discussion.

In using an experimental approach, we are attempting to establish a cause and effect, but in reality, educational research is unlikely to be this clear cut, as we shall see. Suppose that Dr Jones decides to divide her class into two groups of 40 where one half will be asked to take part in the electronic discussion forum and the other half will be given extra reading. This is the simplest type of independent groups design and ensures that, in this case, all students receive some form of intervention, which is an important ethical concern.

A more sophisticated design might involve three or more groups. Dr Jones might, for example, wish to examine the effects of extra reading as well, so she would need three independent groups: two with the different seminar preparation conditions and one where there is no experimental condition, referred to as the control group. How Dr Jones allocates the students to each group is crucial to avoid any 'extraneous' or 'nuisance' variables such as self-selection might cause. It would not be a good design, for example, if all the students in one group happened to be of one gender or one ability level.

The experiment also needs to be carefully devised so that an appropriate measure of effect is formulated; this is called the dependent variable. In this case, Dr Jones might decide to use the overall examination grade, which would be a fairly crude measure. She might prefer to use the marks given to specific examination questions, which were the focus of a given seminar. This would be a slightly more sophisticated measure, but it still has the disadvantage that it allows for many other explanations for enhanced performance.

Another measure might be some analysis of the examination scripts themselves for quality of thinking, perhaps using Biggs and Collis' (1982) SOLO taxonomy, for example (see Chapter 7 for a description of this taxonomy).

As I mentioned earlier, what we are looking for in an experimental design is to establish a cause and effect by testing a hypothesis. You will need, therefore, to analyse your results statistically to find out if your hypothesis is supported and how significant this is. More details on hypothesis testing are given in Chapter 8. Should Dr Jones find that her electronic discussion group does do significantly better than the extra reading group, then this informs her practice immediately and she may wish to share this intervention with other colleagues.

What is more likely to happen in your own pedagogical research is that you find your results are not that clear-cut, so you would then undertake a second cycle of action research, possibly refining your design and/or improving your intervention. One of the potential difficulties with interpreting Dr Jones' findings, if there is a difference, is that one group may simply be more able or more motivated than the other, and that it is that rather than the intervention which has caused the improvement in examination performance. One solution to this problem is to use another experimental design called the matched participants design.

2. Matched participants design

In order to take care of nuisance or extraneous variables such as ability or motivation, you can allocate your students to each group, matched on these two variables (i.e. ability and motivation) as far as you are able. This sounds deceptively simple, but is in fact fiendishly difficult to do, which is why this design often features one variable only.

Let us imagine that Dr Jones is testing her same hypothesis:

> Students who prepare for seminars by taking part in an electronic discussion forum will perform better in the examination than students who prepare by extra individual reading without discussion.

Let us also suppose that she wants to match her students first for ability.

The immediate problem is: how will she measure 'ability'? She could give them all an intelligence test or some other test of intellectual ability or, more practically, she might consider their past academic performance so far. Again, there are a number of choices she can make. She could use A-level grades or their overall performance in year one, or perhaps some formula calculated on an aggregate of the two.

If Dr Jones decides on first-year overall grades as an indicator of her students' abilities, she then needs to rank order her students from highest performance to lowest performance and then to systematically go through the ranked list allocating them into her two groups. To illustrate how this works, I have devised Table 6.1, which shows just the top eight out of 80 students.

If, however, Dr Jones wants to take both ability and motivation into account, assuming she has been able to give the students some sort of motivation test, she will need to do a similar ranking and then a composite ranking (assuming she thinks both variables are equally important) before she allocates to the experimental groups. I have illustrated what this might look like in Table 6.2.

Once again, I have done this to show only eight students but I have taken hypothetical rankings from all 80 students, as it would be extremely unlikely that the same eight most able students would also get the eight highest scores in the motivation test. Then, on the basis of the composite rankings, the students can be allocated to the experimental groups. Such a procedure, while time consuming, would be rigorous and ensure an even match of ability and motivation in both groups as far as possible.

Should Dr Jones think that gender or age was an important influencing factor, then the process would be a little easier as there are only two categories (male versus female or traditional versus mature), but the principle is the same, i.e. she would be trying to even up, as far as possible, extraneous variables that might affect the results of her experiment.

Table 6.1 Allocation to experimental groups based on ability

Student	Grade	Rank	Group allocation
Andy	A	1=	Electronic discussion
Sylvie	A	1=	Extra reading
Joanne	A-	3	Electronic discussion
Gary	B+	4=	Extra reading
Jack	B+	4=	Electronic discussion
Hakim	B	6	Extra reading
Greg	B-	7	Electronic discussion
Colin	C+	8	Extra reading

Table 6.2 Calculation of composite ranking for ability and motivation

Student	Grade	$Rank^1$	Motivation (out of 20)	$Rank^2$	Composite ranking $(^1+^2)$ for allocation to experimental groups
Andy	A	1=	10	30	31
Sylvie	A	1=	15	7	8
Joanne	A-	3	11	23=	26
Gary	B+	4=	12	14	18
Jack	B+	4=	8	42	48
Hakim	B	6	11	23=	29
Greg	B-	7	6	67	74
Colin	C+	8	17	8	12

Ethical issues

Both these experimental designs sit very uneasily in a higher education context because of the obvious ethical issues they pose. The whole area of ethics in educational research is discussed in full in Chapter 10. Involving students in research that might potentially disadvantage them in work that counts is not a defensible option, so how do you get round it? There is an argument to say that we do not know which method will work best, so, provided students know that this is the case and agree to being selected for either group, then that is reasonably fair. You could not, however, justify a control group using this argument.

This is one of the difficulties of carrying out experimental (laboratory-style research) in a naturalistic educational setting. If you divorce the experiment from the students' course and set up an artificial context where nothing counts, these problems do not arise but the findings will not necessarily relate to the real context, which is the very point of doing pedagogical action research. The third experimental design is perhaps the best solution, where you use the same students before and after the intervention. This is known as the repeated measures design.

3. Repeated measures design

Sometimes this is also known as a within-subjects design, where the same participants are measured twice, thus there is no worry about differences between the groups. At first glance, this might seem the best of the three designs as it also effectively sidesteps the ethical issues that the other designs raise. But it too has some disadvantages, such as order effects or carry over (meaning that participants tend to improve with practice).

I shall assume that Dr Jones' is using the same hypothesis:

> Students who prepare for seminars by taking part in an electronic discussion forum will perform better in the examination than students who prepare by extra individual reading without discussion.

Then her research design might look something like the following.

Semester One:
Stage 1   Examination performance[1] (baseline measure)
Stage 2   Discussion forum (intervention/first part of independent variable)
Stage 3   Examination performance[2]
Stage 4   Difference in examination scores (first part of experimental measure/dependent variable)

Semester Two:
>   Stage 5   Examination performance[3]
>   Stage 6   Extra reading (intervention/second part of independent variable)
>   Stage 7   Examination performance[4]
>   Stage 8   Difference in examination scores (second part of experimental measure/dependent variable)

Dr Jones would then need to compare the difference in examination marks between performance on examination[1] and examination[2] in Semester One with the difference in examination marks between performance on examination[3] and examination[4] in Semester Two. If her hypothesis is supported, there will be a greater difference in Semester One than in Semester Two.

Of course, such a hypothetical design has many problems, including the need for multiple examinations, but this could be simplified to class tests rather than formal examinations, but there is still the problem, as with any repeated measures design, of order effects. In this case, students may be getting better at examinations, or may simply be more knowledgeable and do better in Semester Two regardless of the intervention.

One way you can deal with this is by counterbalancing the interventions. This would mean that half Dr Jones' students would take the discussion intervention and the other half the extra reading in Semester One. This would then be reversed in Semester Two. She could then confidently expect that any differences in examination performance were as a result of the intervention rather than as a result of order or practice effects. Such a design does, however, bring us back to the problem of independent groups or matched participants. Dr Jones could therefore decide to circumvent such complexity by testing a simpler hypothesis that 'Students who prepare for seminars by taking part in an electronic discussion forum will show an improvement in examination performance.' In this case, there would be no need to investigate the effects of the extra reading intervention, or it could be tested with another cohort in a second cycle of action research.

Summary

If you decide to take an experimental approach in your pedagogical action research, the benefits are that you will have a research study where the evidence will be quantitative, and statistical analysis will allow you to interpret the statistical significance of your findings. You will still need to be very careful though in not overgeneralising from your findings, as no matter which basic experimental design you choose, you are not working in a laboratory with inert substances but in the field where educational research with human participants is never straightforward and rarely produces clear-cut findings which cannot be challenged.

This is one of the reasons why action research is so powerful, for a whole series of experiments with statistically significant results may provide a convincing argument for the efficacy of an intervention or a modification to practice.

Observational research

Another way of finding out the effects of an intervention is to carry out an observational study. Dr Jones will have to think very hard about what evidence she wants to collect and whether or not she wishes to test a hypothesis. Let us imagine that she decides to see if her discussion forum intervention affects student engagement in seminars and lectures.

When carrying out observational research you have to decide what behaviours you will observe, who will actually carry out the observations and how they will be recorded. In Dr Jones' case, we will suppose that she has decided she wants to observe the number of questions asked in each one-hour lecture over a semester, and that in seminars she wants to observe the contributions made in each seminar over a semester. There are basically three types of observation that can be used.

1. Direct observation
   This is where people know you are observing them, so students would understand that in the course of the lecture or seminar they were being observed. This has the advantage of no deception, but has the disadvantage of students behaving artificially in a way they would not necessarily behave if they were not being watched. In the teaching situation this is not too much of a problem, as the very nature of teaching and learning implies some sort of observation to see how students are learning by watching their behaviours.

2. Naturalistic observation
   In this type of observation, people do not know you are observing them so they are likely to behave much more spontaneously, which makes for more ecologically valid data. However, with this type of observation, consent cannot be obtained and there are ethical issues around infringement of personal freedom and confidentiality.

3. Participant observation (direct or naturalistic)
   In this set up, the observer is actually one of the group of people she is observing, so Dr Jones would need to employ some of her students as participant observers. The advantages of this approach is that it gives an 'insider's' view and so there is less chance of the observed behaviour being misinterpreted as the observer is part of the group and engages in the same behaviours she or he is recording. The disadvantages are that the participant observers may well be too tied to their group to make objective recordings.

The observation process

You can carry out an observation process in any of the three types by:

a. Continuous mentoring (for the whole of the lecture/seminar session). This has the advantage of capturing all the occurrences of the behaviours that are being looked for, but has the disadvantage of being time consuming.

b. Time sampling where you record observations for five minutes in every 15 minute period, for example, or whatever time schedule suits your purposes. This has the advantage of being more manageable, but lacks completeness.

c. Event sampling where you simply record the occurrence of the specific behaviour you are interested in, for example, questions that ask for:
more information
clarification
guidance on further reading.

Recording observations can be done by simple paper and pencil means, but it is far more effective to video record where possible, as this enables you to playback and be more accurate in your recording. It also enables you to have more than one observer so that you can calculate a measure of inter-rater reliability for at least a sample of the behaviours of interest, to address the problem of observer bias.

The two most commonly used methods are percentage agreement and Cohen's (1960) kappa coefficient. The first method is the ratio of the number of times the two observers agree divided by the total number of ratings performed, so this measure can be calculated by hand but it does not correct for the possibility that your agreement has happened by chance. Generally speaking, 70 per cent agreement is considered necessary, 80 per cent is adequate and 90 per cent is good (Hartman, 1977; House, House and Campbell, 1981).

For Cohen's kappa, it is advisable to use a statistical package, but basically it is calculated by the observed agreements minus the expected agreements divided by 1 minus the expected agreements. According to Landis and Koch (1977), more than 0.8 is a good agreement 0.6–0.8 is substantial, 0.4–0.6 is moderate and 0.2–0.4 is fair.

Summary

If carried out well, through careful planning and taking a systematic approach to objectively observing and recording behaviour, observation studies can be both valid and reliable because of their high ecological validity.

Correlational studies

Suppose Dr Jones has neither the time nor the inclination to actually do any research at this stage, then she could decide to use data that already exists, see Figure 6.1. This might be a precursor to some action research study in the future. She might, for example, wish to find out if there are any relationships between lecture attendance, seminar attendance, average hours a week spent socialising, examination marks and coursework marks.

Correlational research is not a research method but a statistical technique. It is used to show if there is a relationship between two independent behaviours or measures. This relationship can be positive where you would expect a high score in one to be related to a high score in the other. I have constructed Table 6.3 to illustrate some potentially important variables.

For example, Dr Jones might expect a positive relationship between the number of:

- lectures attended and examination marks;
- lectures attended and coursework marks;
- seminars attended and examination marks;
- seminars attended and coursework marks.

Correlations may also be negative, where you would expect a high score in one measure to be related to a low score in the other. For example, Dr Jones might expect a negative relationship between the number of:

- average hours a week spent socialising and examination marks;
- average hours a week spent socialising and coursework marks;
- average hours a week spent socialising and number of lectures attended;
- average hours a week spent socialising and number of seminars attended.

The degree of the relationship can be displayed visually in a scattergram which will also enable you to estimate the strength and direction of positive or negative correlations or if there is no correlation at all. See Figures 6.2, 6.3 and 6.4, for an example of each.

The strength of a correlation can be calculated statistically, which gives you the correlation coefficient. The nearer the correlation coefficient is to +1 the stronger the positive relationship, and the nearer the correlation coefficient is to -1, the stronger the negative relationship. Where the correlation coefficient is close to 0, there is very little or no relationship. Although it is possible to do this by hand, it is much easier to use one of the statistical packages such as SPSS (Statistical Package for the Social Sciences).

It is also important to be clear that correlations do not imply cause and effect, they can only infer a relationship, but they can be very useful as an

Table 6.3 Dr Jones' records on attendance, socializing and examination performance

Student	No. of lectures attended	Examination performance marks	No. of hours per week socialising	No. of seminars attended
1	15	85	5	10
2	12	78	4	2
3	15	72	3	4
4	14	68	9	9
5	8	65	8	6
6	6	62	5	14
7	5	58	7	8
8	4	55	8	1
9	4	52	16	13
10	3	48	15	11
11	5	45	20	3
12	6	42	18	7
13	2	38	21	5

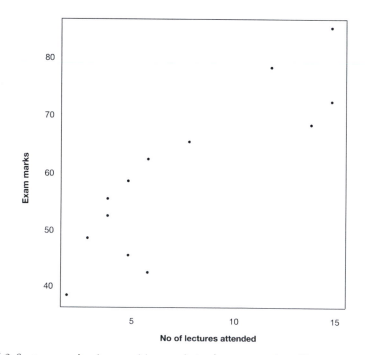

Figure 6.2 Scattergram showing a positive correlation between number of lectures attended and coursework marks

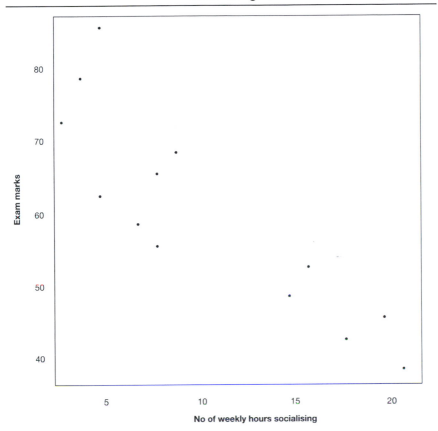

Figure 6.3 Scattergram showing a negative correlation between average number of weekly hours socialising and exam marks

indicator of what elements might be useful to research in an experimental design. If Dr Jones discovers a link between lecture attendance and academic performance, she might decide to test this out by getting her students to attend a greater number of lectures (through some sort of reward system such as counting it as part of the assessment for the course) to see if academic performance on examination and coursework is enhanced.

Summary

Correlation techniques can be useful when it is not practical or ethical to carry out an experimental or other type of research study. They can also be useful for establishing whether or not your assumptions about what is happening may be borne out sufficiently to warrant further investigation.

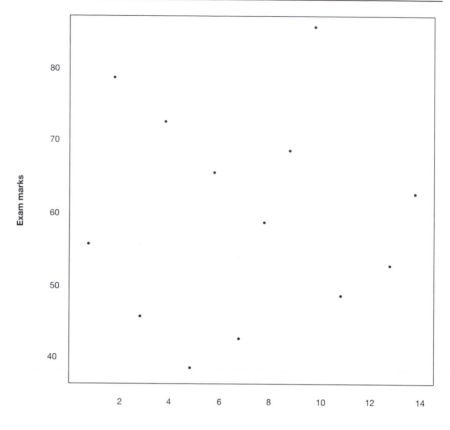

Figure 6.4 Scattergram showing no correlation between number of seminars attended and exam marks

Synopsis

- In this chapter I have described some of the more common research methodologies that you could use in carrying out your first action research study, through using the device of a hypothetical scenario in teaching and learning that most of us will be familiar with, and a decision chart (see Figure 6.1).
- Throughout the chapter, I have stressed the importance of clarity and forward planning and suggested that completing a research protocol would be helpful. To illustrate what is required, I have given an example of a 'real' protocol that I have used for the collaborative research I am involved in (see Appendix B).

- In the section on questionnaire design, I have described the difference between a questionnaire and an attitude or measurement scale, and given guidance on the stages required for both.
- In the interview section, I have described the three basic types: structured, semi-structured and unstructured, and discuss which is appropriate for a given research aim together with some basic advice on interview procedure.
- The experimental design section is probably the weightiest in terms of the detail, as differences between the three types of independent groups, matched subjects and repeated measures need some careful thinking about. By using the hypothetical scenario, I have described the main complexities involved in each.
- Observational research has been divided into three main types: direct, naturalistic and participant, with a brief consideration of their respective advantages and disadvantages. The process has been outlined together with a consideration of how to calculate inter-rater reliability to counteract observer bias.
- Finally, I briefly discuss the correlation technique as although it is not an actual research method but a statistical procedure, it can be a useful precursor or a way of establishing some evidence about the learning and teaching issue you are interested in.
- The aim throughout this chapter has been to provide you not with a definitive textbook account of each method, nor with a complete list of all the research methods available, but with enough information to design a robust study which is publishable.

Further reading and resources

Books

Many of the texts on research methods cover the same ground and are usually available in your own institutional libraries in the social sciences section. The following are recommended as they are written more for academics than for students and are particularly relevant to the context of higher education action research. It can be useful to build up your own personal collection of such books. As your experience in carrying out action research grows, you may well want to expand your repertoire of appropriate research methods.

Bell, J. (2005) *Doing Your Research Project: A Guide for First-Time Researchers in Education, Health and Social Science*, 4th edn, Maidenhead: Open University Press.

This book covers approaches to research, planning the project, ethical issues, managing information, literature searching and reviewing, methods of data collection, analysing documentary evidence, questionnaire design, interviews, diaries, dissertation studies and interpreting the evidence.

Cohen, L., Manion, L. and Morrison, K. (2000) *Research Methods in Education*, 5th edn, London: RoutledgeFalmer.

A well-known and comprehensive best-selling textbook that looks at the nature of research and research paradigms, including a short section on action research. Particularly pertinent to our purposes, the authors, who are experienced teachers, acknowledge the politics of educational research.

Denscombe, M. (2003) *The Good Research Guide: For Small-Scale Research Projects*, 2nd edn, Buckingham: Open University Press.

This is a clearly written and practical guide. It is presented in three reader-friendly sections:

Strategies (surveys, case studies, experiments, action research and ethnography);
Methods (questionnaires, interviews, observations and documents);
Analysis (quantitative and qualitative data and writing up).

Gorard, S. and Taylor, C. (2004) *Combining Methods in Educational and Social Research*, Buckingham: Open University Press.

This book is particularly useful for researchers who want to move beyond the qualitative versus quantitative dichotomy and combine multiple research methods. The authors use examples from compulsory and post-compulsory education in their persuasive case for a richer and more flexible approach to doing research.

Robson, C. (2002) *Real World Research: A Resource for Social Scientists and Practitioner-Researchers*, 2nd edn, Oxford: Blackwell.

A comprehensive text that does what its title says. It has sections on real-world enquiry, approaches to social research, developing your ideas, designing the enquiry, fixed designs (quantitative), flexible designs (qualitative), designs for particular purposes (evaluation, action and change), methods for data collection, and dealing with the data. There are two particularly useful appendices, which make this book distinctive from the others: writing a research proposal, and the role of practitioner-researchers and consultants in real-world research.

Websites

Trochim, W. (2006) *Research Methods Knowledge Base*, 2nd edn. Available: http://www.socialresearchmethods.net/kb/ (accessed 8 March 2008).

A web-based textbook in social research methods mainly aimed at under-graduate and graduate students, but useful for the beginning researcher. It covers research philosophy and practice, research design and analysis in an easy to understand and accessible way.

Chapter 7

How can you analyse qualitative data in pedagogical action research?

Introduction

Deciding on a research method cannot be carried out in isolation from thinking about the kind of research information or data that it will produce and deciding how you will analyse that data. As with everything else, there are paradigms in the field of analysis, the most fundamental of which has been the quantitative versus qualitative debate. This has resulted in some-times bitter divisions, with names being bandied around of 'number-crunchers' for those who favour a quantitative approach and 'storytellers' for those who opt for a qualitative approach.

Such derogatory terms expound very crudely the distinction between the scientific positivist paradigm which assumes that behaviour can be explained through objective measurement in which sources of bias and error can be minimised or eliminated, and the arts paradigm, where the assumptions are phenomenological, meaning that there are multiple realities which are socially defined and, rather than seek to explain, the researcher attempts to describe in rich detail. Just as there are proponents who believe passionately that the two paradigms must be kept separate (Smith, 1986), there are others who believe that a combination of both approaches is appropriate, particularly for educational researchers (Gorard with Taylor, 2004; Hammersley, 1998; Saloman, 1991; Ercikan and Roth, 2006). These refer-ences make a good case for integrating both the objective and the subjective in educational research by considering how the types of research question asked should determine the approach. This view accords well with my own position, where I believe that a multi-methodological approach is best suited to the ultimate goal of pedagogical action research, which is to inform policy and strategic change, and, more immediately, helps us to modify our own practice. An example of how I have used both is given in a case study in Appendix C, and I give some suggested reading for mixed methods at the end of this chapter.

In the course of this chapter and the next, however, I present both meth-ods separately for ease of access. In this chapter I concentrate on qualitatively analysing your data, and in Chapter 8 I describe some of the more commonly used quantitative analyses.

When is qualitative analysis appropriate?

Qualitative analysis is useful in research studies where:

- little is known about the research area, and the research question is being framed to enable the discovery of new information, such as a new way of conceptualising independent learning;
- a richer understanding of the perspective of the person being researched is sought, as is the case with Dr Jones and her efforts to understand her students in interviews and focus groups;
- more in-depth information is needed (which may be difficult to quantify), such as the richer detail that can be obtained from open-ended questions to amplify questionnaire responses;
- there are already existing sources such as diaries, students assignments, video recordings and reports.

Unlike quantitative research where the aim is to be as objective as possible and to minimise error and bias, in qualitative research the aim is to acknowledge fully the subjective part played by the researcher, not only in collecting your data but also in how you analyse and interpret it. This is why, wherever possible, you should make notes in the data collection phase of:

- what you felt was going on;
- what your research ideas were;
- how they are being changed by what you are listening to and/or observing;
- what you are selecting to record and analyse;
- what you are missing out and why.

There are many types of qualitative analysis, including, for example:

- grounded theory (discovering the theory/hypothesis from the data);
- discourse analysis (analysing underlying meanings in speech/text);
- semiotics (study of signs, i.e. words, images, sounds, gestures and objects);
- interpretative phenomenological inquiry (understanding the individual's perspective and experience).

It would be impossible to describe all these different types in sufficient detail in one chapter, so I have provided further sources of information about them at the end of this chapter. Instead of trying to touch on several methods, I am going to concentrate on two commonly used and closely linked analyses that I have found useful in my own action research:

- thematic analysis (searching for patterns);
- content analysis (which I describe as halfway between qualitative and quantitative analysis).

Carrying out a thematic analysis

In order to illustrate the various stages, I am going to use an excerpt from a recent research study on ten new lecturers' views about learning teaching and assessment (Norton and Aiyegbayo, 2005), which I first introduced in Chapter 3.

Reproduced in Box 7.1 are their responses to the first question in the interview schedule:

'What do you think university teaching is all about?'

Box 7.1. Interview excerpt from Norton and Aiyegabo (2005)

Interviewer: What do you think university teaching is all about?'

Lecturer A: 'It depends on the university really. I guess it is about nurturing the students. Getting out their best potential. Working on them. Finding out where they come from and what they know and to treat them as individuals.'

Lecturer B: 'There are three ways I look at it. I think it is about inspiring people especially in an institution like this where the students do not come from a HE background attainment. You have to inspire people to learn, to read, to question, to rebel, to fit. I like to think it is about inculcating them in professional values I learnt as a journalist (that was my previous job). It is a constant evolutionary process of learning for me. It is about learning information and communicating it to the students.'

Lecturer C: 'I think it is about teaching people the skills to carry on learning after university. To develop skills to problem solve and analyse things. I teach a special needs course which is essentially disability studies which is rooted in education.'

Lecturer D: 'I think it is about extending people's interests in what they are interested to a higher level. My view is to get people ready for employment. To give them graduate level skills and I think university performs that.'

Lecturer E: 'I think it is about providing the opportunities for people to develop. Also to provide the opportunities for employment. What I do is to prepare people to be teachers. At the same time, prepare people to be reflective. And to live more fulfilled lives.'

Lecturer F: 'I think primarily it is to facilitate students acquiring intellectual skills as appropriate for them to leave here and find employment. It is to help people engage with the evolving body of knowledge. In a discipline that I am doing (Philosophy) a lot of the arguments are engaging with people's attitudes towards reality. It deals with the students' relationship with the discipline as well.'

Lecturer G: 'I think it should be about helping students to think critically and learn transferable skills that they can use in whatever employment they find themselves.'

Lecturer H: 'I suppose it is about facilitating students' learning in the path towards their future careers. I supposed there has been a change from when I was in university. It is not about delivering truths or information; it is about enabling students to be lifelong learners.'

Lecturer I: 'Our job is to engage the students so they go away with the feeling they have learnt something. The way we teach them should have an effect on the way they learn.'

Lecturer J: 'It is about students finding more about the subject area and also finding more about themselves. To become much more self aware and also becoming much more confident and developing their own knowledge base but not only in the subject but wider than that.'

This research was part of a HEFCE funded consortium psychology project called Assessment Plus, details of which can be accessed from the Write Now CETL website: http://www.writenow.ac.uk/.

Stage 1: Immersion

This is where you read your first transcript and note down any general themes that you notice. Normally, you would do this with the whole of the interview and not just for the responses to each answer. One of the common mistakes of thematic analysis is to look for themes related to the questions asked. This tends to result in a descriptive synthesis rather than an analysis where the so-called themes are no more than extricated quotes under each question heading (see Braun and Clarke, 2006). So here we are going to have to imagine that these ten answers represent ten entire interview transcripts, in order to give you a flavour of the process without producing reams of transcripts. In my first readings of the transcripts I note some general themes:

- academic
- employment
- transformative
- lecturer's own teacher development.

Stage 2: Generating categories

This next stage involves a much closer reading of each transcript, one by one, looking to generate as many categories as possible and to write down a label that best describes each category, before moving onto the next transcript, where you repeat the process but also look for new categories.

This is my list of categories. If you are surprised by, or disagree with, any of them, this is a good illustration of why and how qualitative analysis is subjective and inevitably affected by the values and belief system of the researcher doing the analysis.

Lecturer A
- The institutional context
- Developing students academically

Lecturer B
- Inspiring students academically
- Professional values/vocational preparation/employment
- Lecturer's own teacher development

Lecturer C
- Lifelong learning skills
- Reflection on subject

Lecturer D
- Developing interests academically
- Preparing students for employment

Lecturer E
- Transformative effects of higher education

Lecturer F
- Engaging with knowledge
- Engaging with the discipline

Lecturers G, H, I and J
   No new categories

This process gives me 12 categories, which would be a manageable number (normally between 10 and 15 is considered to be acceptable), but if I were looking at the whole interviews I would have many more than that, possibly running into hundreds). So normally the next stage would be to reduce this number.

Stage 3: Deleting categories

In this stage, I am looking to get rid of any categories that have only one or two examples in them, or any that overlap considerably with other categories. I hesitate to suggest that you should always be as sweeping as this, for it may be that even if only one person has said something that can be described as a category, it might be more true to the research analysis to keep it in; again, this is part of the subjective process and will need justifying. It could be, for example, something that one respondent mentioned over and over again, signalling for that person at least, it is an important part of her or his lived experience.

In my own example presented here, I would not want to delete the category of 'Engaging with knowledge' because although it was only mentioned once by lecturer F, I know that there is much in the pedagogical research literature about epistemological beliefs and the nature of knowledge (see Hofer, 2000; King and Kitchener, 1994) as well as disciplinary epistemologies, so this is a theme I would want to retain.

As a result of this stage I am now left with 11 categories:

1. Developing students academically
2. Inspiring students academically
3. Professional values/vocational preparation/employment
4. Lecturer's own teacher development
5. Lifelong learning skills
6. Reflection on subject
7. Developing interests academically
8. Preparing students for employment
9. Transformative effects of higher education
10. Engaging with knowledge
11. Engaging with the discipline.

This is a manageable number of categories, but if, as mentioned above, I were looking at ten entire transcripts, there would be many more, so normally the next stage would be to reduce this number.

Stage 4: Merging categories

This is where you look again at your categories and try to collapse as many of them as possible, relabelling them as themes. A useful strategy is to go back to the original tentative themes you garnered from your first readings and see if you can refine and describe them more accurately.

In my example, this produces the following themes.

1. Developing students' academic abilities (developing students academically, inspiring students academically).
2. Engaging with the subject (developing interests academically, reflection on subject, engaging with the discipline).
3. Employment (professional values/vocational preparation, preparing students for employment, lifelong learning skills).
4. Transformative effects of higher education (engaging with knowledge).
5. Lecturer's own teacher development.

Stage 5: Checking themes

Reread your transcripts alongside your list of themes and revise them if necessary. One way of checking how accurate your theme labels are, is to ask a willing colleague to allocate quotes from the transcripts to fit your generated themes. I have learned this the hard way in an early research study looking at students' conceptions of learning (Norton and Crowley, 1995), where we soon found how difficult the process was until we resolved the ambiguities by more precise terminology, or sometimes by giving illustrative quotes as examples.

Stage 6: Linking themes

This is possibly the most difficult stage. As Braun and Clarke (2006) caution, one of the major pitfalls in thematic analysis is:

> a failure to actually analyse the data at all! Thematic analysis is not just a collection of extracts strung together with little or no analytic narrative. Nor is it a selection of extracts with analytic comment that simply or primarily paraphrases their content. The extracts in thematic analysis are illustrative of the analytic points the researcher makes about the data, andshould be used to illustrate/support an analysis that goes beyond their specific content, to make sense of the data, and tell the reader what it does or might mean not to analyse the data at all, but simply to describe it.
>
> (Braun and Clarke, 2006: 94)

This is why they advise researchers not to analyse the data under questions as themes, as discussed earlier. In this stage, then, you need to make notes of any relationships or links you see between your themes. Keep in mind your research aim and look for patterns that make sense, in order to tell a coherent and convincing account of what the data tells you.

In my example, I am going to illustrate this by focusing on employment, as it was a finding which surprised me. In this analysis it looks as if employment links with professional values, vocational preparation and possibly lifelong learning skills (but this latter might also link with my transformative theme). The pattern that appears to be emerging from looking at these themes is that these new lecturers most decidedly do not have a 'traditional' view of doing a degree for the love of learning or a passion for the subject; they are much more pragmatic and tuned into higher education in the twenty-first century with its demands from government and consumerism. Of course this is only a brief excerpt and if I was doing it 'for real' it would be much more richly described and articulated.

Stage 7: Presenting your findings

Take the most important theme, select examples of your transcript data and begin to construct an overall commentary on how the data examples are linked together – you can use illustrative quotes to do this. The quotes need to be vivid examples of the argument or case you are making within the overall narrative. The aim is to present an analytical narrative that makes some sort of reasoned case in response to your original research question.

In my example, this might look something like the beginning of a hypothetical analysis presented in Box 7.2.

Box 7.2. An example of the beginning of an analysis (hypothetical)

Researcher notes:
'What struck me most forcibly in this study was that the new lecturers I interviewed thought that teaching in university was much more than just teaching the academic subject, important though that was. I had not expected this, but in view of the changes in the university landscape, I am not sure why I was surprised. The lecturers talked to me about the need to prepare students for life beyond the university and employability was a common theme mentioned by seven out of the ten. Lecturer D talked specifically about graduate skills and clearly saw the role of university to prepare students for employment

> ... to get people ready for employment. To give them graduate level skills and I think university performs that.' (Lecturer D)

Although most of the lecturers who mentioned this, seemed happy with this current situation, there is a suggestion in the transcripts, that Lecturer H does not feel quite the same way as she commented that things have changed and there is an almost resigned acceptance in the way she used the phrase 'I suppose':

> I suppose it is about facilitating students' learning in the path towards their future careers I supposed [SIC] there has been a change from when I was in university. It is not about delivering truths or information; it is about enabling students to be lifelong learners. (Lecturer H)

As well as talking about employment, this lecturer also divulged her own teaching orientation which would appear to be about knowledge transmission, when she talked about *delivering truths or information*. This is an important point, which I will return to later when discussing the theme of lecturers' own development as teachers.'

Summary

The process I have just described has variations but, essentially, the principles of reiteration and careful coding apply. Throughout it is important to remember the part you play in making a subjective researcher interpretation, which should not mean any loss of rigour. This is why, in any account, it is important to specify the stages you took in arriving at your analysis and interpretation.

Carrying out a content analysis

For many years in my own research, I have used this method of analysis as I have found it combines both the search for rich meanings and a deeper understanding of the topic I am researching, together with the ability to carry out some very basic quantitative procedures.

In pedagogical action research, it would be particularly useful if you wanted, for example, to carry out some rigorous analysis on the content of students' written assignments. Perhaps you might want to apply Biggs and Collis' (1982) SOLO taxonomy to essays to see if the level of understanding was related to the essay grade given. This taxonomy is described in five levels of understanding. In such an example much of the decision making about coding and categories is already taken care of, for there is already an existing framework to do the analysis:

> Pre-structural. At this level there is no understanding; students acquire bits of information that are not connected and do not make any coherent sense.
> Uni-structural. Student understanding at this level is to focus on just one element of the task.
> Multi-structural. In this type of response, students may address a number of elements in the task but are unable to make any connections between them or see how they connect to the whole; a typical example is the 'shopping-list' essay.
> Relational. This level of understanding shows that students are able to make connections between interrelating parts of the task and construct some sort of balanced answer.
> Extended abstract. This is the highest level of understanding where students are able to see beyond the parameters of the task and think hypothetically about alternatives in different contexts.

When you do not wish to use an existing framework like this, you have to construct your own categories; so to illustrate this process I will use the same excerpt shown in Figure 7.1.

Stage 1: Deciding on the unit of analysis

Because this analysis is partly quantitative, the very first decision you have to make is what units of analysis will you use? This can be at the level of words, phrases, sentences or paragraphs. Which you choose will be dependent on your research question. For example, if I wanted to find out how many times the lecturers had referred to employability, I could simply look for the word 'employment', which is mentioned four times, but of course I miss phrases which mean the same or alternatives such as 'future careers', but, more crucially, I miss the nuances such as preparing students for employment or helping them acquire graduate skills or giving them opportunities for employment, which could be captured in a longer unit of analysis such as a sentence:

> I think primarily it is to facilitate students acquiring intellectual skills as appropriate for them to leave here and find employment. (Lecturer G)

My own preference has been to go for what I call information units; first described in some research I did in my PhD content analysing examination scripts (Norton and Hartley, 1986). By this I mean a unit that conveys a single discrete concept, thought or idea, which might be expressed in a single word, a phrase, sentence or even a paragraph or two.

Stage 2: Dividing transcript into units of analysis

Taking my information units as the unit of analysis, I now need to divide the transcript as shown in Figure 7.3. which shows the first five transcripts broken down into a total of 25 information units.

Stage 3: Construct categories

This stage is exactly the same as Stages 1–5 in a thematic analysis, as described earlier.

Stage 4: Assign units of analysis to categories (coding)

This is the stage where you have to ensure that all your information units are assigned to one category. It is a fundamental rule in content analysis that no unit can appear in more than one category, nor can any unit remain unassigned to a category. So using my themes and describing them as categories, I am able to assign 20 of the 23 information units as follows.

Developing students' academic abilities
- 'I guess it is about nurturing the students.'
- 'Getting out their best potential. Working on them.'

- 'Finding out where they come from and what they know and to treat them as individuals especially in an institution like this where the students do not come from an HE background attainment.'
- 'I think it is about providing the opportunities for people to develop.'

Engaging with the subject

- 'I think it is about inspiring people.'
- 'I think it is about extending people's interests in what they are interested to a higher level.'

Box 7.3 Five transcripts divided into information units

Lecturer A: 'It depends on the university really. || I guess it is about nurturing the students. || Getting out their best potential. Working on them. || Finding out where they come from and what they know || and to treat them as individuals.'||

Lecturer B: 'There are 3 ways I look at it. || I think it is about inspiring people || especially in an institution like this where the students do not come from a HE background attainment. || You have to inspire people to learn, to read, to question, to rebel, to fit. || I like to think it is about inculcating them in professional values I learnt as a journalist (that was my previous job). || It is a constant evolutionary process of learning for me. || It is about learning information and communicating it to the students.' ||

Lecturer C: 'I think it is about teaching people the skills to carry on learning after university. || To develop skills to problem solve || and analyse things. || I teach a special needs course which is essentially disability studies which is rooted in education.' ||

Lecturer D: 'I think it is about extending people's interests in what they are interested to a higher level. || My view is to get people ready for employment. || To give them graduate level skills and I think university performs that.' ||

Lecturer E: 'I think it is about providing the opportunities for people to develop. || Also to provide the opportunities for employment. || What I do is to prepare people to be teachers. || At the same time, prepare people to be reflective. || And to live more fulfilled lives.' ||

Employment

- 'I like to think it is about inculcating them in professional values I learnt as a journalist (that was my previous job).'
- 'My view is to get people ready for employment.'
- 'To give them graduate-level skills and I think university performs that.'
- 'Also to provide the opportunities for employment.'

- 'What I do is to prepare people to be teachers.'

Transformative effects of higher education

- 'You have to inspire people to learn, to read, to question, to rebel, to fit.'
- 'I think it is about teaching people the skills to carry on learning after university.'
- 'To develop skills to problem solve.'
- 'And analyse things.'
- 'At the same time, prepare people to be reflective'
- 'And to live more fulfilled lives.'

Lecturer's own teacher development

- 'It is a constant evolutionary process of learning for me.'
- 'It is about learning information and communicating it to the students.'

However, having gone through this process of assigning units, I find that I still have three units to allocate, which will not readily fit into any of my existing categories:

- 'It depends on the university really.'
- 'There are three ways I look at it.'
- 'I teach a special-needs course which is essentially disability studies which is rooted in education.'

The first two seem similar and could form another category called 'introductory qualifier', but the third is more to do with the lecturer's own subject influencing her views of education. Reflecting a little more on this, I see some commonality with all three in that they are essentially telling me their personal framework for answering the question, so I now have a sixth category which I have called 'lecturer's personal framework.'

Being unable to code or fit all your units of information is a common occurrence in content analysis, but what you have to be careful about is that new categories do not mushroom. If you find this happening, you have to go back to the stages of deleting and merging until you are left with a manageable number of about 10–15 categories. Because content analysis involves counting units, it is possible to use some measure of inter-rater reliability, as described in Chapter 6, to check whether or not your categories are sufficiently descriptive to allow reasonably consistent allocation.

Stage 5: Calculate the percentage of information units that fall into each category

This is where the quantitative aspect can be applied. Your research question will determine how you do this. In my example, I want to see what proportion of all the lecturers' answers relate to these six categories, which will give me a simple percentage figure as shown in Table 7.1.

Table 7.1 Percentage of total information units (N = 23) in each category, content analysed from responses to the question 'What do you think university teaching is all about?'

Category	N	Percentage
Developing students' academic abilities	5	22
Engaging with the subject	2	9
Employment	5	22
Transformative effects of higher education	6	26
Lecturer's own teacher development	2	9
Lecturer's personal framework	3	13
Total	23	101*

* The total percentages add up to more than 100 because of rounding up.

Interestingly, what this tells me, is that while I thought that these lecturers were actually very focused on employment, the quantitative measure tells me something different, namely that the highest percentage of their comments (26 per cent) related to the transformative effects of higher education (personally, I find this a much more cheering view).

This is the most basic form of quantitative analysis, but I might be interested in looking at the percentage of information units in each category for each lecturer, or I might want to compare them on the basis of the subjects they teach. I could do this by perhaps dividing them into an arts/sciences split, or the number of modules they had completed on the postgraduate certificate programme for learning and teaching in higher education.

To illustrate how this latter suggestion would work, I am going to make up some spurious facts about the five lecturers whose transcripts I have analysed. Let us imagine that lecturers A, B and C have completed the programme (the 'completers') and lecturers D and E are only just beginning (the 'beginners'). I am specifically interested in whether the programme itself has had any effects on their views about the nature of higher education. See Table 7.2 for a comparison of percentages in each category divided into 'completers' and 'beginners'.

Immediately, you can see without doing any statistical analyses that there do appear to be some noticeable differences here. The lecturers who have completed the programme seem to be more diverse in their answers about the nature of higher-education teaching; they are concerned with their own professional development and they see employment as one of the less important elements. The lecturers who have only just begun the programme talk more about employment, with 50 per cent of their responses falling into this category. As far as the transformative effect of higher education is concerned, there seems to be little difference between lecturers who are at the end or the beginning of the programme. This, of course, is a very simple example based on tiny numbers so no statistical comparison is possible, but there are statistical tests that could be applied to these data, and this will be the focus of Chapter 8.

Table 7.2 Comparison of percentages in each category divided into programme completers (15 units) and beginners (8 units)

Category	Completers		Beginners	
	N	Percentage	N	Percentage
Developing students' academic abilities	4	27	1	13
Engaging with the subject	1	7	1	13
Employment	1	7	4	50
Transformative effects of higher education	4	27	2	25
Lecturer's own teacher development	2	13	0	–
Lecturer's personal framework	3	20	0	–
Total	15	101*	8	101*

* The total percentages add up to more than 100 because of rounding up.

Software packages for qualitative analysis

It is possible to use software packages to help you with thematic or content analysis, or any of the other types of qualitative analysis you might want to carry out. Such software cannot do the thinking for you but arguably gives you more time by providing tools to classify and sort your information. Which one to choose is difficult as it is often hard to get unbiased information from the Internet, or from reading the commercial advertisements. The best advice I can give is to seek personal recommendation from a colleague who has used a package and can give you a good idea about what it can do, as well as some of the pros and cons in working with such tools.

Overall summary

As you can see, there are many commonalities between thematic and content analysis. The main differences are that thematic analysis gives you a rich understanding of the topic you are researching from the participant's point of view, whereas content analysis takes a more formulaic objective approach and uses quantitative measures to do so.

In both cases, you have to be scrupulously careful about generating your themes or categories to maintain rigour while maintaining the flexibility that both methods offer. In terms of pedagogical action research, qualitative analysis is particularly effective for gaining an in-depth understanding of the student experience, a strategic mission of the Higher Education Academy. For details of further information on the other types of qualitative analysis that I have mentioned, see the suggestions at the end of this chapter.

Synopsis

- In this chapter I have described two quite closely related methods: thematic analysis (which is commonly used) and content analysis (which also enables you to carry out some basic statistical analyses).
- For both methods I take readers through each stage in the process, using an example from my own research to illustrate this process.
- Throughout the chapter, I have aimed at giving you enough information to start you on a pedagogical action research study that would be of publishable quality.

Further reading and resources for qualitative analysis

Books

Qualitative analysis

Hatch, J.A. (2002). *Doing Qualitative Research in Educational Settings*, Albany, NY: Albany State University, New York Press.

Mason, J. (2002) *Qualitative Researching*, 2nd edn, London: Sage.

Richards, L. (2005) *Handling Qualitative Data: A Practical Guide*, London: Sage.

Silverman, D. (2005) *Doing Qualitative Research: A Practical Handbook*, 2nd edn, London: Sage.

Wolcott, C. (2001) *Writing Up Qualitative Research (Qualitative Research Methods)*, 2nd edn, London: Sage.

Grounded theory

Charmaz, K.C. (2006) *Constructing Grounded Theory: A Practical Guide through Qualitative Analysis: Methods for the 21st Century*, London: Sage.

Strauss, A., and Corbin, J. (1998). *Basics of Qualitative Research: Grounded Theory Procedures and Techniques*, 2nd edn, Newbury Park, CA: Sage.

Content analysis

Krippendorf, K. (2003) *Content Analysis: An Introduction*, 2nd edn, Newbury Park, CA: Sage.

Neuendorf, K.A. (2002) *The Content Analysis Guidebook*, London: Sage.

Weber, R.P. (1990) *Basic Content Analysis (Quantitative Applications in the Social Sciences)*, 2nd edn, Newbury Park, CA: Sage.

Thematic analysis

Boyatzis, R.E. (1998) *Thematic Analysis: Coding as a Process for Transforming Qualitative Information*, Newbury Park, CA: Sage.

Discourse analysis

Potter, J. (1996) 'Discourse analysis and constructionist approaches: Theoretical background', in J.T.E. Richardson (ed.) *Handbook of Qualitative Research Methods for Psychology and the Social Sciences*, Leicester: BPS Books.

Internet resources

Qualitative analysis

British Psychological Society (BPS) (n.d.) *Qualitative Guidelines. Criteria for Evaluating Papers Using Qualitative Research Methods*. Online. Available: http://www.bps.org.uk/publications/journals/joop/qualitative-guidelines.cfm (accessed 27 April 2008).

Grounded theory

Dick, B. (2005) *Grounded Theory: A Thumbnail Sketch*. Online. Available: http://www.scu.edu.au/schools/gcm/ar/arp/grounded.html (accessed 27 April 2008).

Pandit, N.R. (1996) *The creation of theory: A recent application of the grounded theory method*. Qualitative Report, 2(4). Online. Available: http://www.nova.edu/ssss/QR/QR2–4/pandit.html (accessed 27 April 2008).

Content analysis

Stemler, S. (2001) *An overview of content analysis. Practical Assessment, Research and Evaluation*, 7(17). Online. Available: http://pareonline.net/getvn.asp?v=7andn=17 (accessed 27 April 2008).

Semiotics

Chandler, D. (2001) *Semiotics for Beginners*. Online. Available: http://www.aber.ac.uk/media/Documents/S4B/sem12.html (accessed 27 April 2008).

Chapter 8

How can you analyse quantitative data in pedagogical action research?

Introduction

In many action research studies, quantitative analysis would be seen as inappropriately positivist, as discussed in Chapter 4; but for those of you who would like to undertake research that produces quantifiable results, I have described some basic statistical analyses.

When is quantitative analysis appropriate?

Quantitative analysis is useful in pedagogical action research studies where the method is:

- an experiment;
- an attitude scale or questionnaire;
- an observation study which involves counting;
- one that produces any information that is quantifiable (age ranges, number of years teaching etc.).

Regardless of the research method, there are two types of quantitative analysis: statistics for description and statistics for drawing conclusions (known as inferential statistics which I will discuss later). Sometimes you will want to include both.

Descriptive statistics

These are used when you want to present succinctly what your data (information) shows. In the content analysis example described in Chapter 7, for example, it is difficult to get a feel for the importance of the different categories just by looking at the transcripts. In this particular case, examining the codings would actually have given us a pretty good idea, but this is because we were dealing with only 23 information units, but imagine 2,300 or even 23,000 units and it soon becomes clear why we need some way of summarising a large body of information.

Descriptive statistics include measures of central tendency or averages (mean, median and mode), measures of dispersion or variability (range, mean deviation and standard deviation) and frequency counts.

I will use the Dr Jones vignette to explore each of these in a little more detail.

Measures of central tendency

The mean (average)

This is the most commonly used measure and one that we use in our everyday lives. Dr Jones asked her students 'How many hours a week do you read the given readings on childhood disabilities?'. Remembering that there are 80 students in her class, an average would clearly be a useful way of summarising these data. To avoid presenting large quantities of hypothetical data, I have made up numbers for Table 8.1, representing 20 students, to illustrate these statistics.

Before you do anything else, it is always a good idea to have a really hard look at your data (sometimes known as 'eyeballing' the data), as this will enable you to make sense of any statistical techniques you carry out.

As you can see from Table 8.1, the commonest number of hours spent reading that appears to be 1 and the other students do slightly more than

Table 8.1   Raw data on weekly hours spent reading from Dr Jones' research

Student	Hours reading
A	6
B	1
C	1
D	1
E	2
F	1
G	4
H	3
I	2
J	1
K	5
L	1
M	1
N	3
O	4
P	1
Q	12
R	2
S	3
T	1
Total	55

this, all in the range of 2–6 hours. The student who stands out, however, is student Q who claims to do 12 hours a week reading just for this module. We will keep student Q in mind as we proceed.

The mean is calculated by adding up the total number of hours spent reading each student has claimed (55), divided by the total number of students (20), which gives us an average of 2.75 hours a week. This would seem fairly reasonable, given this is only one module that these sports students study. However student Q's claim of 12 hours of reading has grossly inflated the total. This is called an outlier score, and what it means is that, in this case, the mean is not a helpful measure for Dr Jones to consider as it does not represent an accurate picture of what all her students are doing.

CONCLUSION

The mean is very useful for summarising large numbers of scores in a single score. It can be used safely when scores cluster closely together, but is misleading when they are spread out.

The median

This is the midpoint of a range of scores and is obtained by arranging your scores in order of size and then finding out which number falls in the middle. This is the median.

In Dr Jones' study there is an even number of scores so she has to take the average of the two middle scores, which in this case are the same. The median is 2 (i.e. {(2 + 2)/2}).

1 1 1 1 1 1 1 1 1 **2 2** 2 3 3 3 4 4 5 6 12

CONCLUSION

The median is very simple to calculate if you have a small number of scores. Its other advantage is that the size of the outlier does not affect the measure. If, however, you have a very large number of scores, finding the median soon becomes a very tedious process (even Dr Jones' 80 students seems too much to contemplate).

The mode

This is the most frequently occurring score in a set of scores. In our example, you find it by counting the most frequently occurring score, which would be 1. Sometimes you get scores where two or more scores occur equally frequently in which case you have a bimodal or trimodal measure.

CONCLUSION

The mode is another easy measure of central tendency involving a simple count of the score/s that occur most frequently. It is not so useful when there is more than one group of frequently occurring scores, as it is not a representative single figure.

Summary

Dr Jones now has three measures to represent her students' weekly reading hours:

- a mean of 2.75 hours;
- a median of 2 hours;
- a mode of 1 hour.

In this case she may prefer to use the median and the mode as being the most representative single-figure measures of her students' reading time, but because student Q's time is not represented, Dr Jones may wish to go on and look at measures of variability as well.

Measures of variability (dispersion)

In order to give herself a more accurate picture of her students' reading habits, Dr Jones needs to be able to indicate how widely spread their scores are.

The range

This is easily calculated by subtracting the smallest score from the largest (12–1), so the range of students' weekly reading hours is 11.

CONCLUSION

This is a very simple measure to calculate and has the benefit of taking student Q's extraordinary score into account, but this also means you have a somewhat distorted picture. In its simplicity, you do not get a sense of how many students had small or large scores because it does not take all the scores into account.

The mean deviation

This is a number that indicates how much, on average, the scores differ from the mean score. The larger the mean deviation, the greater is the spread of scores.
   It is calculated by taking the following steps (adapted from Clegg, 1983).

Step 1:
Compare each score with the mean score.

$$1 - 2.75 = -1.75$$
$$1 - 2.75 = -1.75$$
$$1 - 2.75 = -1.75$$
$$1 - 2.75 = -1.75$$
$$1 - 2.75 = -1.75$$
$$1 - 2.75 = -1.75$$
$$1 - 2.75 = -1.75$$
$$1 - 2.75 = -1.75$$
$$1 - 2.75 = -1.75$$
$$1 - 2.75 = -1.75$$
$$2 - 2.75 = -0.75$$
$$2 - 2.75 = -0.75$$
$$3 - 2.75 = 0.25$$
$$3 - 2.75 = 0.25$$
$$3 - 2.75 = 0.25$$
$$4 - 2.75 = 1.25$$
$$4 - 2.75 = 1.25$$
$$5 - 2.75 = 2.25$$
$$6 - 2.75 = 3.25$$
$$12 - 2.75 = 9.25$$

Step 2:
Add the differences found in Step 3 (but ignore the signs).

$$1.75 \times 9 = 15.75$$
$$0.75 \times 3 = 2.25$$
$$0.25 \times 3 = 0.75$$
$$1.25 \times 2 = 2.50$$
$$2.25 \times 1 = 2.25$$
$$3.25 \times 1 = 3.25$$
$$9.25 \times 1 = 9.25$$
Total = 36.0

Step 3:
Divide the total found in Step 2 by the number of scores.

{36.0/20} = 1.8

The mean deviation is 1.8 weekly hours reading.

CONCLUSION

The mean deviation is a more stable measure of dispersion than the range as it is calculated using all the scores, whereas the range is just based on two. It is however, a measure that is not much used, because it is a very simple figure and does not have any powerful mathematical properties, unlike the standard deviation.

If you want to read further about the mean deviation, Gorard (2004) has written an interesting paper making a reasoned case for why it should be used more.

The standard deviation

This is similar to the mean deviation but is calculated differently, by using the square root of the variance. This is quite a complicated formula, and there is no need to do it by hand as it is easily done using a scientific calculator or in the Microsoft Office spreadsheet Excel.

The standard deviation is related to the normal distribution which is where the mean, the median and the mode are all the same or very close in value and scores are spread evenly above and below the central value. If you get more scores below the central value, it is called a positively skewed distribution (as is the case with the reading hours example). If there are more scores above the central value, it is called a negatively skewed distribution.

A very large standard deviation, which would be one that was larger than the mean, would indicate a great deal of variability in your scores. If this occurs, you may have to be cautious in any statistical tests you use. Parametric tests, which are more powerful, should only be used when the distributions are normal and the standard deviations are roughly similar, otherwise it is safer to use non-parametric tests. For example, if Dr Jones found in her experiment comparing a group who took part in the electronic discussion forum (group A) with the group who took part in the extra reading (group B) that the standard deviations in the exam results were much larger in group B than in group A and did not show a normal distribution, she would be better advised to use non-parametric statistics. This distinction is described more fully later in this chapter.

CONCLUSION

The standard deviation is the most commonly accepted measure of dispersion as it has mathematical properties and is one of the indicators for choosing an appropriate statistical test.

Frequency counts

This is possibly the simplest method of descriptive statistics and it is useful for displaying your results in a summarised form. This might be in a bar chart or a pie chart, depending on your preference.

Let us take an example from Dr Jones' questionnaire in which one item was:

'We are expected to learn the topics ourselves.'

The responses using a Likert scale were:

Strongly agree (SA)
Agree (A)
Unsure (U)
Disagree (D)
Strongly disagree (SD)

To illustrate how this will work, I have again made up a table of responses to represent the answers of Dr Jones' class. See Table 8.2.

Just looking at such a large number of responses makes it difficult to see what the majority response was, but we might, however, get a sense that the strongly agree response was most often mentioned.

Calculating frequency scores for these data will give us a much clearer idea and can be displayed as a bar chart as shown in Figure 8.1 or as a pie chart as shown in Figure 8.2.

Immediately we can see that actually the picture is a little more complicated than we might have at first thought by just looking at Table 8.2 of the results. Although the 'strongly agree' response occurs the most frequently, if we were to add the 'agree' categories (14) together with the 'strongly agree' categories (26) we would get a total of 40, which is 50 per cent of the total number of responses.

Effectively, this means that only half of Dr Jones' students actually agree that they are expected to learn the topic themselves. 30 per cent of her students disagree (12 strongly disagree + 12 disagree) and the other 20 per cent are unsure (16). This presents a somewhat different picture that Dr Jones may well wish to reflect on.

Table 8.2 Raw data in response to the questionnaire item 'We are expected to learn the topic ourselves.'

Student	Response	Student	Response
1	SA	41	A
2	SA	42	U
3	SD	43	D
4	A	44	SA
5	U	45	SA
6	SA	46	U
7	D	47	SA
8	SA	48	SD
9	A	49	SA
10	A	50	SD
11	D	51	SA
12	U	52	A
13	A	53	U
14	U	54	SA
15	A	55	D
16	D	56	D
17	SA	57	U
18	D	58	SA
19	A	59	SA
20	SD	60	A
21	SA	61	D
22	SA	62	SD
23	SA	63	SA
24	SA	64	D
25	U	65	SA
26	SD	66	U
27	U	67	SD
28	SD	68	SA
29	SA	69	U
30	SD	70	D
31	U	71	SA
32	SA	72	U
33	D	73	SD
34	D	74	A
35	SA	75	A
36	SD	76	A
37	SD	77	U
38	A	78	U
39	U	79	SA
40	A	80	SA

Conclusion

Frequency scores are a useful way of summarising data relatively easily and they are immediately accessible to an audience who might not be mathematically orientated.

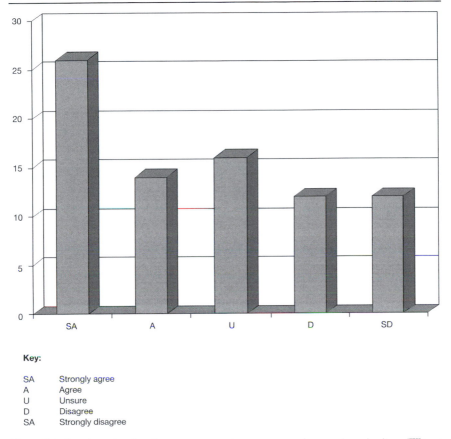

Key:

SA	Strongly agree
A	Agree
U	Unsure
D	Disagree
SA	Strongly disagree

Figure 8.1 Bar chart showing frequency count in response to the questionnaire item 'We are expected to learn the topics ourselves'

Summary

Descriptive statistics offer a clear way of presenting the results of your action research. They have the advantage of being relatively easy to calculate either by hand, or by using a calculator or Excel.

However, there are studies when you want to go beyond describing your data in order to give a cause and effect explanation. This is where inferential statistics are needed.

Inferential statistics

This type of statistical analysis goes beyond the level of description and attempts to draw some conclusions from the data that you have collected. Specifically, this type of analysis would be used when you are testing hypotheses; for example,

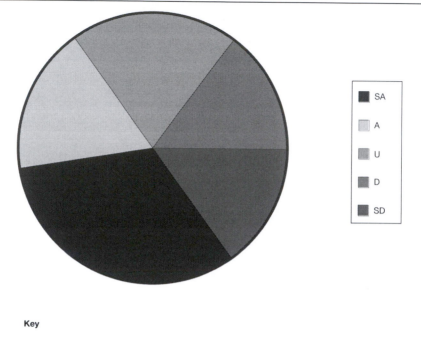

Key

SA   Strongly agree
A   Agree
U   Unsure
D   Disagree
SD   Strongly disagree

Figure 8.2 Pie chart showing frequency count in response to the questionnaire item 'We are expected to learn the topics ourselves'

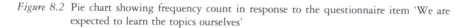

by making predictions such as looking to see if a teaching intervention improves student learning.

There are many inferential statistics, but I am going to concentrate on three main types: tests for correlations, tests for differences in means (from paired and independent scores) and tests for goodness of fit.

Before I do this though, I need to briefly explain the concept of probability and of significance testing, and the broad differences between parametric and non-parametric tests. This is not intended to replace any of the excellent statistics textbooks that are readily available, and some of which I mention at the end of this chapter, but is a basic outline of the most salient points you need to be aware of when designing and analysing your own pedagogical action research studies.

Probability and testing for statistical significance

When researchers use statistical tests they are following a convention to establish the significance of their research findings. 'Significance' in statistical terminology has a precise meaning, which is to do with probability. Very simply it means to what extent we can be confident that the results we have obtained in our investigations have not occurred by complete chance.

In statistics, the level of significance is expressed in terms of a decimal fraction where:

- 0.05 means there is a 5 per cent probability (i.e. one in twenty) that your results arose by chance;
- 0.01 means there is a 1 per cent probability (i.e. one in a hundred) that your results arose by chance;
- 0.001 means there is a 0.1 per cent probability (i.e. one in a thousand) that your results arose by chance;
- 0.0001 means there is a 0.01 per cent probability (i.e. one in ten thousand) that your results arose by chance; and so on.

For the purposes of most social science and educational research, these four levels of probability are commonly accepted as conventions. In cases where human life might be at stake such as in drug testing, for example, the levels of probability accepted as statistically significant are quite rightly much lower (0.000,01, for example). When presenting tables of results, a lower case 'p' represents probability together with the symbol ' < ' which means lower or smaller. The symbol ' > ' means higher or larger.

$p < 0.05$ means that your results are statistically significant beyond the five per cent level of chance, and
$p > 0.05$ means your results are not statistically significant at the five per cent level of chance.

Choosing a parametric or non-parametric test

There are differences of opinion among the statisticians as to whether or not this distinction is important, but when I learned my statistics in my psychology degree, I was taught that it did matter, and so it has stayed with me ever since. Basically, parametric tests are advised when a number of criteria apply, otherwise you are supposed to use non-parametric tests, which are less powerful but do not need such stringent criteria.

As a general rule of thumb, use parametric tests when:

- Data/scores have a true numerical value. By this I mean measures such as length (e.g. centimetres) or weight, (e.g. kilograms), where the differences between the values are the same (sometimes referred to as interval and ratio measurements). When measuring length we know that 8 cm is exactly twice the length of 4 cm. When measuring weight, we know that 6 kg is exactly three times the weight of 2 kg. This enables us to apply mathematical formulae to the data in a way that we cannot do when the measures do not have a true numerical value.

- The spread of scores in your sample/s are clustered around the mean or measures of central tendency (sometimes this is known as homogeneity).
- Your sample size/s are large and roughly equal (e.g. you were attempting to compare exam results from a group of 100 students with another group of 110 students).

Use non-parametric statistics when:

- Data do not have a true numerical value such as that produced by Likert scales where SA = 5, A = 4, U = 3, D = 2 and SD = 1. (This is known as an ordinal measurement where the numbers do not have any mathematical properties.) Here we have no idea at all if the difference of 1 between SA (5) and A (4) is exactly the same as the difference of 1 between D (2) and SD (1), nor could we possibly claim that the score of 4 for A somehow counts twice as much as the score of 2 for D. It has to be said, though, that many researchers do not bother with these finer distinctions and will quite readily use parametric statistics on data produced from questionnaires.
- The spread of your scores indicates a large variability.
- Your sample size/s are small, or unequal (e.g. you were attempting to compare exam results from a group of ten students with another group of 100 students).

Basically my advice is that if you are in any doubt about whether to use parametric or non-parametric tests in your research, it is better to err on the side of caution and use the non-parametric version.

Having briefly described the basic principles of statistical testing, I want to begin this section on inferential statistics by looking at correlation tests.

Correlation tests

We have already looked at correlational research briefly in Chapter 6 when I said it was more of a statistical test than a research method. This ambiguity also relates to whether it is considered as a descriptive or inferential statistic; in fact, it can be both. As I said earlier, even if you obtain a strong correlation, this does not mean that there is a causal relationship, although were you to carry out several correlational studies and the same strong relationship emerged, then you can use them as a satisfactory experimental investigation.

Correlations can also be used to make predictions about scores, a well-known one being the assumed relationship between A-level performance and degree performance, on which we base our admissions policy to higher education.

You will remember from Chapter 6 that Dr Jones was interested in the relationship between the number of lectures her students attended and their exam performance.

The scattergram (see Figure 6.2) indicated a fairly strong positive correlation, but we cannot tell from a scattergram alone, if this relationship is statistically significant or not.

Calculating correlations

Normally, if you have a large number of paired scores (or variables) to correlate I would advise you to use a statistical package, but it is possible to do it by hand and most basic statistics textbooks will show you how.

Spearman's rho and Pearson's product moment correlation coefficient

There are two commonly used statistical tests for correlational analysis: either Spearman's rho, which is a non-parametric test and works on ranking each of the two variables rather than their actual values, or Pearson's product moment correlation coefficient which is the parametric equivalent and does use actual numerical values.

Aside from the criteria outlined above, there is another reason why you might choose Spearman's rho. This is if your scattergram shows that there is not a straightforward linear relationship, but more of a curvilinear one.

Provided your sample shows a reasonably normal distribution, you have used interval or ratio data and your scattergram suggests a linear relationship, Pearson's product moment correlation coefficient would be the better test to use as it provides a more precise correlation coefficient and like all parametric tests it is more powerful (meaning it is more likely to detect a significant relationship).

To illustrate the difference I have ignored all the criteria and carried out both tests on Dr Jones' raw data shown in Table 6.3. I have also looked up the statistical significance of these findings in significance tables (often called tables of critical values) in a textbook. Most statistics textbooks have these, but it is also possible to look up significance tables on the Internet.

This gives me a Spearman's rho of 0.837, which is statistically significant ($p < 0.01$), and a Pearson's correlation coefficient of 0.868, which, although slightly larger, is still statistically significant at the same level of probability ($p < 0.01$). You will remember that a correlation of 1.0 would be a perfect association between the two variables and a correlation of 0 would be no relationship at all between the two variables, so the nearer the statistical value is to 1.00 the more significant it will be.

Because this is such a very small sample (only 13 students) we need a high correlation coefficient to reach significance. If, for example, we had used the data from all of Dr Jones' 80 students, we would have reached the same level of significance with 0.283.

Conclusion

Correlation tests show the strength of the relationship between two factors (variables). When in doubt about which correlation test to choose, it is safer to use Spearman's test and the more paired variables you have the better.

Tests of difference for repeated measures (paired variables)

These are used for when you are looking for significant differences between two sets of scores from the same people.

The sign test (S)

This is a very simple test, which can easily be calculated by hand but which is sometimes forgotten about in this day and age of sophisticated computer analysis. I mention it here because it can be very useful in observation studies, questionnaire studies or any investigation where you obtain a limited number of paired variables.

Let us take Dr Jones' data in Table 6.3 and imagine that she wants to find out if her students attend lectures more often than seminars. This is a repeated measures design as there are two scores from each student. The steps in calculating the sign test are again adapted from Clegg (1983).

Step 1:
Mentally subtract the value of seminar attendance away from the value of lecture attendance, giving each a + sign or a – sign, or 0 if there is no difference:

Student	Lectures attended	Seminars attended	Sign
1	15	10	+
2	12	2	+
3	15	4	+
4	14	9	+
5	8	6	+
6	6	14	–
7	5	8	–
8	4	1	+
9	4	13	–
10	3	11	–
11	5	3	+
12	6	7	–
13	2	5	–

Step 2:
Count the number of times the less-frequent sign occurs, which gives you your S statistic of 6.

Step 3:
Count the number of pluses and minuses to give you an N (take away any 0 differences) of 13.
Step 4:
Consult a table of significance in a statists textbook. For an N of 13 and an S of 6, this is not statistically significant, $p > 0.05$. This is not surprising, given that the signs were almost equally divided. To have reached significance at the lowest level of probability for this small sample, S would have had to have been 3 or less.

Another example of how this test works can be applied to my content analysis data shown in Table 7.2 where in comparing the responses of lecturers who had completed the programme with lecturers who had not, I might hypothesise that I would obtain a greater number of information units from the 'completers' as they have more experience and pedagogical language to articulate their views.

A quick look at this table shows that this does indeed seem to be the case, but how statistically significant is it? Doing the calculations, I have 5 plus signs, 1 minus sign (this is the S statistic) and 1 no difference, which gives me an N of 6. But for this to be statistically significant, I would need an S of 0. Basically, if you have a very small sample as I did, you have to have all the differences in the same direction to be statistically significant.

CONCLUSION

The sign test is simple to calculate and can be useful when you want to carry out a statistical test on paired variables which may not necessarily be derived from an experimental design.

Wilcoxon matched pairs test

A more sophisticated and powerful test to use when testing for differences between paired variables is the Wilcoxon matched pairs test, sometimes known as the Wilcoxon matched pairs signed rank test.

As its name suggests, it works by calculating the differences between each set of pairs, and then ranking them. Then it sums the ranks and compares the two. If the two sums of ranks is large, then the lower the probability level (meaning the more statistically significant it is). Because it works by ranking or ordering data, it is a non-parametric test.

To illustrate this test, I will take the simplest of Dr Jones' repeated measure designs discussed in Chapter 6 where she was interested in testing her hypothesis that the electronic discussion forum would help improve exam performance. The design is simple. Let us suppose that she takes a baseline measure of their exam performance, which becomes the pre-intervention exam score. She then encourages the students to take part in the online discussion forum before their final exam, which becomes the post-intervention measure.

The data she might obtain are presented in Table 8.3. To keep things simple, I have just made up data for 15 students; I have also identified them by name as I want to comment on individual students after I present the outcome of the Wilcoxon test.

Using a statistical package such as SPSS (Statistical Package for the Social Sciences) to compute this statistic, gives us a Z score of -3.215, p < 0.001. (The minus sign simply indicates that it is based on the negative rankings; had the positive rankings been greater, the Z score would have been +.)

Looking at the raw data in Table 8.3 you can see clearly that all the post-intervention exam marks were higher after the intervention, with the exception of two students, Charlene and Jim, whose marks were the same (known as tied scores).

To present your results, I would suggest devising a simple table from the SPSS output as shown in Table 8.4.

This is a very pleasing result, but what the Wilcoxon test does not do is to take into account the size of the differences in the students' exam marks (see, for example, Joe, who has improved by 14 marks, Jane by 23 marks and Sarah by a massive leap of 27 marks, yet most of the other students make only modest improvements, which they might have made anyway).

Student's t-test

Such fineness of detail is lost when you carry out a non-parametric test based on ranking scores. I now want to show you what happens if I use the

Table 8.3 Comparison of examination performance before and after the electronic discussion intervention

Student	Pre-intervention exam	Post-intervention exam
Adam	55	58
Ben	45	48
Colin	62	65
Charlene	52	52
Grace	48	52
Tim	58	65
Pete	42	45
Jim	38	38
Joe	48	62
Jane	42	65
Mark	52	55
Sarah	58	85
Harry	42	45
Lenny	45	52
Ray	52	58

Table 8.4 Results of Wilcoxon test comparing exam performance before and after the electronic discussion forum

Rankings	N	Mean rank
Post intervention: Negative ranking[a]	0	0.000
Pre intervention: Positive ranking[b]	13	7.00
Number of tied rankings	2	
Total	15	

[a]Post-intervention ranking is smaller than pre-intervention ranking
[b]Post-intervention ranking is larger than pre-intervention ranking
Test statistic $Z = -3.215$ (based on negative ranks), $p < 0.001$

parametric version, the rather confusingly named Student's t-test (nothing to do with students but a pseudonym chosen by its creator William Gosset). Nowadays it is more commonly referred to simply as the t-test.

There are two versions: the t-test for related (repeated) measures and the t-test for independent groups, which I discuss a little later. The t-test for related measures works by calculating the means and the distribution of scores around the means for both conditions, see Table 8.5.

Here we can see right away that the mean exam performance after the intervention is larger than it was before the intervention (56.3 as opposed to 49.3), but we can also see that the standard deviations for each condition differ, which means that there is a much larger spread in exam marks after the intervention than there was before, which is why we should really choose the non-parametric test. However, using a t-test still gives us a statistically significant result of $p < 0.01$, but not quite as significant as the Wilcoxon test.

What neither test tell us is why some students did really well, others improved only slightly and two not at all. This is the limitation of all inferential statistics and is one of the reasons why I think we need a combination of qualitative and quantitative analysis (see Appendix C). Imagine what an interesting study Dr Jones could do if she used these findings to carry out a second cycle of action research to interview the students about

Table 8.5 Results of student t-test for related measures comparing exam performance before and after the electronic discussion forum

Condition	N	Mean	SD
Pre-intervention	15	49.3	7.0
Post-intervention	15	56.3	11.4

$t = -3.397$, df = 14*, $p < 0.004$ (conventionally reported as $p < 0.01$)
* df stands for degrees of freedom, which refers to the total number of scores from your samples that have to be known to fill in any missing scores, given that you have the overall total. It is calculated as the total number of scores making up both samples minus 1.

their perceptions of the electronic discussion task and whether or not they felt it had affected their exam performance.

Conclusion

Testing for differences between paired variables can be done very simply with the sign test if you do not have too many scores to deal with. For larger numbers, it is preferable to use the non-parametric Wilcoxon test or its parametric equivalent; the Student's t-test.

Tests of difference for independent groups

The second type of inferential test that I want to look at is concerned with analysing differences between groups.

The Mann–Whitney U test

This is the most commonly used non-parametric test of difference when you have independent groups and it can be applied to groups of uneven sizes. It works by ranking, so it can be used when your samples are very small and/or if the distribution of scores is not normally distributed. It can be calculated by hand but there are plenty of statistical packages that will do it for you. Its parametric equivalent is the t-test for independent groups, which works by dividing the difference between group means by the variability of groups. The formula for calculating it is quite complex, so I would always use SPSS.

In Dr Jones' case, she could choose to test her hypothesis that the electronic discussion forum would help improve exam performance by comparing it with another condition rather than choosing repeated measures as discussed above. The hypothesis will have to be formally stated:

> 'Students who prepare for seminars by taking part in an electronic discussion forum will perform better in the exam than students who prepare by extra individual reading without discussion.'

I have made up some more scores to illustrate how both tests work (see Table 8.6).

I will again ignore assumptions about the data and use both the non-parametric Mann–Whitney test and the parametric t-test on SPSS. When entering the data on SPSS, on the view that says 'variables', you will need to put both groups' data into the first column headed exam performance, and for the second column give a 1 to group A and a 2 to group B. (This is because SPSS works on what it calls a grouping variable for independent groups, rather than on two separate columns representing each of your groups.)

Table 8.6 Comparison of exam performance between groups with different interventions

Group A: discussion forum	Group B: extra reading
65	48
58	55
62	78
85	55
72	52
65	58
78	52
62	62
65	48
62	58
72	68
68	65
55	58
78	58
42	45
52	55
58	38
68	45
65	42
78	58
65	48
58	55
62	78
85	55
72	52
65	58
78	52
65	62
65	48
62	58
72	68
68	65
55	58
78	58
42	45
52	55
58	38
68	45
65	42
78	58

The Mann–Whitney U test resulted in a U value of 326, which is significant (p < 0.0001).

The t-test resulted in a t value of 4.968, which is significant (p < 0.0001).

As before, I suggest making a table where you can report what you need, see Tables 8.7 and 8.8.

Perhaps, not surprisingly, the two tests come up with a level of significance that is the same. Looking at Table 8.8. we can see that the standard deviations are similar and the sample size is reasonably large, so the parametric test would have been perfectly appropriate in this case.

Dr Jones' hypothesis is supported, so what might this mean to her in terms of her action research? The first thing to note is that she has a finding which suggests she should modify her teaching to ensure that all her students take part in the electronic discussion forum. In terms of an action research cycle, she may now want to look at coursework, to see if a electronic discussion forum has the same beneficial effect, and report her findings at a learning and teaching conference; or she may wish to use this as a pilot study to use as a basis for seeking some external funding. Action research is often collaborative, so another course of action for Dr Jones to consider is to present her findings to colleagues in her department to see if others are interested in developing and researching the electronic discussion forum.

Conclusion

When comparing the scores from two independent groups, you have the choice of the Mann–Whitney (non-parametric) or the t-test for independent

Table 8.7 Comparison of exam performance between electronic discussion and extra reading using Mann Whitney

Group	N	Mean rank
Electronic discussion	40	52.35
Extra reading	40	28.65

Mann Whitney U = 326, $p < 0.0000$* (conventionally reported as p < 0.0001)
*In SPSS it is actually reported as 0.000 which means it is more significant than the four conventional levels of significance used in social science and educational research.

Table 8.8 Comparison of exam performance between electronic discussion and extra reading using Student's t-test

Group	Mean exam score	Standard deviation
Electronic discussion	65.58	9.96
Extra reading	54.90	9.24

Student's $t = 4.968$, df = 78**, $p < 0.0001$
**df stands for degrees of freedom, which refers to the total number of scores from your samples that have to be known to fill in any missing scores, given that you have the overall total. It is calculated as the total number of scores making up both samples minus 1.

groups (parametric). Either test is best carried out using a statistical package although it is possible to calculate them by hand.

Tests of goodness of fit

Finally in this chapter I want to discuss the goodness of fit tests. These tests are somewhat different from the ones I have already described in that they can be used in situations where you do not have measures or scores, but simply observations or categories.

Chi-square

The most commonly used goodness of fit test is chi-square (χ^2), which is particularly useful when carrying out observation studies or for other studies where you are simply getting categorical data (for example simple yes/no answers in a questionnaire study). The usual way of dealing with these data is to put them into what is called a contingency table and then, using chi-square, you can work out if your observed values are significantly different from values you would expect to have happened by chance.

Let us suppose Dr Jones has carried out an observation study to test her hypothesis that:

'Students ask questions for further information more frequently in seminars than in lectures, where they tend to ask more questions for clarification'.

She carries out this observation over the course of ten lectures and ten seminars, and then puts her results into a two by two contingency table (see Table 8.9).

Because this is an easy test to calculate by hand, I will describe the steps (again, adapted from Clegg, 1983), but the test is also available on SPSS.

Step 1:
To calculate the expected frequency for each of the four cells, multiply the row total with the column total and divide by the overall N.

Cell A: $\{(77 \times 40)/107\} = 28.8$

Table 8.9 Contingency table based on type of questions raised in lectures and seminars

Type of question	Lectures	Seminars	Total
Further information	(Cell A) 21	(Cell B) 56	77
Seeks clarification	(Cell C) 19	(Cell D) 11	30
Total	40	67	107

Cell B: {(77 × 67)/107} = 48.2

Cell C: {(30 × 40)/107} = 11.2

Cell D: {(30 × 67)/107} = 18.8

Step 2:
Find the difference between the observed (recorded) frequency and the expected frequency (taking the smaller from the larger) and then subtract 0.5.

Cell A: 28.8 − 21 − 0.5 = 7.3

Cell B: 56 − 48.2 − 0.5 = 7.3

Cell C: 19 − 11.2 − 0.5 = 7.3

Cell D: 18.8 − 11 − 0.5 = 7.3

Step 3:
Square each of the values obtained in Step 2 and divide the answer by the expected frequency for the cell.

Cell A: $\{7.32^2/28.8\}$ = 1.85

Cell B: $\{7.32^2/48.2\}$ = 1.11

Cell C: $\{7.32^2/11.2\}$ = 4.76

Cell D: $\{7.32^2/18.8\}$ = 2.83

Step 4:
Add the four values obtained in Step 3 to give you the value of chi-square (χ^2).

1.85 + 1.11 + 4.76 + 2.83 gives you χ^2 = 10.55

Step 5:
You have to consult a statistics textbook for the significance levels for chi square, which must be equal or bigger than the stated value, but since the degrees of freedom in a simple chi-square are always 1, I have presented the χ^2 value needed to be significant here at the following levels of significance.

0.05	0.01	0.001
3.841	6.635	10.83

Looking at our χ^2 value of 10.55, we can see that it is not quite large enough to be significant at the highest level ($p < 0.001$). Therefore we conclude that it is significant beyond the 0.01 level ($p < 0.01$).

What this test does not tell you, however, is where the significant differences lie. Like correlations tests, goodness of fit tests do not imply causation, so all we can conclude here is that proportionately fewer questions asking for further information and proportionately more questions asking for clarification were made in lectures than in seminars, so Dr Jones' hypothesis is supported. Chi-square is also available to take care of multiple observations, known as complex chi-square, which is usually best calculated on a computer.

CONCLUSION

Goodness of fit tests such as chi-square are useful for establishing if there are significant differences between categories of data.

Overall summary

The basic tests described here will carry you a long way with your pedagogical action research, and, as I have demonstrated, they can actually be calculated yourself with the aid of a good simple textbook like Clegg (1983).

Throughout, my intention has been to give you enough knowledge to carry out a publishable action research study. By tackling your research in this way, using simple statistics first, you can pick up more sophisticated knowledge and understanding as you become more experienced and confident. In this digital age, there is a great temptation to go for the most sophisticated analysis possible. In my view, it is much better to choose a simple statistical method that you really understand and can report with confidence when you are embarking on pedagogical action research.

Synopsis

- In this chapter I have presented the most commonly used descriptive statistics, describing the basic measures of central tendency, dispersion and frequency counts.
- In drawing the distinction between descriptive and inferential statistics, I have briefly touched on the basic principles of statistical testing, specifically testing for significance and probability, as well as giving some basic guidelines for helping you choose whether to use a parametric or a non-parametric test.
- I then describe the three main types of inferential statistics: correlation tests, test of differences in means and tests of goodness of fit. Where I think the tests are reasonably easy to calculate by hand, I have presented a step-by-step procedure. In other cases, I refer readers to statistical software packages such as SPSS.

Further reading and resources for quantitative analysis

Books

Field, A. (2005) *Discovering Statistics Using SPSS (Introducing Statistical Methods Series)*, 2nd edn, London: Sage.

Field, A and Hole, G.J. (2002) *How to Design and Report Experiments*, London: Sage,

Heiman, G.W. (2003) *Essential Statistics for the Behavioral Sciences*, Boston, MA: Houghton Mifflin.

Rowntree, D. (1991) *Statistics Without Tears: An Introduction for Non-Mathematicians*, London: Penguin Books.

Salkind, N.J. (2004) *Statistics for People Who (Think They) Hate Statistics*, 2nd edn, London: Sage.

Chapter 9

How can you develop and adapt pedagogical research tools?

Introduction

Wherever possible in carrying out your pedagogical action research study, it is a good idea to use instruments that are already published, and there are a good many of them that are readily available, such as the Approaches and Study Skills Inventory for Students (ASSIST), the Assessment Experience Questionnaire (AEQ) and the Approaches to Teaching Inventory (ATI), although sometimes it can be laborious to track down the latest version. Others, such as the Reflections on Learning Inventory (RoLI©) and the Reasoning about Current Issues (RCI) Test, require fees. In all cases you need to acknowledge the authors of the instruments that you are using and cite where they are published.

However, by their nature, existing measures are not designed for your own specific pedagogical action research study, so the purpose of this chapter is to describe how you can develop and adapt your own tools to address your specific research issues. The chapter begins with a section in which I describe three of my own questionnaire-based research tools, the Ideal *** Inventory, the Learning Objectives Questionnaire (LOQ) and the Essay Feedback Checklist (EFC), which you are welcome to use and adapt.

In the second and third sections I draw on my own experience in carrying out pedagogical action research to illustrate how you can adapt both quantitative and qualitative instruments that have been published. In the further resources section at the end of this chapter, I give information on how to access some of the better-known and widely used questionnaires for those readers who would prefer to use established instruments.

Questionnaire-based research tools

A generic pedagogical research tool: The Ideal *** Inventory

I want to begin this chapter with describing a very simple generic research tool, known as the Ideal *** Inventory, that is easily adaptable for pedagogical action research.

Background

An earlier brief description of this tool can be found on the Higher Education Academy's website (Norton, 2001a). It originated as the Ideal Self Inventory (Norton, Morgan and Thomas, 1995), which was designed as an alternative to the published self-esteem questionnaires by providing a constructivist measure of what respondents themselves thought were salient to their self-esteem. Since its original formulation, the Ideal Self Inventory has been used in research in higher education and is now called the Ideal *** Inventory in which the stars are simply meant to represent the topic of investigation.

The original idea for the basic design drew on principles of Kelly's (1955) personal construct theory by asking respondents to describe their ideal self in terms of what they personally thought was important to them. As such, it was a variation of the self-grid used by Button (1994), who asked people to elicit constructs and then to rate themselves using the concepts of 'present self' and 'ideal self'.

In our version we used a variant of the Osgood semantic differential scale to ask participants to generate characteristics using two poles: the 'ideal self' and the 'not-ideal self'. The distinctive feature of the Ideal Self Inventory was that not only did participants decide for themselves what features were salient to them in relation to self-esteem, but they were also asked to rate themselves in terms of where they actually felt themselves to be on each dimension. See Figure 9.1.

Using the Ideal Self Inventory in this way enables you to get a qualitative measure in terms of the dimensions the participant generates, which might tell you something interesting about how that individual conceptualises self-esteem. In the example given in Figure 9.1, this particular individual is concerned with intelligence, taking a conscientious approach to life, being contented and confident – and being slim.

The inventory also yields two quantitative measures, an overall self-esteem score and scores for each of the dimensions. In Figure 9.1 the individual has a total score of 18 out of a possible 25, and so would seem fairly high in self-esteem.

Ideal Self	5	4	3	2	1	Not ideal self
Intelligent and quick to grasp things		✓				Stupid and slow learning
Slim	✓					Fat
Conscientious	✓					Couldn't care less
Contented with life			✓			Never satisfied, always wants more
Confident					✓	Full of doubts

This represents a self-esteem score of 18/25, but also each dimension has its own score out of 5.

Figure 9.1 An example of the ideal self inventory

But when you look at her scores on each dimension, you can see some large variations particularly on the last dimension where she sees herself as 'full of doubts' rather than 'confident', and where she scores only 1 out of a possible 5.

Using the Ideal *** Inventory for pedagogical action research

This flexible tool can be adapted to suit your pedagogical research topic, which might be discipline specific, such as students' conceptions of the ideal way to teach:

- bioethics;
- fluid mechanics in engineering;
- legal information research skills.

Equally, it can be adapted for more generic pedagogical topics such as the ideal:

- lecturer
- student
- lecture.

The best way to illustrate some of its potential is to describe some ways in which you can develop it. In my example, I have chosen the ideal lecture (see Figure 9.2).

Step 1: Constructing an individual Ideal Lecture Inventory
Ask your participants to generate their own characteristics of the lecture using the concept of an 'ideal/not-ideal' dichotomy. The number of

Ideal lecture	5	4	3	2	1	Not ideal lecture
Interactive and involves students	✓					Delivers information
Well-prepared	✓					No effort
Interesting			✓			Boring
Relates to students' previous knowledge			✓			Does not build on anything
Inspirational	✓					No enthusiasm for topic
Informed and up to date		✓				Second hand
Applies theory to real life examples		✓				Theoretical

This represents a total score 29/35

Figure 9.2 An example of a completed ideal lecture inventory

dimensions you want depends on the nature and purpose of your research, but usually I have found between five and ten works well.

It is important to tell participants to do this row by row by thinking first of a word or short phrase to capture the essentials of an 'ideal' lecture and then doing exactly the same to capture the opposite end of the dimension, the 'not-ideal' lecture. When row one is complete, participants move onto row two and so on until all the dimensions are complete.

It is also important to tell them that when they are thinking of how to describe the 'not-ideal' pole for each dimension, their word or phrase does not have to be a literal opposite, as it is how they conceptualise the dimensions that you are interested in.

Step 2: Self-rating an individual ideal lecture inventory

When all the dimensions have been completed, ask your participants to think of the last lecture they delivered and rate this particular lecture on each of their dimensions.

Step 3: Constructing a composite Ideal *** Inventory

This can be done by collating the responses on the individual inventories and carrying out a content analysis (see Chapter 7) on the inventories in order to arrive at a composite list of the most frequently mentioned dimensions. Since the inventory allows participants to use words or phrases, you will have to make a number of judgements on meanings, so establishing a measure of inter-rater reliability is a good idea.

If you are interested in using the Ideal Inventory as a staff-development exercise, you can ask colleagues to share, discuss and come up with their own composite list. I have found this works very well in workshops and can be used either with staff from the same department or in an interdisciplinary context. This variation was first introduced by Williamson (2002), who actually used it with his students to engage them in understanding through group discussion what was required in a finance and accounting programme.

Step 4: Self-rating a composite ideal lecture inventory

Before asking your participants to complete a composite inventory, make sure that it appears as neutral as possible to guard against getting socially desirable responses. The following hints may be helpful.

- Do not title the columns 'ideal' and 'not ideal'.
- Construct the inventory so that all the 'ideal' poles of each dimension do not appear in the left-hand column and all the 'not-ideal' poles do not appear in the right-hand column.
- When scoring the inventory, give 5 to the point nearest to the ideal pole and 1 to the point nearest to the not-ideal pole, but remember to reverse the scoring where appropriate.

- Give neutral instructions such as: 'Circle the point that is closest to your experience/attitude/belief for each dimension.'

Step 5: Qualitative analysis

Analysing the data depends very much on the purpose of your research. If you are interested mainly in lecturers' conceptions of an ideal lecture, for example, you may want to report on the content analysis as an analysis in its own right as representing a departmental view.

Step 6: Quantitative analysis

Let us imagine that you are interested in the relationship between lecturers' perceptions of their own lecture and the amount of time they felt they had to prepare that lecture. You could carry out a simple correlation between the overall score on each lecturer's ideal lecture inventory and the number of hours' preparation time. Alternatively, you might want to use a composite inventory and ask each lecturer to rate his or her lecture against this composite version and then carry out the correlation. Another way you can use the data is if you were interested in individual lecturer scores on specific dimensions. Supposing, for example, that you obtained a composite dimension of 'well prepared' versus 'poorly prepared', you could use this for descriptive statistics or inferential statistical analysis as described in Chapter 8.

Summary

The Ideal *** Inventory is a generic tool for pedagogical research. Its particular advantages lie in its flexibility and how it can be adapted to suit a number of different research and teaching purposes. Its disadvantages lie in its very flexibility, which sometimes means the analysis can be tedious and time consuming (Perrin, Busby and Norton, 2003). Another disadvantage is that it requires a considerable amount of interpretation from a limited number of words or phrases.

A tool for evaluating your teaching: The Learning Objectives Questionnaire

Background

This next instrument is also a generic tool and is offered as a possible module-based alternative to many of the existing student-evaluation questionnaires that have become an integral part of university life, not only within subjects but at institutional and national level.

Probably the best known of these is Ramsden's Course Experience Questionnaire (CEQ), which was designed to evaluate student perceptions of their learning environment over a whole programme rather than individual modules or courses at the University of Sydney (Ramsden, 1991). It is now:

funded by Graduate Careers Australia (GCA), an organisation with representation from employers, universities and government which aims to
provide authoritative information on the supply of, and demand for new
graduates in Australia. As part of its activities, GCA receives information
and feedback from recent graduates through the Graduate Destination Survey,
and the Course Experience Questionnaire (CEQ), which are mailed together.

(Richardson, 2007: 4)

The Course Experience Questionnaire was the basis for the UK National Student
Survey as it was psychometrically sound and had a solid research base. However,
questionnaires such as these are not intended to be used at the module level and
so are difficult for the individual practitioner to interpret and use to modify their
own teaching.

In the second edition of his well-known book *Learning to Teach in Higher
Education* (2003) Ramsden comments that evaluation in higher education has
been debased so that it refers principally to the collection of data rather than
its interpretation; in the short term to modify teaching and in the longer
term to redesign the curriculum.

> Evaluation of teaching in its true sense is no more or less than an inte-
> gral part of the task of teaching, a continuous process of learning from
> one's students, of improvement and adaptation.
>
> (Ramsden, 2003: 99)

If we accept then that the purpose of student evaluation is to improve our
teaching, it follows that the questionnaires we use must be pedagogically sound,
but are they? Sometimes the questions are too general for an individual teacher
to know what specific modifications need to be made. Sometimes questions are
directed at areas of the student experience that the individual teacher has no power
to change (such as timetabling resourcing and rooming). Often course evaluations are carried out at the end of the course, when it is too late to change anything, and sometimes students' ratings can be affected by factors such as their
own preferred methods of studying (Entwistle and Tait, 1990) and teaching
(Hativa and Birenbaum, 2000) and also lecturer charisma (Shevlin *et al.*, 2000).

The Learning Objectives Questionnaire (LOQ) was designed to overcome
some of the difficulties associated with course evaluation by focusing on lecturers' pedagogical aims expressed as learning objectives (Norton, Horn and
Thomas, 1997). The advantages of this instrument were:

- It encourages lecturers to think closely about what they actually want
  students to achieve.
- By focusing on the lecturer's pedagogical aims, it is more effective in
  providing data/information on what needs to be done to make teaching or
  assessment modifications.

- Since it can be focused on just one element of a course, it is possible to administer while the course is ongoing and to make changes immediately.

Constructing the Learning Objectives Questionnaire for pedagogical action research

The following steps show you how to construct your own LOQ and are adapted from information on the Higher Education Academy's Psychology Subject Centre website.

Step 1:
Decide on the element of your course or assessment practice that you want feedback on. I have chosen seminars as my example (see Figure 9.3).

Step 2:
Formulate your learning objectives. In my example, this will be what I want my students to learn/achieve by taking part in my seminars.

This questionnaire has been designed to find out how successfully you think you have achieved specific aims on the seminar element of this course. Please be absolutely honest so I can make changes before the course ends, if necessary. For each objective circle the one response that most accurately represents your experience, where VS = Very Successful, S = Successful, U = Unsure, US = Unsuccessful, VUS = Very unsuccessful.

Learning objectives for seminars	VS	S	U	US	VUS
To develop your skills of finding out more information about the topic					
To develop your skills of presenting a reasoned argument to your fellow students					
To enhance your understanding of the lecture topic					
To apply theoretical knowledge to an applied context					
To critically evaluate your fellow students' views about the topic					
What is the single most important thing you feel you have learned from the seminars so far?					
What is the single most important thing I can do to improve the rest of the seminars for this course?					

Figure 9.3 An example of a learning objectives questionnaire on seminars

Step 3:

Decide on your response set. Traditionally this has been a five-point Likert scale where:

Very successful (VS) = 5
Successful (S) = 4
Unsure (U) = 3
Unsuccessful (US) = 2
Very unsuccessful (VUS) = 1.

You may wish to adapt this to suit your own context.

Step 4:

Give some form of general instruction at the beginning of the LOQ to explain to your students the rationale, which shifts the focus from more traditional course evaluation to their perceptions of how successfully they think they have achieved your stated learning objectives. It also helps if you can say that the information they give will result in changes for the rest of the course, if there is a need.

Step 5:

At the end of the closed-response items, add two open-ended questions adapted from Angelo and Cross (1993):

What is the single most important thing you feel you have learned from the seminars so far?

What is the single most important thing I/we/your tutors can do to improve the seminars for the rest of this course?

Summary

The LOQ is a tool for evaluating elements of the course that you consider to be pedagogically important. It enables you to take action and to change your teaching and/or assessment if your results warrant it. It also limits the effect of student characteristics by being phrased in terms of learning objectives. Its main disadvantage, I think, is that it has not been widely published and so may be viewed with some scepticism. This might make it difficult to adopt as a departmental initiative.

A tool for both pedagogy and research: The Essay Feedback Checklist

Unlike the two tools described so far, this next one is one that I have used a great deal with my students to try to improve the feedback I give them and help them write better essays. The Essay Feedback Checklist (EFC) has been, therefore, not just a research tool, but also a pedagogical one.

Background

This tool has been well documented as it has been used in action research designed to help students improve their essay writing (Norton *et al.*, 2002) and it is described fully in Campbell and Norton (2007), so it will only be briefly described here. There is a version available on the Higher Education Academy's Psychology Subject Centre website which gives details of how it was successively refined in three cycles of action research.

Basically, the EFC is a tool that lists the assessment criteria for a specific task and then asks students to rate the assignment for each assessment criterion and then to hand it in with their assignment. In this way it is meant to act as a reminder to students about the essential elements of their assignment that they should be focusing on while they are actually writing. Many such feedback sheets are commonly used, of course, but where the EFC differs is that there is a space also for tutors to give their rating for each of the assessment criteria. So where there is a difference between student and tutor ratings, the tutor can spend more time giving specific feedback on that particular criterion.

I mention it here because it is an example of how you can design a simple tool with a pedagogical purpose – that of improving your feedback to students – but you can also use it for research – that of comparing students' ratings with tutor ratings. See Table 9.1 for an example.

As you can see, the findings generated by completion of the EFC can be used descriptively and inferentially to find out where students appear to be having the greatest difficulty. In this example, the biggest mismatches between students' and tutors' ratings were in matters of referencing, spelling and grammar. This could then lead to a further wave of action research where some action could be taken to help students with these specific aspects of their writing.

Summary

The EFC is a dual-purpose tool designed to help students improve their essays by enabling tutors to give targeted feedback. It gives students practice at judging the worth of their own work, as well as acting as a reminder to them about what to focus on when writing their essays. It can also be used as a research instrument for pedagogical action research to alert tutors to the need for interventions. Although termed the Essay Feedback Checklist, it can easily be adapted to any assignment. Its disadvantages are that students might feel concerned that if they give an honest rating this will affect the tutor's marking. This can be dealt with by assurances that you will not look at it until you have marked the essay. The other disadvantage is that some staff do not like giving feedback in this way but prefer to write on the essay itself, so completing the EFC afterwards makes for additional work.

Table 9.1 Comparison of 3rd year psychology student's with tutors' ratings

Assessment criterion	Students (N=40)			Tutors (N=2)			p
	C	P	N	C	P	N	
Addressed the question throughout the essay	35	60	5	43	48	10	NS
Organized essay clearly with structure appropriate to the question	55	40	5	35	53	13	<0.05
Put forward a relevant argument of good quality	15	78	8	30	63	8	NS
Synthesized a range of material into a coherent whole	28	65	8	38	43	20	NS
Shown depth of understanding relating to underlying psychological issues	33	60	8	25	60	15	NS
Evaluated theoretical concepts and research evidence	25	65	10	10	63	28	<0.05
Referenced according to psychology requirements	65	28	8	28	33	40	<0.001
Checked for spelling and grammar	80	20	0	38	55	8	<0.001
Written in an appropriate academic style	68	33	0	45	45	10	<0.05

Key: C = Completely confident; P = Partially confident; N = Not at all confident;
p = significance level of difference between paired ratings using Wilcoxon Signed Ranks test.
Note: Percentages have been rounded so not all totals are 100

Designing your own pedagogical tools by developing and adapting published instruments

Of course it is perfectly possible to 'start from scratch', and I have described this process in Chapter 6. In my view, it is better, if at all possible, to build on what already exists, especially if you are aiming at publishing your research study in a peer-reviewed journal. There are hundreds of questionnaires, inventories and interview schedules in the research literature on teaching and learning which you can use. Some places to start looking for them are suggested in the further reading and resources section at the end of this chapter, but you do have to be careful in selecting them, as some may be poorly designed and not tested for reliability and validity. Generally, it is a good idea to check the publication for details of how they have been constructed, as even published instruments may not have been rigorously developed.

For the rest of this chapter I am going to show you how I have used and developed two examples of published questionnaires and two examples of published qualitative measures to give you some idea of what can be done in your own pedagogical action research.

I will begin with the quantitative measures. If you want to develop new items, ideally you should develop, test and pilot your new items in the way I described in Chapter 6. If you are going to adapt actual items from an existing questionnaire you will need to approach the authors for permission. In my first example, I have adapted some of the items in the Approaches to Studying Inventory (ASI). In my second example, rather than adapt the instrument in any way, in this case the Reflections on Learning Inventory (RoLI), I have adapted the way it can be used.

Adapting quantitative measures: The Approaches to Studying Inventory

Background

For many years, the ASI was a frequently used questionnaire appearing in countless pedagogical research studies. It was devised by Entwistle and his colleagues (Entwistle, Hanley and Hounsell, 1979; Entwistle and Ramsden, 1983; Ramsden and Entwistle, 1981) and was designed to measure deep and surface approaches to studying. In a study carried out to see if lecturers actually rewarded students for showing evidence of a deep approach in their assignments (Steward, Norton, Evans and Norton, 2003), we used the 32-item version of the ASI (recommended by Richardson, 1990) as a starting point for developing our own questionnaire for lecturers. This can be seen in Figure 9.4.

What we did here was to select the essential elements of a deep approach, partly drawn from the meaning orientation scale of the ASI and partly drawn from the characteristics of a deep and a surface approach as described by Entwistle (1987), as could be evidenced in an assignment. This resulted in nine items reflecting a deep approach and two reflecting a surface approach that we believed could be evidenced in an assessed assignment. The imbalance was because we were interested in only a deep approach, but knew that memorisation was an important strategy in some of the five disciplines involved in the research (biology, information management and communications, management and business, sociology and psychology).

Our findings showed that lecturers did reward a deep approach; memorising was seen by some subjects as part of a deep approach and only management and business did not reward it.

Summary

This is an example of how you can use a standardised questionnaire, such as the ASI, as a springboard for your own research, where it is the meaning of the items you want to use rather than the items themselves. Creating item stems for a questionnaire can come from the broader literature or from your

1.   Please identify each assessment task for this module together with a brief description of its purpose (space has been provided for up to 3 assessment tasks; if you set more than this number, please choose the three that carry the most weighting in your module)

Brief description and weighting of assessment task A....

What do you believe the purpose of this assessment task is?...

Brief description and weighting of assessment task B....

What do you believe the purpose of this assessment task is?...

Brief description and weighting of assessment task C....

What do you believe the purpose of this assessment task is?...

2.   Please consider each of the assessment tasks in your module and tick which of the following you actually <u>reward</u> students for demonstrating

	Assessment		
	A	B	C
Understanding of theories/concepts			
Understanding of practical applications of theory			
Active engagement with module content			
Evidence that student has built on what s/he already knows in the subject			
Application of understanding of module content to everyday life			
Relating evidence to conclusions			
Examining the logic of arguments			
Memorizing theories/concepts			
Memorizing practical applications of theory			
Evidence of ability to distinguish principles from examples			
Integrating/synthesizing information from different sources			
Other? Please state			

3.   If you have any other comments please write them here....

Figure 9.4 The module assessment questionnaire (adapted from Steward, Norton, Evans and Norton, 2003)

own practitioner experience, but it is likely to be a sounder instrument if you can develop it from existing questionnaires.

Adapting quantitative measures: The Reflections on Learning Inventory RoLI©

Background

The next quantitative measure I want to discuss is an example of a copyrighted instrument that cannot be adapted, but which can be used in a number of different pedagogical ways to build students' meta-learning capacity. The Reflections on Learning Inventory (RoLI©) originated as a measure of conceptions of learning (Meyer, 1995), and has subsequently been developed by Meyer (2004) over many years, being produced in at least ten versions.

The RoLI© is now a web-based tool; see further resources section at the end of this chapter for more information.

For a number of years, my university used the RoLI© as part of a first-year generic personal development planning (PDP) programme to help students adapt to the demands of higher education by reflecting on their own approaches to and understandings of learning as measured by their RoLI© profiles. See Figure 9.5 for an example of a completed hypothetical profile of a student called Suzy.

In this initiative, which was part of a series of pedagogical action research studies, students were asked as one element of their PDP module to complete the RoLI©, and then to discuss the implications of their resulting RoLI© profile with their PDP tutor, an academic tutor responsible for about 12 students pastorally and academically.

This institutional initiative was inspired by the work of Lindblom-Ylänne (2003), who used a study-counselling approach to help students to interpret their own approaches to their RoLI© profiles. In our case, PDP tutors helped students to reflect on their own RoLI© learning scores in the context of their academic subjects. Students were then required to write an assessed reflective essay about what they had learned from their RoLI© profile and their discussion with their PDP tutor.

The next year, as a further stage in the action research, I gave a lecture to the first-year cohort explaining what the various subscales meant so that they could have more detailed information before going to discuss their profiles with their PDP tutor and writing their reflective piece. Students were required to attend the lecture and bring their completed RoLI© profiles with them. In the lecture, I used Meyer's analogy of traffic lights where 'green for go' subscales (black bars in Figure 9.5) indicate approaches or beliefs that would help them do well in higher education, so a high score on these in their profile would be encouraging.

The 'amber for proceed with caution' subscales (grey bars in Figure 9.5) indicate approaches or beliefs that sometimes help and sometimes hinder students from doing well in higher education. Students were told that if they score highly on these, they may want to think about changing them only if they are not doing as well as they expected for the effort they are putting into their studies.

The third category consists of the 'red for stop' subscales (white bars in Figure 9.5) and indicate beliefs or approaches that will hinder students from doing well in higher education, even if they are putting in a lot of effort.

Looking at the hypothetical student Suzy's RoLI© profile in Figure 9.5 suggests someone whose approaches and beliefs are largely in tune with the expectations of higher education. If I were Suzy's PDP tutor I would have wanted to explore with her the belief she appears to have that knowledge is fact based (this may be perfectly fine in some subjects but would be

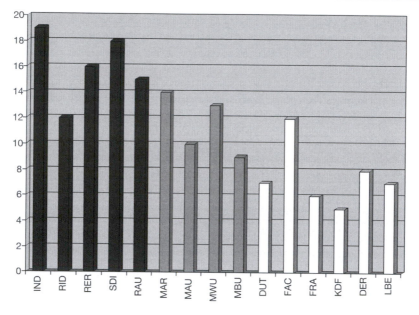

Key

High scores on these subscales indicate an approach that fits well with degree level study:

IND   Thinking independently

RID   Relating ideas

RER   Rereading a text

SDI   Seeing things differently

RAU   Repetition aids understanding

Figure 9.5 Hypothetical example of a RoLI profile for 'Suzy'

epistemologically at odds with others). I would also have discussed whether or not Suzy saw her low score on relating ideas to be a difficulty in her studies and, if so, what strategies she might use to improve on this aspect.

Summary

This example shows how you can sometimes adapt the context in which you use a published tool that cannot itself be altered, and there are a number of them. If you plan to introduce an institutional initiative, such as the one described, this would inevitably have a considerable impact on the student-learning experience. It would be important, therefore, to use a reliable and valid measure that has a good research base. It would also be helpful to have some input and advice from the instrument's authors. In the PDP initiative, Professor Jan Meyer was invited to lead two staff-development sessions in my university on the RoLI© and how it could be used to build students' meta-learning capacity. Using a published measure like the RoLI© also has the advantage of enabling you to generate sound research data (with students' permission) in your action research studies.

Adapting interview methodology

In the two examples that I discuss here, I describe how you can adapt an interview methodology to an open-ended questionnaire method in the specific context of assigning students to developmental stages. In my first example, this worked quite well, but in the second it was less successful. In both cases, as in the development of all research tools, more work is needed to progressively refine these methods.

Conceptions of learning

Background

Ever since Säljö (1979) categorised students' conceptions of learning, there have been attempts to produce quantitative measures such as in the RoLI© just described and, most recently in the ASSIST, where the conceptions of learning measure are still under development. In Säljö's original research, he interviewed 90 people ranging in age from 15 to 73 about their approaches to learning. When he analysed these transcripts he was able to identify five conceptions, which were developmental and hierarchical. These were later confirmed in a study by Marton, Dall'Alba and Beaty (1993) who added a sixth conception (see Figure 9.6).

Adapting the categorisation

In thinking about how this hierarchical categorisation might be measured, I explored some different methods myself (see Appendix D), but I never used them in any research, preferring instead to go for a qualitative approach, as this more closely matched Säljö's original research.

Phenomenographical research means taking a rigorous approach to establish categories and the relationships between them (Marton, 1994), but how do you do this as a hard-pressed academic/pedagogical researcher? One way is to make modifications, so, for example, rather than interview, which takes time not only to carry out, but also to transcribe before you even get to the stage of analysing your information, I would suggest an open-ended question

Conception	Description	Characteristics	Illustrative quotes
1	Learning as the increase of knowledge	Answers are characterized by vagueness, taken for granted nature, synonymous phrases for learning	" ...it's to learn new things, other things you did not know before...."
2	Learning as memorizing	Answers refer to the reproduction of the learning material, often orientated to some kind of test or performance	"...learning it up for exams, drumming it into the brain and reeling it off...."
3	Learning as the acquisition of facts or procedures which can be retained and/or utilised in practice	Answers include phrases such as applying what is learned when the need arises, retrieving what is learned and using it	"...take in information, see how it can be used, it's being able to put it into use"
4	Learning as the abstraction of meaning	Answers relate to understanding or gaining meaning, grasping the sense of something	"...seeing things in a different light, gain more insight, grasping new ideas"
5	Learning as an interpretative process aimed at the understanding of reality	Answers refer to changing your thinking about something, seeing the whole and how parts are related	"...opening your mind a little bit more so you see things in different ways... a different view of the world"
6	Learning as changing as a person (added by Marton, Dall'Alba & Beaty, 1993)	Answers are sophisticated and multi-layered, referring to developing insights into the phenomena dealt with in the learning material, one develops a new way of seeing those phenomena and seeing the world differently means that you change as a person	"sometimes if you learn something you may actually lose something ...some of my hide-bound ideas that I've had in the past, I lose them, they've changed. I think any type of learning is going to have to change you...you learn to understand about people and the world about you and why things happen and therefore when you understand more of why they happen, it changes you..."

Figure 9.6 Säljö's (1979) hierarchical conceptions of learning (adapted)

to which your participants can write a reply. These responses can then be content analysed into the already defined categories.

An example of this methodology was used in some early research we did to see if psychology students would show more sophisticated conceptions following an 'approaches to learning' programme (Norton and Crowley, 1995; Norton, Scantlebury and Dickins, 1999). According to Gibbs (1992), there is a strong link between the first three levels of conceptions of learning and a surface approach to studying. We described this in our paper as an 'inchoate' conception of learning. The last three levels are closely related to a deep approach to studying. We described this as a 'developed' conception of learning.

In order to see if our students would change from an inchoate to a developed conception of learning, we asked them at the start of the course to write as much as they could in answer to the question

'What do you actually mean by learning?'

They were then asked to do exactly the same at the end of the course. Each written response was broken down into information units, which were individually assigned to one of Säljö's conceptions.

The process differed from our usual content-analysis process in that we categorised the student into the highest conception that their response had shown evidence of, following the 'priority rule' described by Marton, Dall'Alba and Beaty (1993). This led us to making some difficult decisions, such as when 90 per cent of the response was at a lower-level conception and there was just one small part which fell into the higher conception. Another case was where the students might write a sentence that seemed to fit easily into a higher conception but the whole sense of the rest of their answer did not; almost as if they were parroting some 'truth' that they did not really understand. In both these instances, we made a subjective decision taking the sense of the whole answer as our guiding principle.

As always, to safeguard rigour, the analysis was done by two researchers and inter-rater reliability calculated. In the event, our findings from the first study showed a move from inchoate to developed conceptions, but we were unable to replicate this finding in our second study, which was rather disappointing. Normally this would have led to a further research study, but the 'approaches to learning' course was withdrawn from the psychology programme.

Summary

In terms of adapting an interview methodology, the written-question format appeared to work well. However, the process of reliably analysing content and assigning students responses to a predefined framework, such as the conceptions of learning categories, took a great deal of developmental work, so it is not a quick and easy method to use. Its main disadvantage for us was that some students wrote relatively little, which made it difficult to accurately assign them to a conception.

If you are interested in trying this approach for yourself, it might be helpful to ask your participants to write a specified number of words in response to your open-ended question, as described below.

Reflective Judgement

Background

In my final example of adapting existing tools and methodologies, I have chosen King and Kitchener's (1994) work on reflective judgement. King and Kitchener describe a developmental progression that occurs between childhood and adulthood by which they mean how people understand the process of knowing and how they justify their beliefs about what are described as ill-structured problems, to which there is no single easy answer.

In their model they describe seven stages, which represent distinct assumptions about knowledge and how it is acquired. Like Säljö's conceptions of learning, the stages are hierarchical. Each successive stage represents a more complex and effective form of justification with more inclusive and better-integrated assumptions, or evaluating and defending a point of view.

In their model, stages 1 to 3 are identified as 'pre-reflective thinking' where knowledge is thought of as almost always stable and certain, gained either by direct personal observation or through authority figures.

Stages 4 and 5 are called 'quasi-reflective thinking' where knowledge is conceived as uncertain and contextual. People at this stage have difficulty in understanding how to then make judgements in the light of this uncertainty. They typically argue that judgements ought to be based on evidence, but their evaluations are often idiosyncratic and individual.

Stages 6 and 7, according to King and Kitchener, are the only stages that are truly indications of reflective thinking and are even more advanced, they claim, than Perry's (1970) top stage of intellectual development. Reflective thinking reflects epistemic assumptions that our understandings of the world are not given, but must be actively constructed by understanding knowledge in the context in which it was generated. People at this stage understand that, while there is no absolute certainty, some explanations can be evaluated as more reasonable than others.

In order to establish what stage an individual is at, King and Kitchener devised the Reflective Judgement Interview (RJI), which was designed to elicit rateable data about peoples' fundamental beliefs about knowledge and how it is acquired. This was a measure with psychometric properties, as interviewers had to be trained and certified and responses were analysed according to a set of standardised scoring rules (Wood, 1997). Like many instruments, the RJI has undergone substantial development and can now be obtained on a fee-paying basis as an online questionnaire (see further resources).

Adapting the ill-structured problem interview

We were interested in exploring whether students' levels of reflective thinking would develop over the course of the first year using King and Kitcheners' (1994) model (Norton *et al.*, 2001).

Instead of using their RJI, we adapted the open-ended questionnaire format described above for conceptions of learning, but this time we used the principle of an ill-structured problem (in our case an ill-structured question about their own discipline) and a justification.

Students in psychology, mathematics and music were asked to take part in the research, which involved completing an open-ended questionnaire twice; once at the beginning of their first academic year and once at the end. The questionnaire had only two questions:

1. 'What do you think the study of psychology/mathematics is about?' (Please answer in around 150 words.)
   Music students had a slightly different version:
   'What do you think instrumental practice is about?' (Please answer in around 150 words.)
2. 'Please explain (in around 150 words) why you hold this view.'

The questionnaire scripts were read and reread by a research assistant to get a feel for the depth and quality of the thought processes used in the responses. Next, he assessed each script using both the answer to question 1 and, more importantly, the second question which explained their reasoning, in order to compare with King and Kitchener's criteria for each stage.

See Figure 9.7 for some examples of responses and their categorisation.

A small sample of 28 questionnaires was independently rated by one of the other researchers, which gave an inter-rater reliability of 61 per cent. This was not sufficiently reliable as we found it difficult to make fine distinctions between the stages in the students' responses. When we used instead

---

Pre-reflective thinking

Example of stage 2 thinking:

Explanation: *'I feel that the study of psychology is about the mind i.e. how the brain responds to different influences that are placed on the body. Things like alcohol as this slows reactions etc.'*

Justification: *'I hold this view as I have a small amount of knowledge on sport psychology having studied this for two months at college.'* (Participant 19)

Quasi-reflective thinking

Example of Stage 4 thinking:

Explanation: *'Psychology is the study of the mind. I think it looks at animal behaviour and it compares it to the human behaviour. It tries to explain our behaviour – why we do certain things; if they are learned or genetic determined. With psychology various experiments are conducted to study and to try to find out why we do certain things.'*

Justification: *'I did do an access course with psychology. We looked at the different perspectives and all the perspectives had a different theory why we do things. Also if there are programms on the TV about psychology I will sit down and watch them. Most of the programms try to explain behaviour.'* (Participant 62)

Reflective thinking

Example of Stage 6 thinking:

Explanation: *'The **word** 'psychology' covers a lot of areas and may be described as an extremely profound word. Personally I interpret the word psychology to mean an exploration if the human mind and how and why it provokes an individual to act in the way that they do. Psychology can also involve the study of animals and the way in which they behave too. Environmental factors are involved in Psychology. the reason being that to some extent our surroundings effect the ways in which we act. Psychology is discovering yourself by learning about others and the way in which they act. Psychology is what you make it and it can be personal, social. Psychology involves cognitive development.'*

Justification: *'I believe that the interpretation of the word 'psychology' is thoroughly personal. At this stage, I am aware that Psychology involves humans and animals and the way in which they behave and the reasons why they behave in such a manner. It would be interesting to see how I would interpret the word Psychology after I have completed my journey of learning on this psychology course. Perhaps I would hold a slight different view then?'* (Participant 17)

Figure 9.7 Sample of data showing stages of reflective thinking in psychology students at the beginning of the year (adapted from Norton *et al.*, 2001)

the three main levels of pre-reflective, quasi-reflective and reflective, the inter-rater reliability increased to 86 per cent, which was considered satisfactory.

This open-ended questionnaire was followed up with a small sample of telephone interviews. Our findings showed that most of the students from all three subjects gave answers at the pre-reflective stage of thinking at the start of their undergraduate study and there was little progression to higher stages at the end of the year. Some small differences were observed between the disciplines, with psychology students having slightly higher percentages operating at the quasi and reflective stages than mathematics and music students.

Summary

In this example, the open-ended questionnaire format was perhaps too crude an instrument to measure the complexity of critical reasoning and reflective judgement. This was apparent in the low inter-rater reliability when attempting to use all seven stages. If we had been able to use these finer distinctions, we may have detected more movement overall at the end of the year. If we were to replicate this study in a further wave of action research, we would need to develop the open-ended questionnaire by making the questions relate more specifically to the seven stages for each discipline.

If you were thinking of adopting a methodology like this in your own action research, it would be a good idea to run a pilot study first to see how the analysis process works. This enables you to make changes in the questions you are asking before you expend a considerable amount of time and effort in a main study, which might not give you the clear-cut results you were hoping for.

Synopsis

- The purpose of this chapter is to demonstrate some of the pedagogical tools that can be used in pedagogical action research. Since it is not possible to describe the hundreds of published instruments in any detail, I have drawn on my own research tools, which are more modest in terms of rigour and scope, but may be a helpful starting point.
- In the first section, I describe the Ideal *** Inventory which is a generic questionnaire designed to allow participants to generate their own characteristics of whatever topic is being researched and then to rate themselves.
- This is followed by the LOQ which provides an alternative form of course evaluation, designed to focus on what the lecturer considers to be pedagogically important.
- The third measure is the Essay Feedback Checklist, which can be used to target more effectively tutor feedback, as well as to reminding students about the assessment criteria as they write their essays.

- In the next sections, I have taken examples from my own pedagogical action research work to give readers an idea of what is involved in adapting and develop published tools and methodologies. To do this, I look at two examples of quantitative measures and two examples of qualitative measures.
- In the first of the quantitative measures, I have described how the Approaches to Studying Inventory (ASI) was used as a resource for generating items in another questionnaire with a different purpose.
- In the second example, I have taken a different approach by showing how the Reflections on Learning Inventory (RoLI©) can be used as part of an institutional initiative to help students understand themselves as learners. In this example, I am trying to demonstrate what can be done with a published measure that cannot itself be altered.
- In the qualitative measures, I describe how an interview methodology can be adapted to a questionnaire methodology. Using the examples of conceptions of learning and reflective judgement, which both produce hierarchical categorisations indicative of student development, I show how written responses can be categorised into existing frameworks.
- Throughout the chapter, the emphasis has been on showing what can be done by building on existing instruments and methodologies in pedagogical action research.

Further reading and resources

How to find published instruments

These can be found most easily in learning and teaching journals. See for example:

- Assessment and Evaluation in Higher Education
- Higher Education
- Innovations in Education and Teaching International
- Research in Higher Education
- Studies in Education
- Teaching in Higher Education

They can also be found using Internet resources. See, for example, large research project websites such as:

Enhancing Teaching–Learning Environments in Undergraduate Courses project (funded by the ESRC Teaching and Learning Research Programme). Online. Available: http://www.tla.ed.ac.uk/etl/publications. html#measurement (accessed 27 April 2008).

This is a particularly rich resource as it makes available four instruments that are particularly relevant to pedagogical action research:

- Experiences of Teaching and Learning Questionnaire (ETLQ);
- Shortened Experiences of Teaching and Learning Questionnaire (SETLQ);
- Learning and Studying Questionnaire (LSQ);
- Approaches and Study Skills Inventory for Students (ASSIST).

Higher Education Academy research and evaluation web page. Online. Available: http://www.heacademy.ac.uk/ourwork/research (accessed 27 April 2008).

This contains many resources, which may yield instruments such as:

- Downloadable recent publications, an example of which is the report by Nixon, Smith, Stafford and Camm on work-based learning in higher education which contains an interview schedule and a survey instrument. Online. Available: http://www.heacademy.ac.uk/assets/York/documents/ourwork/research/wbl_illuminating.pdf (accessed 27 April 2008).
- Literature reviews commissioned by the HEA.
- Observatories which aim to identify, collate, assess and disseminate research for different themes (such as widening participation and e-learning).
- Surveys, an example of which is the Postgraduate Research Experience Survey. Online. Available: http://www.heacademy.ac.uk/assets/York/documents/ourwork/research/surveys/pres/web0591_pres_questionnaire_jan_2007.pdf (accessed 27 April 2008).

Higher Education Academy's Subject Centre Network. This requires some diligent searching, as not all the centres publish their own journals, but those that do can yield substantial instruments, such as in the Biosciences Centre for example, where you can access:

- Brown, Gibbs and Glover's (2003) Assessment Experience Questionnaire (AEQ). Online. Available: http://www.bioscience.heacademy.ac.uk/journal/vol2/beej-2-5.htm (accessed 27 April 2008).
- Hughes' (2006) assessment audit tool. Online. Available: http://www.bioscience.heacademy.ac.uk/journal/vol7/beej-7-1.htm (accessed 27 April 2008).

Centres for Excellence in Teaching and Learning (CETL) websites are developing pedagogical research so may well be worth exploring but again this will need quite a bit of persistence.

For example, I started with the largest CETL, LearnHigher, which is a network of 16 institutions working on various aspects of learner development and found a useful link to:

- Image-based research. Online. Available: http://iirc.mcgill.ca/txp/?s= methodologyandc=aboutpercent20imagepercent20basedpercent20research (accessed 27 April 2008).

Write Now is a CETL that has a number of pages on its website devoted to pedagogical research studies large and small in the area of student writing and assessment. Online. Available: http://www.writenow.ac.uk (accessed 27 April 2008).

I happen to know of this one specifically as I am involved as its research director, but I am sure there are many other CETLs engaged in pedagogical research, and these would be worth contacting for advice and potential research collaborative opportunities.

Specific instruments

Reflections on Learning Inventory

Author: Meyer, J.H.F.

RoLIspsTM is managed by the University of South Australia, which provides a variety of fee-paying services to institutions, subject and course coordinators, and individual students. Online. Available: http://www.rolisps. com/0Page.htm (accessed 27 April 2008).

Reflective Judgement

Authors: King, P.M. and Kitchener, K.S.

This website gives details of the Reasoning about Current Issues Test, which is now available on a fee basis as on online tool. Online. Available: http://www.umich.edu/~refjudg/index.html (accessed 27 April 2008).

Approaches to Teaching Inventory

Authors: Trigwell, K. and Prosser, M.

The latest version is downloadable as a pdf file. Online. Available: http:// www.learning.ox.ac.uk/files/ATI22.pdf (accessed 27 April 2008).

Revised Two-Factor Study Processes Questionnaire (R-SPQ-2F)

Authors: Biggs, J., Kember, D. and Leung, D.P.

This is reprinted in full in an appendix to the paper. Online. Available: http://www.itl.usyd.edu.au/programs/3day/BiggsrevisedSPQ.pdf (accessed 27 April 2008).

Reflective Thinking Questionnaire

Authors: Kember, D., Leung, D.Y.P., Jones, A., Yuen Loke, A., McKay, J., Sinclair, K., Tse H., Webb, C., Wong, F.K.Y., Wong, M. and Yeung, E.

Online. Available: http://teaching.polyu.edu.hk/datafiles/R144a.doc (accessed 27 April 2008).

Chapter 10

What are the ethical issues involved in pedagogical action research?

Introduction

Researching into learning and teaching practice within your own institution raises a number of ethical dilemmas. It is relatively easy to convince ourselves that the research we do on students' learning and on teachers' teaching at university is for the greater good of improving both. But what happens if such research shows the institution where we work in a bad light, or the students, or our fellow colleagues, or the subject? How do we know we are not abusing our power as a teacher by researching the very people we are supposed to be teaching?

These, and other questions, will be explored in this chapter. Throughout, I am going to use the word 'participants' for those who agree to take part in our research studies rather than the demeaning but frequently used term 'subjects'. The British Psychological Society advised this change many years ago and would not accept the 'subject' terminology in their publications any more than they would accept gender discriminatory terms. I would like to suggest that the action research movement should follow the same terminology to accord with the often quoted maxim in most, if not all, of the published codes of conduct about respecting human dignity.

Types of research

I also want to explain the subtle differences between research, teaching and learning research (pedagogical research), pedagogical action research and the scholarship of teaching and learning, as these terms are used commonly in the literature, often interchangeably, but there are some implications, particularly when thinking about ethics.

In reading the codes of practice such as those produced in psychology and sociology, the emphasis is on research with human participants, so much of what is said in these discipline-related codes apply equally well to research in learning and teaching. This is sometimes referred to as pedagogical research and can itself be subdivided into two interrelated areas: pedagogic development

(PedD) and pedagogic research (PedR). These are described in a useful report on research in the scholarship of teaching and learning (SOTL) to the Higher Education Funding Council for England (HEFCE) by Gordon *et al.*, (2003). Briefly, they see each as not representing opposite poles on a continuum but much more overlapping, and which can be used to describe features of enquiry that contribute to the field of the scholarship of teaching and learning.

PedD tends to include activities that have a practical focus rather than a theoretical one, and where dissemination may be presented as examples of good practice to one's colleagues or perhaps in workshops. PedR tends to be a more formal enquiry with accepted research methodology, and is likely to be aimed at a wider audience, often through conference papers and publications. I want to add the subject of this book as a third category to Gordon *et al.*'s typology. In my view, pedagogical action research (PAR) is a third overlapping form of enquiry, which includes some elements of both PedD and PedR (see Figure 10.1).

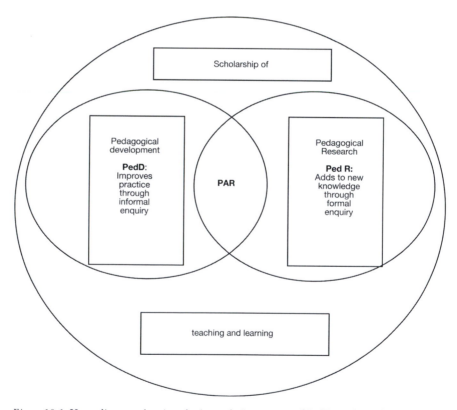

Figure 10.1 Venn diagram showing the interrelating aspects of PedD, PedR and PAR within the scholarship of teaching and learning

Not everyone in higher education is familiar or comfortable with these terms, sometimes regarding them with some suspicion and scepticism, but for the purposes of this chapter I am going to use them in order to discuss specific ethical issues.

Fundamental principles of ethical research

No matter which code of practice you look at (and I give several at the end of this chapter), they nearly all agree on three basic principles:

- informed consent;
- privacy and confidentiality;
- protection from harm.

I have drawn mainly on the British Educational Research Association's revised ethical guidelines (2004) and the ethical standards of the American Educational Research Association (2000) for this chapter. (See the further reading and resources section at the end of this chapter.)

Informed consent

This principle involves two equally important elements: 'consent', which means asking people to agree to take part in our research without any coercion; and 'informed', which means giving them sufficient information on which to make a realistic judgement on the possible consequences of taking part.

Consent from students

In pedagogical research, we tend to think of participants as students, but they can equally be lecturers or staff related to learning support or services. If you carry out research on your own students' learning, you have to be careful of undue influence or coercion, given your power and authority as their teacher or the person closely involved with supporting their learning. In our Dr Jones scenario, for example, which was described in Chapter 6, do you think she is using undue influence to get her students to take part in an interview or questionnaire study and how freely would her students be able to decline to take part? In her experimental research looking at the effects of the electronic discussion forum, there is no option for students to decline as the intervention is designed as part of the course.

We can encourage students to take part in our research believing, as we do, that there will be some pedagogical benefits, but in making students aware of potential benefits of pedagogical research we have to be careful not to use our authority to coerce them or use our authority unfairly to convince them to take part. Let us take the example of a professor in music who is interested in the effects of journal keeping on first-year students' motivation to regularly practice. She decides to carry out a study in which she will analyse their journal records against performance measures at the end of the year. She addresses a class of first years in the first couple of weeks of their degree, suggesting that they keep a journal of their instrument practice, and telling them that this is likely to lead to increased motivation and more rapid development of their musician skills. It is very likely that at this stage of their degree, as they are just starting at university, that they will implicitly trust her and comply with any demands she makes. Is this unfair coercion?

We might be so convinced of the benefits to our students that we over-power them with justification and make it very difficult for them to refuse. Even when we assure students that if they do not want to take part in our research, this will in no way affect the teaching or the quality of the learning they experience, nevertheless there are other social penalties. For example, what sort of pressure do we put on students if we want to administer a questionnaire in class time and say 'Participation is entirely voluntary, so anyone who does not want to complete the questionnaire can leave now.'?

There is plenty of research in social psychology to show how human beings are reluctant to flout authority or act in a non-conforming way, par-ticularly when peer pressure is great. Paradoxically, the reason we know so much about these powerful pressures that influence us to comply when we do not want to comes from the classic research experiments of Asch (1955) on conforming to group pressure and Milgram (1974) on obedience to authority, both of which are nowadays cited as research studies that contravene most ethical principles.

Consent from staff

When our research is concerned with lecturers and/or learning-support col-leagues, the power/authority element does not have the same impact that it does on students unless it involves high-status staff and junior colleagues, in which case the risk of coercion might be quite similar. There are, however, other pressures to take part, such as research that might be exploring a departmental culture. Let us imagine that the researcher wants a rich phe-nomenograhical portrait of the staff who work in a department or faculty or school, from the head to the graduate assistants. By declining to take part, staff will readily become visible, which might not just disappoint the researcher who is not getting the full picture (particularly if the member of staff who declines is a key person in the organisational structure), but it might also cause ongoing irritation and resentment amongst other members of the department who have agreed to take part.

If you are the researcher and it is your colleagues who are unwilling to take part, there may be scepticism, spoken or unspoken, about the value of your research (sometimes seen in academic attitudes to scholarship of teaching and learning), which does not make for good long term working relations. In my first ever research study as a psychology lecturer I carried out an interview study with all the members of the psychology department including the head of department, which, understandably, I was rather nervous but delighted about. Unfortunately, for some unfathomable reason which I still do not understand to this day, his interview was the only one where my tape recorder did not work and I had to rely on a few written notes, as I did not dare approach him to repeat the interview. Involving colleagues in your pedagogical research is not always easy, even when they are willing, particularly if there is a difference in status.

Information

How can we be sure that we give fair information in pedagogical research to potential participants about the study, and what form should that information take? It can be an oral statement in a lecture to students, or on a one-to-one basis with your colleagues, but for most research studies it tends to be a participant information sheet and a consent form. For an example of a completed participant information sheet see Appendix E and for a consent form template see Appendix F.

Participant information tends to follow a similar pattern consisting of the following elements.

- Statement and explanation about research aims, expected duration, description of what will be involved and what will happen to the findings.
  The aims of the study have to be written in clear non-specialist terms, and details about the input from the participants have to be expressed as accurately as possible. (I recently received an angry email from a lecturer in another institution to tell me that completing the questionnaire I sent her took much longer than the 20 minutes I had estimated.) We also need to be as clear as possible about how we will use the information they give us, a point I will return to in the section on privacy and confidentiality.
- Description of any possible discomfort or risks and any possible benefits.
  It is quite difficult to judge this one, as you do not want to exaggerate the risks and frighten your participants. I have seen examples of this in some of the advice given to students on research-methods courses, where they are advised to tell their participants that if the research causes emotional distress, they can be referred to the university counselling service. If overused, this may cause your participants to be fearful where there is no need. Similarly, with the possible benefits of taking part in the research, you have to be very honest, and this is particularly so with pedagogical research where you are likely to be committed to your proposed intervention and

personally convinced that it will enhance your students' learning – but it might not.

- Disclosure of appropriate alternative procedures that might be advantageous to the participants.

  In an action research study to help students write better essays, the ethical issues of which are discussed in Norton (2008), I told my students that I was testing out three different types of written feedback to see which might be the most useful, but because I did not know which would be the most effective, anyone taking part in the research could also have face-to-face individual feedback from me if they wanted it.

- Statement that all information collected as part of the research study will be retained for xx years and details of where the information will be stored and the form in which it will be stored.

  This might be data in hard copy, electronically stored data or video/audio tapes.

- Statement about steps taken to protect confidentiality.

  This is particularly tricky in pedagogical action research and will be discussed in the next section. If there is a difficulty, a statement should be included that makes your participants aware of this.

- Statement about participation being voluntary and the right to withdraw at any time.

  This should also include the right for participants to withdraw their data, but the timing could be problematic if you are on the point of publishing, for example.

- Details about how and when participants will be provided with either a copy of the final research report or a summary of the research findings.

  This might be especially relevant and of interest to your participants if they are colleagues but in any case is a matter of common courtesy to your participants.

- Email or Internet distribution arrangements.

  Include a statement to the effect that you will take every care to remove any identification from the responses as soon as possible and that each individual's responses will be kept confidential by the researcher/s and will not be identifiable in the publication of any findings. However, you also have to be honest and state that you cannot guarantee the confidentiality or anonymity of material transferred by email or the Internet.

- Use of experimental and control groups.

  In research that uses this type of methodology, you should include a statement that participants may be allocated to either a control or experimental group, and that they may not be told which of these groups they are in.

- Collection of data on audio or videotapes.

  Participants should be made aware of the following.

  Information will be taped. Participants should also be reminded of this before data are collected.

The tape or a certified transcript of the tape is raw data and will be securely retained for xx years.
Their identity can be masked if they request this.

Anonymity and confidentiality

Sometimes both researchers and participants confuse these two concepts.

'Anonymity' means that the researcher/s will conceal the identity of the participants in all research findings (including research seminars, conference papers, journal papers and book chapters). This can, however, be particularly problematic with pedagogical action research if you plan to disseminate your research findings in the same institution where you carried out the research. This is quite likely, given that one of the aims of such research is to alter or change existing practice.

The term 'confidentiality' means making clear who has the right of access to the data provided by the participants. Usually, it is the researcher or researchers alone, but what exactly is it that they keep confidential? It is common, for example, in reporting on qualitative studies such as thematic analysis (discussed in Chapter 7) to use excerpts or quotes from interviews in reporting your findings. In such cases, while you can protect anonymity, you are not, strictly speaking, protecting a participant's confidentiality.

We have to be cognisant of the implications of the Data Protection Act (Great Britain, 1998) which has changed the traditional way we used to publish students' examination results and coursework results in lists on notice boards which were publicly available for all to view. This act also affects how we publish such results in our research studies.

A further troubling example in relation to who has right of access concerns the commonly used current practice of using students' work for other students as models or exemplars. Sometimes this has been done without asking for permission, but even when you do ask, it is perfectly understandable that those students who have done really well are willing to have their work used in this way, but what about those who have done badly or failed? These latter students might actually be the ones whose pieces of work you are keen to use as exemplars, as they are the most instructive for other students. In a similar vein, peer assessment poses some similar issues, and can be seen by some students as intrusive and threatening, but in this case, if it is part of the course, they do not have much choice. Interestingly, peer assessment is much less of an issue when it comes to certain disciplines such as creative and performing arts, for example, where peer criticism is part of the disciplinary context.

The fundamental principles of anonymity and confidentiality that individual participants will not be identified in any reporting of your study and that their data are privileged to the researcher are not quite as straightforward as they seem. There may be cases where you have to decide whether or not you should break that confidentiality, such as research in which you might discover frequent occurrences of cynical plagiarism among your student participants, or you uncover racism in marking practices in your fellow lecturers, for example. In a way, these are the easier ethical dilemmas to deal with as they are overt and require a decision about what action you should take. The British Educational Research Association's revised ethical guidelines for educational research (BERA, 2004) tackle this point in their section on disclosure (p. 9) in which they advise researchers to think very carefully about disclosing illegal behaviour to the appropriate authorities, and that, where possible, they should tell the participants of their intentions and the reasons why they must disclose this information.

More difficult to deal with are the covert breaches of confidentiality. For example, when you publish your research, and name yourself as the author, you are immediately giving away, without even deliberately doing so, information about your institution, colleagues and students. In pedagogical action research, the methodology is often qualitative/phenomenographical where we are actually looking to include all the rich contextual detail in our interpretation, so it becomes very difficult to keep our participants' privacy. An example of this situation would be any study where members of an institution's senior management team or other key staff are involved. In such cases, it is impossible to maintain confidentiality or even anonymity.

In most cases, though, anonymity is usually fairly easy to preserve. It is standard practice to use pseudonyms for excerpts from interview transcripts, but again care has to be taken, if you want to give, perfectly reasonably, some basic descriptive information about your interviewee. An example that comes to mind is taken from a research study that was carried out as part of a collaborative HEFCE-funded FDTL 4 (fund for the development of teaching and learning) called 'Assessment Plus', the website of which can be accessed through the Write Now CETL (see Chapter 9). The study involved carrying out research interviews with lecturers from three universities about their views on marking (Harrington et al., 2006).

When reporting excerpts from their interviews, we were keen to provide some descriptive information about our participants, such as the length of teaching experience that they had but, of course, this makes it relatively easy to work out who some interviewees are (the part-time hourly paid assistant who has had less than six months or the reader who has had over twenty years, for example). Perhaps what we should have done was to change the precise details, so as to protect the individuals from being identified by deduction.

Whenever possible, it is a good idea to collect your information without names or unique identifiers attached to the data or known to the researcher. When this is not possible because, for example, you need to re-contact your participants for follow-up information or for a further phase of research (common in pedagogical action research), you can take steps such as using codes for names. Student identification numbers are often used in this way. If this is not possible, you can ensure that names are removed from the records as soon as all the data are collated. In some cases where videotapes or audiotapes are used, you must take steps to ensure these are stored safely, preferably with the researcher having access to them but not the lecturer. This can be problematic when the researcher is also the lecturer.

In some pedagogical action research studies students become co-researchers so it is only natural and right that they receive credit and acknowledgement of their efforts. While this compromises their confidentiality and anonymity rights, the benefits for them may well outweigh the disadvantages (see the case study in Appendix G). Interestingly, Grinyer (2004) has argued that we make assumptions that anonymity is always desirable, yet some research participants would prefer their own names to be used rather than pseudonyms as it gives them some ownership of their information. Finally, in the digital age in which we live, technology is breaking down privacy in ways we have not begun to understand yet, such as wikis, blogs and social networking – all of which are fields of interest to the pedagogical researcher.

Protection from harm

Protecting your participants from harm in pedagogical research is not likely to be about physical harm, as is the case with some medical research, but it might be psychological harm, such as effects on self-esteem and academic confidence. Unpalatable as it is, I think we must acknowledge that pedagogical research on students could potentially harm their learning and academic performance, although this is likely to be relatively minor. Is it appropriate, for example, to use class time for research, which has no direct pedagogical benefits to the students themselves? What about the instances when we might ask them to give up to an hour of their time, which they might have set aside for study, to take part in focus groups, which again, are unlikely to benefit them directly?

Evaluation and student feedback has become a major issue in higher education with the influence of the Higher Education Academy (HEA) on foregrounding the student experience, the influential National Student Survey and the ubiquitous use of course and module evaluation. Perhaps we should be concerned that our students are not being 'questionnaired to death'. Is it right then to add even more surveys or enquiries onto an already overburdened population, many of whom have precious few hours working, studying and often with domestic and family responsibilities?

Throughout this book, I have argued that the purpose of pedagogical action research is to carry out systematic research enquiry in order that we discover something that will enhance our students' learning experience. This seems a morally justifiable and praiseworthy stance, yet in seeking to improve their learning experience, we are actually intruding on that very learning experience by the research we do. We have to recognise that there is an inevitable tension between researching students' learning with the goal of improving it, while at the same time actually interfering with that learning with no guarantees that their learning will improve.

Even when we choose to rely totally on non-intrusive investigations such as correlational research on naturally produced and available data, we may be dealing with issues of confidentiality, which might relate to students, to subjects or departments and to the institutions in which we are carrying out this research. Publishing such results might, by deduction, harm the reputation of our students, colleagues or institutions. Imagine, for example, a correlation study where we found that the number of face-to-face class contact hours was positively related to improved academic performance. The implications of such findings could potentially damage the reputation of those subjects that traditionally have low contact hours, such as arts, humanities and social sciences, as opposed to those that traditionally have high contact hours, such as the sciences and vocational degrees.

The pedagogical action research context

Having sounded all these cautions, I do not think that the pedagogical action researcher should be put off introducing and researching innovation in the learning environment. This is, in essence, what any good teacher does. Shulman (2002) describes it well in his foreword to Pat Hutchings' (2002) book on *Ethics of Inquiry, Issues in the Scholarship of Teaching and Learning*:

> teaching is an intentional, designed act undertaken to influence the minds of others, and to change the world in an intensely intimate, socially responsible manner. Such work brings with it inexorable responsibilities. Having engaged students through an act of instruction, the teacher becomes at least partially responsible for its efficacy. It is unimaginable that a teacher could teach with no concern for whether students had learned, how well they had learned, or whether their learning was appropriate to the field.
>
> (Shulman, 2002: v)

Here Shulman touches on an issue which is fundamental to pedagogical research: that of efficacy. In my career, I have had the pleasure of listening to enthusiastic and committed colleagues talking about their innovative practices at learning and teaching conferences and other related pedagogical events, sometimes put on by the Higher Education Academy, the Subject Centre Network and sometimes by institutions themselves. The question I always want to ask the presenters is:

'How do you know it works?'

Not answering this simple question is, I think, one of the great weaknesses of educational innovation and change. There is often insufficient empirical evidence to show that a specific innovation has the desired benefits. In all the education sectors, including higher education, there is a tendency to adopt practice without testing it. The problem-based learning wave, which started in the medical schools in the 1960s, is a case in point. In a pilot systematic review Newman (2004) concludes that:

> the limited high quality evidence available from existing reviews does not provide robust evidence about the effectiveness of different kinds of PBL in different contexts with different student groups.
>
> (Newman, 2004: 7)

Another example is the ubiquitous assumption that 'transferable skills' is an essential graduate attribute, which is even more accepted now post the Leitch report (Leitch, 2006) than it was post the Dearing report (National Committee of Inquiry into Higher Education, 1997). The concept of 'transferable skills' is in itself questionable (Hyland and Johnson, 1999) and the research evidence is far from robust (Yorke and Knight, 2003). Barnett (2004) describes the idea of skills as a 'cul-de-sac' and argues that learning for an unknown future has to be seen instead in terms of human qualities and dispositions.

Fortunately, the position regarding educational innovation and evidence is slowly changing as can be seen from the research pages of the HEA website, the relevant web pages in the Subject Centre Network, and the increasing influence of the SOTL movement. In my view, pedagogical action research is a particular kind of research which establishes efficacy in a practice focused way, so for this reason alone it is worth wrestling with the ethical issues that inevitably arise.

In a recent chapter that I wrote on ethical issues facing the practitioner-researcher in higher education (Norton, 2008), I suggest that it is the responsibility of the educational researcher to think ethically rather than merely go through an institutional ethics procedure. (To give you an idea of what such a process might involve, I have presented a generic ethics submission template in Appendix H.) What I meant by this was that it can sometimes be an almost formulaic process to go through the steps of gaining permission from an ethics committee but, as I hope I have illustrated above, many of the statements we make about informed consent, confidentiality and protection from harm actually have complex implications and, in the end, it comes down to moral responsibility and integrity. This is what Hutchings (2002) calls a reflective approach but it is more muscular than that because it has practical consequences and we are required to be ethically responsible throughout the course of our research study, rather than just accepting it once we have had the necessary approval. As Susanna Davis (n.d.), research ethics manager for the University of Technology, Sydney says:

Often there's no right answer, just a least wrong one. But there are always choices.

The politics of pedagogical action research

Up until now, most of my discussion has focused on the ethical implications of carrying out pedagogical action research involving either students or staff colleagues as participants. I want to turn my attention to a wider ethical issue: the politics of action research. I have briefly touched on the broader reach of pedagogical action research earlier in the book (in Chapters 3 and 4), but there I do not explicitly refer to it as political.

Pedagogical action research has, as described in Chapter 4, emerged from a broader field of educational action research and specifically the teacher-researcher model as advocated by Carr and Kemmis (1986). Kemmis (1993) has subsequently made some interesting comments about how action research can be a force for social change, but, he says, it depends on the choices we make:

> Our task as educational researchers involves us in taking concrete and explicit steps towards changing the theory, policy and practice of educational research, as well as participating in the work of changing educational theory, educational policy and educational practice more broadly.
>
> (Kemmis, 1993: 6)

What he was referring to here is how the different facets of action research can be seen as working at the micro-level which might be about the here and now of the teacher-researcher, or at the macro level which might be about large-scale policy research. In Kemmis' view, critical action research is connected to social change; it is about trying to understand and improve the way things are. Research itself is, he argues, a social practice, which like other social practices contributes to and serves bureaucracy, such as disciplinary fields. Researchers can however influence and change bureaucracy and the status quo by making different decisions about how they will participate in various research studies and on whose behalf.

For Kemmis, making the connection between social research and social action is achieved by making connections with different people in the service of different interests, which for pedagogical action researchers might be with educational administrators and policy makers as well as with students and fellow teachers. The point is picked up by both Carr and Kemmis (2005) who, in an article reflecting on their book nearly 20 years later, say how important it is to stay critical in the postmodern world, where social inequality worsens and research becomes increasingly restricted.

If we take this view seriously, then as a pedagogical action researcher you may find yourself with divided loyalties. What, for example, do you do, if your research findings show unacceptable bad practice within a department in your university? Carrying out pedagogical action research to change policy at the macro-level might put your own institution or colleagues in certain fields at risk if, for example, your research was used by government bodies to support the current emphasis on science and employability skills. It is important to remember that once you have published your research, you no longer have any say in how your findings might be interpreted, studied or reported in other publications.

An example of a classic research study comes to my mind, that of Marton and Säljö's (1976) deep and surface processing. The deep and surface metaphor was one that really took hold of the higher-education community, probably because it made intuitive sense and was an attractive and easily understandable way of describing the sort of approach we expected of university students. Yet, over the course of time, the original research findings became distorted from a description of students' intentions when they read a piece of text to sometimes being perceived as a description of students' personal characteristics. Such a distortion misses the pedagogical power of the deep and surface distinction, for it is how the student perceives and understands the learning environment and its concomitant assessment tasks that will determine whether she or he takes a deep or a surface approach. The point I am making here is that your research can be misunderstood or misappropriated once it is in the public domain, so sometimes thinking ethically means carrying out more research and writing more publications to influence policy making at the macro level.

Overall summary

Acting ethically involves making some careful and considered decisions at the research design stage, as well as in seeking formal ethical approval from our relevant instructional bodies. However much of the standard advice given in the various codes of practice poses its own particular problems in pedagogical action research, given its characteristics of being 'insider' research, where the practitioner-researcher has a dual role. To illustrate this in some detail I present a case study of some collaborative research I did, asking my students to be co-researchers. I reflect on the ethical dimensions of this study in Appendix G.

Students are often asked to be participants in research because they are relatively easy to access, are inexpensive and there are large numbers of them in the same location. The fact that students tend to be overused in research puts additional pressure on us as pedagogical researchers as we cannot carry out our research without them. This means we have to be extra vigilant about our enthusiasm and commitment to our learning and teaching initiatives leading to any element of coercion. This applies equally to involving staff colleagues in our research. The BERA (2004) guidelines make a particular statement about our responsibilities to participants:

the participants in research may be the active or passive subjects of such processes as observation, inquiry, experiment or test. They may be collaborators or colleagues in the research process or they may simply be part of the context e.g. where students are part of the context but not the subjects of a teacher's research into his or her own professional practice.

(BERA, 2004: 5)

Throughout the entire research process, we need to be aware of these and other ethical issues that are specific to pedagogical action research.

Synopsis

- In this chapter I have discussed ethical issues in carrying out educational research from the perspective of the pedagogical action researcher. In doing so I have argued that the dual role of practitioner and researcher leads us to making decisions not purely on research grounds but equally on pedagogical outcomes, indeed this is the very cornerstone of pedagogical action research.
- In the section on fundamental principles, I describe informed consent, anonymity and confidentiality, and protection from harm, considering how these principles can raise ethical issues that are particularly problematic in pedagogical research.
- In the section on the pedagogical action research context, I briefly discuss its political aspect and ethical implications.
- Throughout the chapter I have argued for an approach to ethics that is 'muscular' and active rather than pragmatically conforming to published codes of practice or institutional processes, by which I mean ticking the boxes without carefully thinking about the implications of doing insider research.
- Finally, I describe (in Appendix G) a case study of an action research study, co-authored by students, and I reflect on the ethical issues raised by this study as a way of illustrating some of the difficult dilemmas which face us.

Further reading and resources

Codes of practice

American Educational Research Association (2000) 'The Ethical Standards of the American Educational Research Association'. Online. Available: http://www.aera.net/aboutaera/?id=222 (accessed 27 April 2008).

American Psychological Society (2002) 'Ethical principles for psychologists and codes of conduct'. Online. Available: http://www.apa.org/ethics/code2002.html (accessed 27 April 2008).

American Sociological Association (1999) 'Code of ethics'. Online. Available: http://www.asanet.org/page.ww?section=Ethicsandname=Ethics (accessed 27 April 2008).

Australian Association for Research in Education (1993) 'Code of ethics'. Online. Available: http://www.aare.edu.au/ethics/ethcfull.htm (accessed 27 April 2008).

BERA (2004) 'Revised ethical guidelines for educational research'. Online. Available: http://www.bera.ac.uk/publications/pdfs/ETHICA1.PDF (accessed 27 April 2008).

British Psychological Society (2006) 'Code of ethics and conduct'. Online. Available: http://www.bps.org.uk/downloadfile.cfm?file_uuid=5094A992–1143-DFD0–7E6C-F1939A65C242andext=pdf (accessed 27 April 2008).

British Sociological Association (2002) 'Statement of ethical practice for the British Sociological Association, plus updated version in Appendix (2004)'. Online. Available: http://www.britsoc.co.uk/equality/Statement+Ethical+Practice.htm (accessed 27 April 2008).

Books

As far as I am able to discover, there are no books specifically written about the ethics of research in higher education. The following are a representative sample of books, which offer something to the pedagogical action researcher:

Burgess, R.G. (ed.) (1990) *The Ethics of Educational Research*, London: FalmerPress.

McNamee, M. and Bridges, D. (2002) *The Ethics of Educational Research*, Journal of Philosophy of Education Book Series, Blackwell.

Mauthner, M.L., Birch, M., Jessop, J. and Miller, T. (eds) (2002) *Ethics in Qualitative Research*, London: Sage.

Simons, H. and Usher, R (2000) *Situated Ethics in Educational Research*, London: Routledge Falmer.

Zeni, J. (2001) *Ethical Issues in Practitioner Research*, Practitioner Inquiry Series, New York: Teachers College Press.

Chapter 11

Going public: How can you grow the influence of your findings?

Introduction

In this final chapter we have reached the point which is the most important of all, that of disseminating your findings. This has been described in the scholarship of teaching and learning (SOTL) movement as 'going public'. No matter how good your research study is, it will, like any pedagogical project, perish unless you can disseminate it as widely as possible. Going public is vital as it opens up your research to peer scrutiny and this is what makes pedagogical action research distinct from introspective, reflective practice or from the usual curriculum development.

Pedagogical action research is in a unique position when it comes to dissemination, as it is research that has a dual aim. It informs policy making and adapts existing practice, as well as contributing to new knowledge making. This will affect your decisions about where and how to share your findings. In the first part of the chapter, by using a hypothetical case study, I will discuss the options for publication that are available to you. I will then describe how you go about seeking funding to further your action research. In this respect, research publications are significant evidence of a track record that will help you in the bidding for funding process (internal or external). And so this chapter comes full circle, like pedagogical action research itself, to another beginning, more questions to answer and further research studies to carry out.

Dissemination

Although the purpose for which you carried out your study will largely determine where you choose to disseminate your findings, it is a sound principle to try and report them as widely as possible. This will inevitably mean adopting different formats. A conference paper is different, for example, to a publication in a journal, which will in turn be different from a report in a professional body's magazine or newsletter, but the more outlets you can use the more effect your research will have. Figure 11.1 is a simple

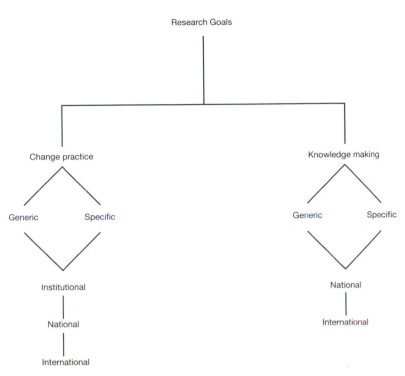

Figure 11.1 Decision chart for deciding on appropriate methods of disseminating an action research project

decision chart to aid your thinking about the purpose and range of your pedagogical research. Figure 11.2 shows some of the most common methods of dissemination.

In this section I will describe some of these more common methods using the following hypothetical vignette.

The case of Maureen and Mike: The wiki enthusiasts

Dr Maureen Lombard is the newest lecturer to be appointed to the School of Mathematics and Statistics in a traditional redbrick university, working in the Department of Applied Statistics. She is on a fixed-term, three-year contract and has just successfully finished her higher-education teaching certificate. The department is large, consisting of more than 40 academics, most of whom have been in post for ten or more years. The department is proud of its last Research

Goals	Focus	Dissemination methods
Changing subject specific practice	Institutional	Presentations to: Department, school or faculty; Written report circulated to subject colleagues (hard or electronic copy) Collaborating with CETL (if subject appropriate)
	National and international	Presentations/reports/workshops via: HEA Subject Centre network; Subject professional body; Subject specific practice-based pedagogical events/conferences; Subject specific practice-based pedagogical journals
Changing generic practice/ informing policy making	Institutional	Presentations/reports to the institutional senior management team or academic committee Presentations/reports/workshops via: Institutional learning and teaching events
	National and international	HEA (including the HEA annual conference) Practice-based teaching and learning conferences National practice based pedagogical journals Press articles Newsletters Chapters in edited books (may be on education rather than specifically higher education) Authored books
Contributing to subject specific new knowledge	National and international	National/international peer reviewed subject-specific journals Chapters in edited books Authored books
Contributing to generic new knowledge	National and international	National/international peer reviewed subject-specific journals Chapters in edited books Authored books

Figure 11.2 Suggested methods of disseminating pedagogical action research

Assessment Exercise (RAE) rating, which was a 5 and the fact that the Royal Statistical Society accredits their undergraduate programme.

Maureen is responsible for a second-year optional module called 'Statistical reasoning and philosophy'. Enthused by her experience on the teaching certificate programme, she decided to incorporate a wiki to replace the traditional assessment. She sought the help of one of the postgraduate assistants, Mike Mantoni, who was in the last stages of completing his PhD and who was keen on developing technology to facilitate learning basic statistical concepts. Together they designed an action research project to see if using a wiki environment on the school's VLE (virtual learning environment) would enhance students' critical thinking skills about statistics.

Students were asked to use the wiki environment to discuss causality and statistics as a group assessed project. They were required to write consecutive drafts of their thinking, exchange opinions on each other's drafts and publish their final agreed version on the wiki. Mike and Maureen analysed each draft for evidence of progression in critical thinking and sent the final version to a national leader in statistics and philosophy for an objective appraisal. To their delight, his report stated that in his view the evidence of thinking exhibited was at postgraduate level.

A further unexpected bonus was the students were so enthusiastic about this way of learning that they wanted to establish a wikipedia for the whole department, which would have contributions from both the staff and the students to develop a glossary of statistical terms and concepts.

Mike and Maureen are keen to take this idea forward, but the head of the department, Professor Roe, has advised Maureen that in terms of her career path she would be better concentrating on maintaining a track record of RAE-assessable publications in her subject rather than 'be diverted by pedagogical research'.

This scenario has a number of crucial factors in it.
On the positive side:

- a good pedagogical idea using inexpensive technology;
- action research findings which suggest evidence of efficacy;
- an outside objective positive report from a nationally recognised expert in the field;
- enthusiastic student feedback;
- a level of student engagement, which is a strong indicator for further development.

On the negative side:

- Mike and Maureen work in a traditional department where most of the staff have many years teaching and research experience and so may be reluctant to change their approaches.
- The department is very proud of the fact that its undergraduate programme is accredited by the Royal Statistical Society, so any proposed changes in curriculum are difficult to get approved.
- The department has a strong RAE reputation, which does not include pedagogical research.
- Professor Roe has given a clear signal to Maureen to concentrate on her subject research, a particularly significant pointer as she is on a fixed-term contract.

I have written this scenario to represent what is often the real situation in universities today. Unfortunately, pedagogical research is frequently not seen as important as subject research. Similarly, teaching itself may not be seen as important as doing research. This is a regrettable state of affairs and one that I oppose. Nevertheless, if we are to promote the cause of pedagogical research it is important to be aware of some of the obstacles that face us, so we can be better prepared to deal with them.

In using this vignette, I hope to illustrate how the different ways of publishing a pedagogical action research study might help you to progress your work despite some of these obstacles.

Reporting within your institution

Impacting on practice within the subject department/school/faculty

One of the goals of pedagogical action research is to have an immediate effect on practice, so it is likely that if your research findings show some benefit to student learning, then it may well have implications for the teaching of your subject by your colleagues. But how do you persuade them to adopt an initiative such as Maureen and Mike's wikipedia?

A good first step would be to have some informal chats with those colleagues that you know are interested in teaching or in your specific pedagogical issue. You might persuade them there and then to join your research. One of the characteristics of action research is that it is collaborative, and it takes only a small number of extra colleagues to grow an action research study and increase its scope and influence. This would then enable you to further the research by seeking some external funding to support it (this will be discussed in detail later). Even if you are not successful in getting their active involvement, you have prepared the ground for the next step, which is presenting your findings at a departmental meeting, and you may be able to look to them for some support.

Different institutions have their own organisational structures, but in Maureen and Mike's case they would need to ask Professor Roe, as head of the Department of Applied Statistics, if they could give a brief presentation on their findings at one of his regular departmental meetings. This can be a very effective way of finding out in a more formal setting, rather than anecdotally or by word of mouth, what the consensus reaction is to your initiative.

Departments, schools and faculties are powerful organisations, the nature of which are described by Becher and Trowler (2001), who use the term 'academic tribes' to capture their essence (see Chapter 1). Since Maureen is the newest member of the applied statistics 'tribe' and Mike is yet to be considered a full member, they have an uphill battle to change the prevailing culture. However, by presenting their findings formally to their colleagues, they are at the very worst keeping them informed and at best they might persuade a few colleagues to contribute to their wikipedia initiative.

Impacting on practice at a generic level within the institution

It is perfectly possible, of course, that Maureen and Mike do not get the sort of interest they were hoping for, but they may still be able to develop their idea from an interdisciplinary perspective. This would involve them giving some sort of research presentation at an institutional learning and teaching event.

The longer I have been involved in pedagogical action research and academic development, the more I realise that while subject and discipline differences are crucial, and indeed this is why the HEA Subject Centres Network have been so successful, there are more commonalities than one might at first suspect. Pedagogical issues of student engagement, widening participation, assessment, employability, skills development and group teaching have their own subject context but raise common areas of concern. This is why it can be an effective strategy to give a research presentation on your study at an institutional level.

Universities have different arrangements, but many have learning and teaching-related events, such as learning and teaching days, and internal learning and teaching conferences. Most have some sort of academic/staff-development unit, which may organise events for continuing professional development in learning and teaching. Institutional events such as these would be an ideal venue to publicise your action research and interest colleagues in becoming research collaborators to develop the pedagogical project in different disciplines and contexts.

Some institutions have dedicated some of their HEFCE funding (such as the Teaching Quality Enhancement Fund (TQEF), e-learning and research-informed teaching) to support pedagogical research studies. If your university has a centre for excellence in teaching and learning (CETL) there may also be opportunities for dissemination and research funding, provided your study is consonant with the overall aims of the CETL.

In Maureen and Mike's case we will assume there is no CETL, but that their university does have an annual learning and teaching weekend organised by the Centre for Academic Staff Development and Human Resources. By promoting their research findings at this event, or, better still, by running a workshop where participants can actively contribute, they are likely to get involvement from colleagues in other subjects who are interested in the pedagogical potential of developing a wikipedia.

The most common mistake with running a workshop is that presenters use it as an alternative to a research presentation. This is not the purpose of a workshop, which should be about getting your participants involved. In Maureen and Mike's case they may want to briefly talk about their initiative and why they think the idea of a wikipedia will be worth developing, and then, ideally, they should demonstrate what has been done so far and allow the workshop participants to have hands-on experience of seeing how this tool can be developed.

The workshop might also include opportunities for the participants to brainstorm ways in which an action research project might be designed to further explore the benefits of a statistics wikipedia, perhaps for students in those disciplines where statistics is part of the course (such as geography, agriculture, biology and medicine, for example). It may be that this has the effect of somewhat changing the direction of their original research study by not confining it to statistics students.

This sometimes happens with action research (or indeed with any type of research) and means you then have to make decisions about whether you want to continue with something with a much larger reach and scope, but at the same time which will lose the focus of your original subject-specific pedagogical issue.

Reporting beyond your institution

As well as impacting on practice at the institutional level, you will want to broaden the reach of your research. This may be to change practice, or to contribute to new knowledge, or, as is common in pedagogical action research, to be a combination of both.

Figure 11.2 outlines some of the more common outlets for dissemination, of which I am going to concentrate on two: disseminating at conferences and disseminating through journal publications.

Giving a conference paper

The benefits of giving a conference paper are threefold.

1. If you are aiming at a journal paper, presenting your findings at a conference first will give you some valuable peer feedback which will help you develop your paper.
2. Writing for publication, such as for a journal, usually has no deadline attached to it, which means that often it is your writing that gets pushed to the bottom of the pile in the numerous tasks we all face as academics in our daily working lives. Giving a conference paper, however, does have a deadline attached to it, so it is a powerful motivator for you to make progress on disseminating your findings. It is always a good idea to have a written version of your conference paper to use as a handout in your session. Extra copies left on the conference reception desk will enable your research to reach a wider audience. Doing this means you are three-quarters of the way there in getting your paper submitted to a journal, or to having it published in the conference proceedings if this is offered.
3. Conferences are invaluable places for networking, inspiration and encouragement, which is often invaluable as pedagogical research can sometimes be an isolating occupation.

If you have never presented a pedagogical paper before, you may feel more comfortable in the first instance in choosing a subject-specific event such as those run by the Subject Centres Network. Since Maureen and Mike are relatively inexperienced in the field of pedagogical research, they could aim for the CETL–MSOR (Continuing Excellence in the Teaching and Learning of Maths, Stats and Operational Research) conference (see http://www.mathstore. ac.uk/conference2007/index.shtml (accessed 27 April 2008)).

The Subject Centres Network conferences are excellent places to start, as you will have the experience of meeting colleagues in your discipline who have the same enthusiastic commitment to the teaching of your discipline as you do. If you prefer to give your paper at one of the generic learning and teaching conferences, there are many to choose from, ranging from national to international (see the further resources section for some of the best-known ones).

Getting your conference paper abstract accepted may not be an easy process. Depending on the status and reputation of the conference, there will be different acceptance rates. Generally speaking, the larger international conferences will have more stringent criteria than the smaller conferences. In all cases though, there are a number of steps you can take to give yourself the best chance of having your conference paper proposal accepted.

Step One: Plan ahead

Although this is a counsel of perfection, it really does pay well to think about where you are going to present your findings at the starting point of designing your action research project. This is why a research protocol is such a useful 'map' as it has a section on disseminating your findings and will get you thinking about this very important end point before you begin (see Chapter 6).

If you do not think this through first, and in reality this happens to a number of pedagogical research studies, you may find that the deadline for submitting your proposals comes before you have analysed your data. If you do not have data already collected, the conference committee is taking a chance on whether you will have anything to report by the time of the conference. Sending in premature proposals is, therefore, one of the most frequent reasons for having your submission rejected. An illustration of this is shown in the appendices, where I have included an example of an abstract that was rejected for an international learning and teaching research conference (see Appendix I) and an abstract that was successful for the same conference (see Appendix J).

Knowing which conference you are aiming for at the design stage of your study and when the deadline for submission is will avoid this potential pitfall.

Step Two: Writing a good conference abstract

There are really two audiences for your conference abstract; firstly the conference reviewing committee who will accept or reject your proposal and, secondly, if it is accepted, the conference delegates who will choose whether or not to hear your presentation. I will take each of these in turn.

1. Writing your abstract for the conference reviewing committee

   a. Reviewers will usually, but not always, review your abstract blind, which means in a very limited space (typically about 300 words) you have to make a good case for why your proposal should be accepted, rather than relying on your name or your reputation. Your abstract, therefore, needs to summarise your key contributions in terms of what is new, different and, most crucially, applicable about your work to the conference themes.

   b. Sometimes you are asked to structure your abstract according to given headings. This is likely to be the case for conferences where you are asked to submit an extended summary (typically about 1000 words) as well as an abstract. Even if you are not asked to do this, it is a good idea to have the following in mind when writing your abstract.

      Title. This should provide a clear indication of what your research is about. If possible, the title should show how the study connects to the conference themes.

      Aims. Tell the reviewers the purpose of your research, and make sure you set it in a theoretical literature review context. (All research builds on research that has gone on before, and you need to demonstrate this.)

      Methodology/research design. Depending on the conference, reviewers may be looking for evidence of a substantial research project, which might mean large samples or inter-institutional research, or depth of analysis. This is generally the case if you are aiming at a large international, research-intensive conference. For practitioner conferences, you are unlikely to need to present such large-scale research, but that does not mean you should be any the less rigorous. In pedagogical action research we are trying to get away from what are sometimes known as 'show and tell presentations' to studies that are carefully designed (as described in Chapter 6).

      Research findings. You may not have completed the analysis of your findings when you have to submit your abstract, but the further on you are the better. The more detail you can give about your proposed analysis on already collected data, the more likely your abstract will be accepted (see Appendix J).

      Theoretical and/or educational significance of the research. This is a good place to explicitly refer to the theme/s of the conference in terms of the implications of your findings.

      References. You should include a small number of key references to demonstrate you know the field, but do not include a lengthy list, as space is precious. It is safer to include your references in the word count if you are not sure, but you might want to check this with the conference reviewers.

c. Finally, it sounds obvious, but make sure you scrupulously follow all the instructions for submitting your abstract, including meeting the deadline for submission and not exceeding the word allowance.

d. If the conference organisers have not announced a notification date, you should contact them to find out when to expect a reply. If you do not hear from them by the specified date, you must get in touch with them immediately. It is a rare occurrence, but sometimes abstracts can go missing, so you must not assume that because you have not heard anything your abstract has not been accepted.

2. Rewriting your abstract for the conference delegates
Once your abstract has been accepted, some, but not all, conference organisers give you the opportunity to modify your abstract for the conference programme. Usually, the timescale for this is quite tight, however it is well worth doing because no matter how good your research, if nobody comes to listen to your presentation your efforts will be wasted.

a. Rewriting your title. If it is possible, try and make your title appealing, so that people will want to hear what you have to say. Avoid titles that are too long, as they can appear dreary. Equally be careful of the too short title, which might be snappy but does not give any information. Some of the more successful titles have the catchy part in the first clause and then a subtitle. Here are two examples of abstract titles taken from a parallel session on e-learning at the Science Learning and Teaching Conference 2007 (http://www.sltc.heacademy.ac.uk/programmedetail.htm#sessions1 (accessed 27 April 2008)).

Beyond Entertainment: Web 2.0 and Science Education, Alan Cann

Research Skills Audit Tool: An Online Resource to Map Research Skills Within Undergraduate Curricula, Gillian Fraser

b. Potential audience. It also helps if you think about your potential audience and show in your abstract how your research will be of particular interest to them. Although not many conferences specify this, it is a useful mental reminder to think through what your audience will gain by coming to listen to your paper, for example:
By the end of our research paper, delegates will:
1. ....
2. ....
3. ....

Giving a conference poster

Many conferences have sessions for posters in their programmes and you may want to consider this as an alternative to a research paper. Generally speaking, you will be asked to submit a poster proposal abstract, so the above principles for research paper proposals apply equally to this type of submission. Occasionally, you may have your research paper proposal rejected but be offered a poster presentation instead. Naturally, this is a disappointing outcome but rather than rejecting it out of hand, it is in fact a good opportunity to get your research disseminated as you can seize this chance by preparing a written paper to go with your poster to give to delegates who are interested in your research.

Posters offer different advantages to formal research presentations by enabling the presenters and the audience to talk with each other much less formally, so they can be a very useful way of getting feedback on your developing work. Typically, there will be an exhibition area in which each presenter is provided with a free-standing bulletin board on which to display his or her poster. Sizes vary, so it is important to check with the conference organisers what size your poster should be.

A certain time will be set aside for poster presentations and during that time the delegates will move around the exhibition area stopping to talk to the authors of those posters that particularly interest them. Advice on how to produce good quality posters is given in the further resources section at the end of this chapter.

Publications from conferences

Some conferences offer presenters the opportunity of publishing their paper in a book of conference proceedings. This usually involves giving you the opportunity to rewrite your paper to a fairly tight deadline but, unlike the abstract reviewing process, there is generally no further peer review, as that is assumed to have taken place in your presentation. You need to think carefully about whether or not you want to take this opportunity, which is a guaranteed publication, or whether you would prefer to aim for a journal instead where there is no guarantee that your manuscript will be accepted. What you cannot do is publish the same paper in both.

Unless you feel you have a groundbreaking research study to report, I would advise you to take the conference proceeding option. Even though it is regarded as less prestigious than a paper in a peer-reviewed journal, it is still a publication and will give you valuable experience in writing in this field, as well as giving you some evidence of a track record if you are seeking funding to further your research.

Writing a journal paper

This is the medium that still carries the maximum esteem and for many disciplines is considered RAE assessable. Getting research published in a journal takes a very long time and is hard work. Never get put off or discouraged, but use the rejections and the comments of colleagues and/or reviewers as a way of helping you improve your paper. It is best to think of it as a process in which many drafts will be needed rather than as a single version. For your first paper, it is helpful to find someone who has had considerable experience in getting published to advise you. Preferably this should be someone in the area of pedagogical research rather than subject research, but if this is not possible, ask a colleague with a solid publications' track record because the principles of getting published are the same, no matter what the field.

Step One: Target your journal before you start writing

This is a vital step, yet it is surprising how many of us write our study first and then look for somewhere to publish it. This is time wasting and lacks focus. There is a list of journals which publish pedagogical research in the further resources section at the end of this chapter. Another useful resource is Tight's (2003) book on the principal areas of research in higher education, in which he has written a chapter analysing 17 selected journals that specialise in publishing higher-education research.

You should look at several journals and find out as much as possible about each of them, before deciding which one to aim for. Nearly all journals have electronic websites, so finding information about them is very easy these days. Here are some general questions to consider.

I. WHAT IS ITS PURPOSE?

This is described in the aims and scope of the journal. What sorts of contribution are the editors looking for? Do they welcome empirical reports or do they prefer more discursive theoretical papers? Some journals are multidisciplinary; others are not. What readership is the journal aiming at? As well as reading the aims and scope, you will get a good feel for a journal by browsing back issues, most of which are available to you or your institution online. This will give you an idea of whether the articles contain a high proportion of tables and statistical data, or whether a qualitative methodology is preferred. Some journals will be more geared towards applied research, others towards more theoretical and/or empirical research.

2. IS IT REFEREED AND HOW?

This is an important index of quality. There are four basic levels.

Editor alone. This is the most basic level as the editor acts, as the gatekeeper in deciding whether or not others will consider your manuscript, unless she or he has commissioned your paper, perhaps for a special issue of the journal. An editor's review would mean a fairly swift response but usually not much feedback if she or he turns down your paper as not being suitable for publication in that journal.

Editorial board. This is not often used today, as the publishing market has become so competitive, but some journals may still rely on their editorial board for a decision on whether or not to publish your manuscript. The feedback you get would tend to be limited but you would receive a fairly swift response.

Peer reviewed. This is the standard for the established journals and is a mark of rigour, because your work will be reviewed independently by at least two colleagues who are experts in the field. In practice the pressure on editors to find suitable reviewers who are willing and able to respond in the six to eight weeks usually allowed makes finding such reviewers sometimes difficult. This might mean that reviewers are not always expert, and/or, quite often, that there is a long delay in hearing from the journal as to what has happened on your submission. It is not unusual to have to wait several months. Some journals are quicker than others. The more prestigious, the more competitive it is to get a paper accepted, so this will mean more throughput and possibly longer delays. Check to see how many issues a year the journal produces, as this will be another indication of how long it might take to get published.

Blind peer reviewed. The most rigorous of all the reviewing systems, as your manuscript is anonymised so that the reviewers will not be influenced by your status or reputation in the field and will judge the worth of your work on its own merits. Most peer review, whether it is done blind or not, tends to be done anonymously, as the consensus view is that reviewers will be more honest if they are not named. Some journals have a policy whereby the reviewers can identify themselves if they wish.

3. HOW PRESTIGIOUS IS IT?

The most commonly used indicator is Thompson's Journal Citation Reports® (JCR) (http://scientific.thomson.com/products/jcr/ (accessed 27 April 2008)), accessible on the ISI Web of Knowledge. This gives information about academic journals in the sciences and social sciences, including a measure of the journal's impact factor which represents the frequency that an 'average' article has been cited in a particular year. For this reason, JCR always operates a year behind the current year.

If your institution does not have access to JCR, there are other ways in which you can gauge the prestige of a journal. Some publishers, such as Taylor and Francis, give the JCR ranking (see, for example, the Journal of Geography in Higher Education at http://www.tandf.co.uk/journals/journal.asp?issn=0309–8 265andsubcategory=ED300000 (accessed 27 April 2008) which has a ranking in the 2006 JCR: 15/39 (Geography); and an Impact Factor of 1.321.

Such indicators of esteem may change, given the current UK situation where the RAE is currently being transformed to a Research Excellence Framework (REF), but at the time of writing it is unclear how this will play out across the sector (see HEFCE, 2008).

Other useful indicators are to look at who is the editor and who is on the editorial board. Finally, you can ascertain whether the journal is national or international. If the latter, it is more prestigious, but you may find you are asked to draw on a wider literature base and write in a simpler more easy-to-understand style for those whose first language is not English.

Step Two: Follow the instructions for authors

Once you have decided on your journal, you should read, digest and follow exactly the instructions for authors. Each journal has its own way of doing things but you should follow the guidelines exactly. If the editor wants you to send in five hard copies with double-line spacing, and tables and illustrations on separate pages, then that is what you have to do. If the editor wants a version on a certain size disc using certain software, then again that is what you have to do.

One of the most frustrating and time-consuming but essential things you have to do is to reference in exactly the way the journal requires and there often seems to be minuscule differences in conventions. With the increasing use of software to help, this task is much easier. Two examples of available reference management tools are EndNote and Reference Manager. If your institution does not already have a site license for these, it would be well worth your while making the case to the relevant research committee.

Step Three: Write your paper

Write your paper, being careful to use a similar style to that used in your targeted journal. Ask your mentor for feedback on your first draft. If you can get feedback from more than one colleague, so much the better. Some university departments set up writing-for-research networks where manuscripts are circulated between members of the group. This is an excellent way to help each other get published and has the added advantage of keeping you on track with your writing when other pressures intrude. You might want to consider establishing a pedagogical action research network for this purpose.

Once you have received feedback from your colleagues, you will need to revise your draft until you are satisfied that it is ready for submission. Make sure that each draft is numbered, dated and saved in several different places and that you have clearly labelled the version that you have submitted to the journal you have chosen.

Step Four: Submit your paper

Following the instructions, submit your paper to the relevant editor. Some journals have specified editors for certain types of submission or to cover geographical locations. It is a usual practice to write some brief letter or email to the editor as follows.

> Dear Professor/Dr (make sure you know who the latest editor is)
>
> Please find enclosed four copies of our paper 'Enhancing statistics students: Critical thinking skills using a wiki.' by Maureen Lombard and Michael Mantoni.
>
> I should be grateful if you would consider this for publication in your journal *Pedagogical Action Research in Mathematics Teaching*.
>
> As first author, I will handle all correspondence and can be reached as follows.
>
> Postal address: Dr Maureen Lombard, Department of Applied Statistics, University of ...
>
> Email:
> Telephone:
> Mobile:
> Fax:
> I look forward to hearing from you.
> Yours sincerely,
> Maureen Lombard

Usually, the editor will acknowledge safe receipt of your manuscript and if she or he judges it suitable will say that it has been sent off to the reviewers and she or he will get in touch with you, when the reviewers' reports have been received. Most turn-round times are supposed to be within the region of six to eight weeks, but in my experience, it is often a great deal longer than that. If you have not heard from the editor after about three months, it is a good idea to send her or him a polite reminder asking how far the reviewing process has got.

Occasionally the editor will send your manuscript back saying it is not suitable for the journal. This is naturally disappointing but the best action to take is to submit it right away to another journal, even if this does mean extra work in tailoring it to different requirements. The worst response is to feel so demoralised that you consign the paper to never being published, which is a waste of time, energy and commitment. If, however, after submitting to a second journal, you still get another rejection, it might be a better option to accept that your research is premature for journal publication and concentrate on disseminating it in another type of publication, as detailed below in the section on other publications.

Step Five: Responding to the reviewers

When you do hear from the editor it is likely that you will receive her or his editorial decision together with copies of the referees' comments. This will usually take one of the following forms:

1. Accept without any revisions
   This does not happen very often, but is very nice when it does.
2. Accept with minor revisions
   This tends to mean you need to do some more work involving responding to all the referees' comments and paying particular attention to anything the editor wants you to take account of. In my view, if you get a decision like this, it is always worth doing, as your paper will very likely be published as long as you do what has been asked. In order to give yourself the best possible chance of having your revised manuscript accepted, make sure you send an additional letter to the editor (see Appendix K for an example), showing how and where you have made the necessary changes. Appendix L is an example of the kind of document that should also be sent to the editor, in which you highlight the referees' comments and show how you have responded to them, giving as much detail as possible (such as page and line numbers) in order to save the editor's time and hopefully make for a swift decision to publish your revised manuscript.
3. Accept with major revisions
   This is quite common and it is quite difficult to know what to do as it usually involves asking you to get more data, which is not always possible, or to reanalyse your data and substantially rewrite the paper. It is likely that the same reviewers who commented on your original manuscript will be asked to review your revised paper.
   If you have been asked to reanalyse your existing data and rewrite, this would be worth doing as it means you have a strong chance of getting your paper accepted. If you are asked to collect more data, this can be much more difficult as pedagogical action research tends to involve students, so usually the opportunity has gone by as they have moved on. In these cases I would take note of all the referees' comments, and rewrite what was possible, before submitting it to another journal.
4. Rejection
   This is the most discouraging response but happens to all of us. The best thing you can do here is to use the referees' suggestions to write a better paper to submit elsewhere. The worst thing you can do is to give up.

Step Six: The final stages

Having had your article accepted, complied with the required changes, you submit it again in the requested format and then you have to be patient and wait. Some journals have a period of several months before they can fit your paper in and usually the editor will tell you roughly how long. You will be sent various legal forms to sign to say it has not appeared anywhere else and to sign various copyright agreements, then you wait again. Then quite unexpectedly, you will get the proofs of your paper, when you tend to have about three days to check them and return to the editor or person dealing with your paper. The instructions will tell you that changing the proof at this stage is very expensive so they want you only to change mistakes, not rewrite anything. It pays you to go through your proofs very carefully, as typesetters often make very tiny but important mistakes that can be very difficult to spot. Make sure you use conventional proofreading symbols. A copy of these can be found online at http://www.jou rnalismcareers.com/articles/proofreadingsymbols.shtml (accessed 27 April 2008).

When your article is published, some journals offer you 20–30 free reprints, free online access to your article and sometimes a hard copy of the journal issue in which your paper appears.

Other publications

Depending on your purpose, you may decide to publish your research in other types of publication.

These might include:

- in-house journals (good for disseminating pedagogical research across the institution and for making yourself known, as it is likely to be read by your institutional senior managers);
- chapters in edited books (usually you are approached by the editors to contribute);
- conference proceedings (as described above);
- newsletters, such as those produced by many of the HEA Subject Centres.

These are particularly appropriate if you want to change subject-specific practice. Maureen and Mike, for example, might choose to write an account in MSOR-Connections, which is a quarterly newsletter distributed in hard copy and electronically in pdf format from the HEA Subject Centres website at http://mathstore.ac.uk/newsletter/index.shtml (accessed 27 April 2008).

- the Subject Centres' journals: most, but not all, of the Subject Centres have their own journals or other outlets for dissemination (see further resources);
- the HEA's magazine Academy Exchange. Online. Available: http://www. heacademy.ac.uk/resources/publications/exchange (accessed 27 April 2008). This would be a good outlet if you are concerned with informing policy making in higher education, as it is circulated to senior managers, vice-chancellors and pro-vice-chancellors, deans of faculty, and heads of academic development, staff development and quality management units.

- the HEA also commissions monographs, research reports and literature reviews.

Some of these publications are more stringent in their requirements than others, but use the same broad principles described for getting a journal paper published.

Summary

Getting published is key to growing the influence of your pedagogical action research study, and to building your profile in this area. If you have never published in the field before, it might be helpful to start with your Subject Centre Network if your research is discipline specific. If it is more generic, my advice would be to aim first for a conference paper, and then develop that into a journal paper or newsletter article or both.

Sometimes colleagues are uncertain about whether or not they can publish the same piece in more than one place. Unless you have specific permission from the editor of your original publication, the answer is no. However, it is perfectly possible to publish different versions of the same study suited to different publications. So you might say in your journal article that an earlier version of the paper was given at a conference; or you might in a newsletter give a broad outline of the study, concentrating perhaps on the pedagogical implications and referring the reader to your journal article. Always check beforehand with the editor of each publication that this is acceptable.

The main point is you should aim to make your research impact as widely as possible – for your own reputation, for pedagogical change and for building a track record that will help you in any bidding for funding you might undertake. This is the subject of the next section of this chapter.

Seeking research funding

This is a process not to be entered into lightly as it is extremely time-consuming and highly competitive. Anecdotally, experienced researchers have told me that you can expect to have one success for every seven applications. So you may ask is it worth it? The answer is yes, for four main reasons.

1. If you want your action research to grow, you will need funding to support further research cycles.
2. Success breeds success, so you are more likely to win further funding if you have been successful in the past.
3. Attracting funding is a major indicator of research prestige, so it may well be a good move for your academic career.
4. Bringing in external funding for pedagogical action research will do much to raise its status, and yours, within your institution.

Internal funding

Depending on your institution, there may be funding set aside to support pedagogical research, particularly since the recent allocation by HEFCE of funds specifically for research-informed teaching, but it is more likely that you will have to compete with more traditional subject-research bids for available monies. This situation has improved in recent years with the establishment of learning and teaching enhancement or academic development units which may fund small-scale learning and teaching projects, and with the development of the CETLs which again may well support pedagogical research connected to their areas of interest.

It is always worth exploring the possibilities within your own institution, especially if you want limited funds, perhaps to employ research assistance on analysing your data, as the process of bid writing is probably going to be easier and quicker.

External funding

The range of opportunities for large-scale research funding in higher education are considerable, ranging from the Teaching and Learning Research Programme (TLRP) of the Economic and Research Council (ESRC) to government initiatives such as the CETLs.

One of the best places to start is the HEA, which has a web page on funding opportunities for learning and teaching projects in higher education (http://www.heacademy.ac.uk/funding (accessed 27 April 2008)), including their online services for funding, which enables you to search by amount, keywords or region which is useful if you want to go beyond the UK (http://www.connect.ac.uk/funding?session=vPAljnGgci4 (accessed 27 April 2008)).

Many of the Subject Centres offer small amounts of funding for pedagogical projects, some of which may be up to £5000, and/or for case studies, which tend to be no more than £500. They also have good subject-specific links to other sources of funding, so they can be useful for subject-specific pedagogical research.

Whether you are going for a small grant such as from the Subject Centres or for a much larger one, you will need to follow the instructions and criteria very closely, but there are some general principles that are common to all, which I outline below.

Identifying your funding source

First of all you have to decide what you need the money for. This may sound obvious, but there is a lot of work involved in developing a research bid, so you need to be clear in your own mind that you actually need the money. In Maureen and Mike's case, they have a pedagogical initiative that they want to develop and to research its efficacy, but being busy academics they realise that they will not have time to collate and analyse the data for their wiki research. Funding of £5000 would enable them to employ a research assistant on an hourly basis who could carry out a qualitative analysis on students' wiki entries and on their assignments to see if there was evidence of advanced critical thinking.

Secondly, you have to focus on why your research is important and what relevance it will have for the funding agency. Let us suppose Maureen and Mike decide to apply for a mini-project from the Maths, Stats and OR Subject Network. Their proposed research study would closely align with the type of projects that this Subject Centre supports (http://mathstore.ac.uk/lateryears/index.shtml (accessed 27 April 2008)).

This is the most important part of the bidding process. Unless you can align your research with the funder's aims, it does not matter how worthwhile your proposal is, as it will not get funded. Colleagues who are successful in winning research funds will also advise you to try and build up some sort of rapport with the funding agency beforehand, and seek their advice informally before you actually start developing your bid. With the HEA Subject Centres you can contact authors of projects that have been successful in the past and ask if they will share their application form with you to give you an idea of how to stand the best chance of success.

Preparing your proposal

Once you have identified a possible source of funding, the most important thing to do before anything else is to read any advice or instructions that they give you and be sure to follow the application guidelines exactly. In the case of the HEA Subject Centres, the application forms are usually fairly simple, but each has their own criteria and ways of selecting successful bids.

In most cases they will include the following sections.

Contact details. Make sure you include all the requested information and identify who is the person to communicate with. It is helpful if the lead researcher already has a proven track record in research and/or in managing projects. This is where building up a publications record in pedagogical research comes in useful.

Title of project. This should be explicit and summarise what the project is about.

Summary of project. Think of this as an executive summary, which will give your reader their first impression of the project. It needs to be succinct and written in easy-to-understand, non-specialist language.

Aims. These need to fit very closely with the criteria and objectives of the funding body, and should be written in a clear style that can be understood by non-experts. This is the place where you are justifying why there is a need for the research to be done and so should be situated in the appropriate literature.

Methods/activities. In this section you must show a well-thought out project that addresses the aims and gives a feasible timescale for completion. A Gantt chart can be very useful for indicating activities during the project's lifetime.

Outcomes. Many funding bodies will set out what they expect, so be sure to put in writing that you will meet these specified outcomes as a minimum. Be specific in your outcomes if you are aiming for a publication in a journal and name two or three possibilities. Do not promise an unrealistic number of outcomes.

Budget details. These need to be as specific as possible (see Appendix M for an example of a simple itemised budget). Projects are often turned down because the proposed expenditure is not itemised in sufficient detail or inflated amounts are asked for.

It does not look good if you claim huge amounts of money for photocopying, for instance, just to claim the maximum funding possible. It is far better to claim exactly what you need and be prepared to give precise details (such as hourly rates for research assistance, properly costed requests for conference attendance and subsistence, details of exact equipment costs and so on).

It can be very helpful to acquire matched funding if possible, as value for money is an important factor.

Managing your research funding

If you are successful, the work begins. If you are not successful, the same principles apply as with a rejection for a publication – you need to take account of any feedback and apply again, preferably to the same funding body if it is allowed.

Managing a research project can be somewhat daunting, particularly if it is a collaborative inter-institutional study. The key to success is clear communication and a well-defined structure so that everyone understands who is responsible for which element of the task. Videoconferencing and telephone conferencing are good ways of keeping everyone involved in touch.

Some of the more common mistakes in managing research projects, even very small ones include not:

- allowing sufficient time at the start of the study to recruit research assistants;
- contacting the funding agency soon enough if the research study has been held up for some reason;
- having a contingency plan if research assistants leave before the project is completed;

- allowing flexibility if the research changes direction (sometimes serendipitous findings turn out to be more important than your original research aims, but you need to keep your funding agency fully briefed);
- completing the project on time (if this looks likely to be the case, let the funding agency know with a re-profiled and realistic timeline);
- delivering the promised outcomes.

Careful planning at the outset should reduce the possibility of these glitches and ensure that you keep to your project deadlines.

Summary

Extending the influence of your pedagogical action research may well need funding to support further cycles. I have briefly touched on the basics of identifying funding agencies and putting a funding proposal together but have not gone into detail, since funding bodies tend to give their own specific instructions. Managing a research project may seem at first sight to be rather forbidding, but it just needs careful planning and regular communication within the team and, equally important, with the funding agency. Building up a good reputation in this way will help your future bids and will also enhance your professional prestige.

Synopsis

- In this final chapter I have come full circle, like action research itself, by describing how you can disseminate your findings and bid for funding which then provides the basis for the next wave or cycle of action research.
- In the first section on dissemination, I have used a hypothetical vignette, not only to illustrate the many outlets that are open to you, but also to address the realities of getting support for pedagogical research in a context that is not always supportive.
- Throughout the chapter, I have stressed the importance of dissemination, as without it pedagogical action research is little more than a private reflection or curriculum development. It is essential for your work to be opened up to the scrutiny of your peers.
- Since pedagogical action research has this unique dual role of being carried out specifically to modify the practitioner-researcher's own practice as well as contribute to knowledge, I have organised the chapter accordingly by suggesting that the primary purpose of your research will largely determine where you want to disseminate it.
- Given that conferences and journal publications are the most usual ways of disseminating research, I have concentrated on these two outlets in some detail.

- In the section on applying for research funding, I have given some broad advice, since so much depends on the funding agency itself. In my view, it is often a good idea to start small in order to build your pedagogical action research experience, which is why the HEA Subject Centres are such a useful source of support.
- Finally, I give some basic guidance on managing a funded research project, although here again you will need to build up your own experience, so small-scale projects are a good way to begin.

Reading and further resources

Getting published

Remenyi, D. and Price, D. (2001) 'Getting published for academics'. *The International Journal of Management Education*, 1, 2. Online. Available: http://www.business.heacademy.ac.uk/publications/journal/vol1no2/paper4/remenyi.pdf (accessed 25 April 2008).

A helpful paper for the novice academic researcher, written primarily for business and management academics but equally useful to academics from other disciplines.

Klingner, J.K., Scanlon, D. and Pressley, M. (2005) 'How to publish in scholarly journals', *Educational Researcher*, 14–20. Online. Available: http://www.aera.net/uploadedFiles/Publications/Journals/Educational_Researcher/3408/02ERv34n8_Klingner.pdf (accessed 25 April 2008).

This paper offers some good practical advice.

Conference posters

Hammerling, S. and Higham, N.J. (2007) 'How to prepare a poster'. Society for Industrial and Applied Mathematics. Online. Available: http://www.siam.org/meetings/guidelines/poster.php (accessed 25 April 2008).

The advice given here is clear and straightforward.

Getting and managing research funding

Grant proposals

Jones, S.P. and Bundy, A (n.d.) Writing a good grant proposal. Online. Available: http://research.microsoft.com/~simonpj/papers/Proposal.html (accessed 25 April 2008).

This is an article which gives sensible, straightforward advice.

Grants Information Collection. Online. Available: http://grants.library.wisc.edu/organizations/proposalwebsites.html (accessed 25 April 2008).

An American website with many excellent links to other useful sources of advice.

Books

Henson, K.T. (2003) *Grant Writing in Higher Education: A Step by Step Guide*, London: Allyn and Bacon.

A practical guide with examples, including a good section on preparing a budget.

Kenway, J., Boden, R. and Epstein, D. (2007) *Winning and Managing Research Funding*, London: Sage.

Includes explanations of how university research funding mechanisms work.

Ries, J.B. and Leukefeld, C (1997) *The Research Funding Guidebook: Getting It, Managing It and Renewing It*. London: Sage.

This is a general rather than an education-specific book, but it starts from the point of rejection and shows the reader how to resubmit to make the bid more competitive.

Learning and teaching conferences

The following list is not intended to be an exhaustive one as the number of pedagogically related conferences is growing fast. It includes some of the generic conferences related to learning and teaching, but there are many more related to specific pedagogical issues such as e-learning and assessment. Check the HEA Subject Centres Network for subject-specific learning and teaching events as many of them host their own conferences.

European Association for Research on Learning and Instruction (EARLI). Online. Available: http://www.earli.org/ (accessed 25 April 2008). Biennial conference, usually held outside the UK.

Higher Education Academy Conference. Online. Available: http://www.heacademy.ac.uk/events/conference (accessed 25 April 2008). Annual in the UK.

Improving Student Learning Symposium (ISL). Online. Available: http://www.brookes.ac.uk/services/ocsld/isl/ (accessed 25 April 2008). Annual in the UK.

International Society for the Scholarship of Teaching and Learning (ISSOTL). Online. Available: http://www.issotl.org/conferences.html (accessed 25 April 2008). Annual, usually held outside the UK.

London Scholarship of Teaching and Learning International Conference. Online. Available: http://www.city.ac.uk/ceap/sotlconference/ (accessed 25 April 2008). Annual in the UK.

Pedagogical Research in Higher Education (PRHE) Conference. Online. Available: http://www.hope.ac.uk/learningandteaching/prhe/ (accessed 25 April 2008). Biennial in the UK.

Journals which publish pedagogical research

The following list contains some of the better known generic learning and teaching journals. Not all of them are focused on higher education, nor might they all accept action research, but check the HEA Subject Centres Network as many of them publish their own journals.

Alt-J Research in Learning Technology. Published on behalf of the Association for Learning Technology. Online. Available: http://www.tandf.co.uk/journals/journal.asp?issn=0968–7769andsubcategory=ED250000andlinktype=2 (accessed 25 April 2008). Three issues a year: Routledge.

Assessment and Evaluation in Higher Education. Online. Available: http://www.tandf.co.uk/journals/journal.asp?issn=0260–2938andsubcategory=ED300000 (accessed 25 April 2008). Six issues a year: Routledge.

British Educational Research Journal. Online. Available: http://www.tandf.co.uk/journals/carfax/01411926.html (accessed 25 April 2008). Six issues a year: Taylor and Francis.

British Journal of Sociology of Education. Online. Available: http://www.tandf.co.uk/journals/journal.asp?issn=0142–5692andlinktype=1 (accessed 25 April 2008). Six issues a year: Routledge.

Comparative Education. Online. Available: http://www.tandf.co.uk/journals/titles/03050068.asp (accessed 25 April 2008). Four issues a year: Taylor and Francis.

Educational Action Research. Supported by Collaborative Action Research Network (CARN). Online. Available: http://www.tandf.co.uk/journals/journal.asp?issn=0965–0792andsubcategory=ED200000 (accessed 25 April 2008). Four issues a year: Taylor and Francis.

Educational Research. Journal of the National Foundation for Educational Research (NFER). Online. Available: http://www.tandf.co.uk/journals/journal.asp?issn=0013–1881andlinktype=2 (accessed 25 April 2008). Four issues a year: Routledge.

Educational Studies. Online. Available: http://www.tandf.co.uk/journals/journal.asp?issn=0305–5698andlinktype=2 (accessed 25 April 2008). Four issues a year; Taylor and Francis.

Higher Education. The international journal of higher education and education planning. Online. Available: http://www.springer.com/west/home/education?SGWID=4-40406-70-35693048-0 (accessed 25 April 2008). Twelve issues a year: Springer.

Higher Education Research and Development. Journal of the Higher Education Research and Development Society of Australasia (HERDSA). Online. Available: http://www.tandf.co.uk/journals/journal.asp?issn=0729–4360andsubcategory=ED200000andlinktype=2 (accessed 25 April 2008). Four issues a year: Taylor and Francis.

Innovations in Education and Teaching International. Official journal of the Staff and Educational Development Association (SEDA). Online. Available: http://www.tandf.co.uk/journals/journal.asp?issn=1470–3297andsubcategory=ED250000 (accessed 25 April 2008). Four issues a year: Routledge.

Journal of Further and Higher Education. Published on behalf of University and College Union (UCU). Online. Available: http://www.tandf.co.uk/journals/journal.asp?issn=0309–0877Xandsubcategory=ED300000 (accessed 25 April 2008). Four issues a year: Routledge.

Learning, Media and Technology. Incorporating Education Communication and Information. Online. Available: http://www.tandf.co.uk/journals/journal.asp?issn=1743–9884andsubcategory=ED250000andlinktype=2 (accessed 25 April 2008). Four issues per year: Routledge.

Research into Higher Education Abstracts. Published on behalf of the Society for Research into Higher Education. Online. Available: http://www.tandf.co.uk/journals/journal.asp?issn=0034–5326andsubcategory=ED300000 (accessed 25 April 2008). Three issues a year: Routledge.

Studies in Higher Education. Published on behalf of the Society for Research into Higher Education (SRHE). Online. Available: http://www.tandf.co.uk/journals/carfax/03075079.html (accessed 25 April 2008). Six issues a year: Routledge.

Teaching in Higher Education. Online. Available: http://www.tandf.co.uk/journals/titles/13562517.asp (accessed 25 April 2008). Six issues a year: Routledge.

Some suggested methods of reflecting on practice

The methods described here are drawn from the literature and I offer them here as starting points for those of you who are interested in developing your own reflective practice, either on an individual basis or in collaboration with your colleagues.

Reflecting by writing

In many of the studies on action research and action learning, keeping a reflective journal appears to be crucial to the whole endeavour and may well be used as a source of data for publications which arise out of these processes. These reflections can be used in the group setting to trigger off and stimulate further insights.

Rönnerman (2003) suggests dividing the entries in two. On the left-hand pages you record the processes, your observations and any other factual details, and on the right-hand pages you record your comments and reflections. Rönnerman also suggests dividing these reflections into three types.

> Practical, such as I have to divide the group into two next time, other-wise ...;
> Discussion, such as I want to discuss this matter with Sally and get her experiences because she was going to try something similar;
> Theoretical, such as this reminds me of what that lecturer said based on Piaget, exactly the same reactions in my class or the opposite.
> (Rönnerman, 2003: 14–15)

Goodnough (2003) suggests that keeping a reflective journal can help you to make your thinking explicit, as well as recording how the action research has evolved. In writing a journal you can begin to critically analyse what is happening in the study by reflecting on whether the needs of the group and the individual participants are being met and by deliberating on how to interpret the data and report the findings.

Using a reflective journal which also acts as a research diary can be quite difficult as it requires time, discipline and reflective thought, yet it can help you to develop richer understandings of the phenomenon that you are investigating. It enables you to keep track of emerging ideas, stimulates further analysis and data collection, and helps you in the development of your arguments and theory integration (Angelides, Evangelou and Leigh, 2005).

Reflecting by reading

Watson and Wilcox (2000) suggest two methods of reflecting on practice by reading, which are derived from their own experiences of reflective reading in library-science education and university academic development. Both methods can be used if you are:

- an individual practitioner working independently to study your own practice;
- within a group such as a study group, an action learning group or a collaborative action research group;
- in a mentor–mentee relationship (Hammersley-Fletcher and Orsmond, 2005).

Watson and Wilcox give a detailed step-by-step procedure for both methods, but basically these are as follows.

Capturing and reading accounts of practice

The authors suggest that this is done through the medium of storytelling, as it is likely to include the teller's (practitioner's) emotions, memories and theoretical understandings in what they call 'a synthesis of both the experiential and theoretical worlds'. They then suggest three reflective readings in which the first is a quick impression reading to allow you to react to someone else's forms of expressions. The second reading is described as 'zooming in' in which you might find yourself asking, 'What is going on here?', 'Why are these words being used?' and 'What do they tell me?'. Then the third and final reading is a 'zooming out' where you distance yourself from the detail and where the underlying themes and issues start to appear, as does the complexity. This way, the authors claim, may help to extend understanding in a way that is not possible 'in the heat of the moment of experience'.

In many ways, such a process reminds me of the steps taken to undertake a thematic analysis of text produced by interviews, which I describe in Chapter 7, but this is much more practical and achievable, given the time constraints that face us all.

Collecting and reading conventions of practice

This method involves gathering together a number of colleagues to collect a number of accounts that represent routine aspects of their professional lives. The rationale is that most professionals have little time in their day-to-day lives to stop and question what they are doing. This can be done by collecting existing artefacts such as lecture plans, handouts, course handbooks, examples of written feedback given to students and so on. The next step is to reflect on the convention by again zooming in, the goal being to develop a heightened awareness and deeper understanding of practice by examining the conventions in some detail.

Watson and Wilcox suggest free writing as an effective way of reflecting, by which they mean writing quickly whatever comes to mind and without editing or stopping when reading the artefact. Then, the final step is to see if practitioners think they have gained any new perspectives or insights about their practice and their own role within it.

An example of a research protocol taken from the **Write Now CETL** research programme

The Write Now CETL is at http://www.writenow.ac.uk/.

Title

'New lecturers' perceptions, beliefs and approaches to assessment, marking and feedback'

Description of proposed research

There are three main aims for this research study which focus respectively on creating new knowledge, promotion of the work of the Write Now CETL in informing assessment policy across the sector and facilitating others to carry out pedagogical research using instruments constructed for this study.

1. To build on the existing research work currently being carried out to explore and better understand new* lecturers' understandings of assessment (*defined as lecturers currently undertaking a training programme for university teachers).
2. To promote the research of Write Now through the sector, and ultimately inform policy and decision making in matters relating to assessment practice.
3. To make freely available research instruments that others may use or adapt in their own contexts to improve staff training in assessment, marking and feedback.

Theoretical background

Across the sector there is relatively little in the way of training and development for assessment, despite the generally accepted claim that assessment is fundamental to the learning process (Boud, 1995; Brown *et al.*, 1997; Gibbs, 1992; Ramsden, 1992; 2003). University lecturers tend to assess in the way they themselves were assessed and learn through experience how to give feedback using their own preferred mental model (Norton *et al.*, 2004).

Currently research is being undertaken by Norton *et al.*, (2006) to challenge university lecturers' views about traditional unseen examinations using the 'device' of asking them about assessment criteria. There is some evidence, though, that new university lecturers are more willing to think through their values and beliefs about assessment and teaching but then may become submerged under the weight of traditional departmental cultures and feel powerless to change assessment practice (Norton and Aiyegbayo, 2005; Norton *et al.*, in submission).

Research methodology

The proposed study will be quantitative as it seeks to establish a reliable and robust measure of lecturers' perceptions, beliefs and approaches to the three interrelated areas of assessment design, marking and feedback practices.

Design

There will be two stages in the research study. First a semi-structured interview will be carried out to generate a large pool of items for the questionnaire. This study may well be publishable in its own right. The next stage will be to construct a questionnaire to be used with as many willing institutions as possible who deliver Postgraduate Certificate in Learning and Teaching in Higher Education (PGCLTHE) programmes.

Materials

The interview schedule for stage 1 will be developed from the research literature and from our existing research. Some typical questions taken from Norton, Aiyegbayo, Harrington, Elander and Reddy (paper in submission) will be:

> How do you know your students are learning?
> What do you feel is the best type of student assessment technique to use?
> Do you feel you have the freedom to change your assessment techniques easily?

The questionnaire for stage 2 will be developed from the research literature, from our existing research and from the outcomes of the interviews in stage 1. It will be piloted on a small sample (30 participants who have not been involved in the interview stage) using standard tests (e.g. Cronbach's alpha) for internal consistency and (e.g. test–retest) for reliability. Items are yet to be devised but will include the three areas of assessment design, marking and feedback.

Sample

Thirty lecturers taking the PGCLTHE at LHU, LMU and AU will be approached for the interview in stage 1.

> Another sample of 30 lecturers not involved in the interview will be asked to complete the pilot questionnaire. If it is not possible to draw these participants from the same three institutions, we will approach others where we have established contacts. The final version of the questionnaire will be sent out to all lecturers taking PGCLTHE programs in all the universities in the UK.

Procedure

Initial arrangements and approaches for stage 1will be made by the research assistant, based at Liverpool Hope University, using contacts through the Write Now CETL and arranging interview schedules to suit willing participants. It is envisaged this may well involve two days of interviewing at each of the three institutions. Interviewees will be briefed through email with the details of the research study, and asked to arrange a time with the interviewer. The usual ethical protocols will be employed, using principles from the BPS and BERA codes of conduct, for example, guaranteeing anonymity, informed consent and participants reserving the right to stop at any point in the interview and/or to withdraw their data from the analysis. Interviews will be taped and transcribed, and data will be held for a period of two years after the publication of any results.

For the questionnaire stage, all universities will be approached to ask if participants on their PGCLTHE programmes would be willing to take part. The questionnaire will be emailed, or adapted to be completed electronically on, for example, SurveyMonkey.

Proposed analysis

The questionnaire will consist mainly of closed questions necessitating quantitative analysis using inferential statistics (ANOVA, correlations, etc.), but there will also be some open-ended items that will require a form of thematic analysis (e.g. content analysis). This is the preferred method since it enables both qualitative and quantitative analysis.

Timetable and stages of completion

Dates are yet to be agreed but the phases of the research are as follows.

1. September – November 2007 – Review research literature
2. November – December 2007 – Devise interview schedule
3. January – February 2008 – Carry out interviews
4. March – April 2008 – Devise the pilot questionnaire
5. May – June 2008 – Test and refine
6. July 2008 – Send out the finalised version of the questionnaire first call
7. September – October 2008 – Send out the finalised version of the questionnaire second call
8. November – December 2008 – Analyse data

Dissemination Plans

The research will inform policy and practice across the sector as it will provide a tool that can be used in PGCLTHE programmes to get new lecturers reflecting on the purpose of assessment and its role in supporting student learning. The questionnaire will be made freely available on the Write Now CETL website. The timescale of the research has been devised to meet the deadline for submission to the European Association for Learning and Instruction's conference in August 2009. (Other conferences will include the Improving Student Learning Symposium, the Higher Education Academy's annual conference and the International Society for the Scholarship of Teaching and Learning's conference.) The research will also be submitted to appropriate refereed journals (e.g. Higher Education, Assessment and Evaluations in Higher Education, Innovations in Education and Teaching International).

Continuation Plans

This research will be continued in further waves of action research using the questionnaire to investigate the effects of PGCLTHE programmes, for example. External funding will be sought to continue this work, through the HEA and its Subject Centres Network opportunities.

References

Boud, D. (1995) 'Assessment and learning: Contradictory or complementary?', in P. Knight (ed.), *Assessment for Learning in Higher Education*, London: Kogan Page.

Brown, G., Bull, J. and Pendlebury, M. (1997) *Assessing Student Learning in Higher Education*, London: Routledge.

Gibbs, G. (1992) *Improving the Quality of Student Learning*, Bristol: TES.

Ramsden, P. (1992) *Learning to Teach in Higher Education*, London: Routledge.

—— (2003) *Learning to Teach in Higher Education*, 2nd edn, London: RoutledgeFalmer.

Norton, L., Harrington, K., Norton, B. and Shannon, L. (2006) 'Challenging traditional forms of assessment: university teachers' views on examinations'. Paper presented at the 3rd Conference of the International Society for the Scholarship of Teaching and Learning (ISSOTL), Washington, DC, USA, 9–12 November 2006.

Norton, L. and Aiyegbayo, O. (2005) 'Becoming an excellent teacher: Factors that influence new university lecturers' beliefs about learning and teaching'. Paper presented at the 5th International Conference on the Scholarship of Teaching and Learning (SoTL), London, UK, 12–13 May, 2005.

Norton, L., Aiyegbayo, O., Harrington, K., Elander, J. and Reddy, P. (in submission) 'Becoming a university teacher: Factors that influence new lecturers' beliefs about learning and teaching'. Paper submitted to Innovations in Education and Teaching International.

Norton, L.S., Ward-Robinson, H., Reddy, P., Elander, J. and Harrington, K. (2004) 'Exploring psychology lecturers' view on assessment criteria'. Psychology Learning and Teaching Conference (PLAT 2004), University of Strathclyde, 5–7 April 2004.

Case study showing how qualitative and quantitive data can be combined

This example is taken from a published research study by Norton and Norton (2000) exploring students' information skills and reported as one cycle of a much larger action research study that was carried out over several years and was designed to help students with this particular aspect of their academic skills.

This particular study was designed to compare the induction procedures in four different departments to establish what information-seeking skills undergraduates were expected to have at the start of their degree and what help was actually given to them. It was also designed to provide a measure of how effectively these provisions were working by testing students' knowledge about subject specific materials available in the university library.

Students were set a library quiz relating to their subject and their tutors were then given a copy of this quiz (together with the correct answers) and asked to estimate what proportion of their students would be able to answer the quiz items correctly. Tutors were also asked what their department did to support their students in finding out about these library resources. A further source of information was obtained from departmental handbooks and from personal communications; for example, we obtained the following information in an email from the Head of English, who suggested that we should use second-year rather than first-year students in our research.

> We make a point of discouraging students from using secondary sources in their first year. We concentrate in first year on looking at primary materials and for this reason are thinking of asking for our students' library induction to take place at the beginning of the second year.
>
> In the first year students are provided with a handbook called the Student Companion – a ring binder to which they are encouraged to add information. There is no formal induction apart from this but the department makes a point of teaching all first years in groups no larger than 12. (Head of Department of English)

The results were then presented statistically in terms of students' responses to the library quiz, followed by comments from their subject tutors and relevant information from the documentary analysis. A brief excerpt from the analysis of the English department on one quiz question (see Table C.1) will show you how this worked.

What this table shows is the actual percentage of students who were able to correctly identify the classification numbers for poetry, language and the novel, and the estimated proportion that their two tutors thought would get it right. These statistical findings were then followed with some qualitative analysis.

Both tutors thought students should know the class numbers for the novel and for poetry, but underestimated the percentage that did. Interestingly, while they did not expect students to know the class number for language, they actually overestimated the proportion who would by 35 per cent as no students were able to identify this number correctly. In view of the emphasis that one tutor in particular placed on reading the texts over and above everything else, it is perhaps not surprising that no English students knew this particular class number.

Both tutors were consistent in where they thought students could get help:

> Information from department handbook. Information desk in library. They ask us! (Tutor 1)
>
> Students' handbook. Library information desk. Using their heads? (Tutor 2)

The slightly irritated quality of their responses might be because they were being asked about second-year students and not first years, as the other three subjects in this research had been asked, or it may have been a reflection of a genuine subject-discipline difference operating here.

This format of presentation was carried out throughout the report and it shows how we were able to use the tutors' comments to interpret the statistical findings in order to obtain a clearer and richer picture of each of the participating departments' support systems, together with an analysis of how effective these were in terms of students' actual library knowledge.

Hopefully such an example will encourage you to use both qualitative and quantitative data in your own research studies.

Table C.1 Correct identification of library classification numbers from the English Department, adapted from Norton and Norton (2000)

Subject	Lecturers (N = 2)		Students (N = 59)
	Should students know?	*How many students would know?*	*How many students did know?*
Poetry	Yes	65%	71%
Language	No	35%	0%
Novel	Yes	65%	85%

Exploring ways of measuring conceptions of learning

Method I

Read each of these statements about learning, and tick Yes or No.

Do you think of learning as:	Yes	No
increasing your knowledge?	1	6
memorising knowledge?	2	5
applying knowledge?	3	4
understanding?	4	3
seeing something in a different way	5	2
changing as a person?	6	1

Scoring: The scoring would not be shown, to guard against socially desirable responses. As can be seen it is reverse scored, so the higher the overall score the more 'developed' the conception (maximum score = 21) and the lower the overall score the more 'inchoate' the conception (minimum score = 12). The problem with an overall score would be how to categorise participants whose scores were in the mid range of 9. One solution would be to take the highest conception ticked Yes and use it as the arbiter.

Method 2

Which ONE of the following definitions of learning most closely approximates to your view? Please circle the appropriate letter.

A.	Learning is increasing your knowledge
B.	Learning is memorising knowledge
C.	Learning is applying knowledge
D.	Learning is understanding
E.	Learning is seeing something in a different way
F.	Learning is changing as a person

Scoring: This is a rough and ready categorisation method where the participant is forced into one descriptive category, or if more than one is allowed, the highest conception would be counted using Marton, Dall'Alba and Beaty's (1993) 'priority rule'.

Method 3

To what extent do you agree with the following statements about learning?

SA = Strongly agree
A = Agree
NS = Not sure
D = Disagree
SD = Strongly disagree

Learning is about...	SA	A	NS	D	SD
increasing your knowledge	1	2	3	4	5
memorising knowledge	1	2	3	4	5
applying knowledge	1	2	3	4	5
understanding	5	4	3	2	1
seeing something in a different way	5	4	3	2	1
changing as a person	5	4	3	2	1

Scoring would not be revealed and is reversed as in Method 1. The overall score would reveal where a participant was on the 'developed–inchoate' continuum, but it would also provide individual scores for each of the six conceptions to give a more sensitive measure of change.

Note that whichever of the above methods was used, it would be important to alter the order of presentation of the conceptions so that they did not go from the least to the most developed thus inducing socially desirable responses.

An example of a completed participant information sheet

Study title

'Encouraging meta-learning through personal development planning for first-year undergraduates: first-year students' perceptions of what makes a really good student'

(The second part of the title is simplified to make it easier to understand.)

Invitation

You are being invited to take part in a research study. Before you decide, it is important for you to understand why the research is being done and what it will involve. Please take time to read the following information carefully and ask us if there is anything that is not clear or if you would like more information.

What is the purpose of the study?

The university has been supporting first-year students, through the PDP module, to adapt to the demands of doing a degree. As part of this work, we are now interested in finding out what students themselves think makes 'a really good student' and to analyse how their perceptions of themselves as students change during the course of their first year in higher education.

Why have I been chosen?

We are asking all first-year students taking PDP if they will take part in this research to give us a better understanding of the first-year student experience.

Do I have to take part?

It is entirely up to you to decide whether or not to take part.

Since the research is being carried out using an electronic form and analysed by two researchers, your lecturers will never know whether you decided to take part or not, so it will not affect your study or academic progression in any way.

If you do decide to take part, you will be given this information sheet to keep and may be asked to sign a consent form. If you decide to take part, you are still free to withdraw at any time and without giving a reason.

What will happen to me if I take part?

In the third week of term you will be asked to fill in a simple inventory that is available electronically and which asks you to think of up to five qualities that you think best describes a really good student in university. You will then be asked to rate yourself on each of these qualities.

It is always hard to estimate how long it will take individuals to complete an inventory like this, but most students who have done this in the past have taken about 30 minutes.

Three weeks before the end of the year we will ask you to complete another inventory and rate yourself, using the same process as before. We will then ask you to look at your original inventory and rate yourself again on the original qualities that you thought of.

This second stage will take a little longer but should not be more than 45 minutes.

What are the possible benefits of taking part?

We hope that your taking part in the study will help you to understand yourself as a learner (known as meta-learning) a little bit more than you did before.

Research evidence so far suggests that students with a greater meta-learning awareness tend to be more adaptable when studying gets more difficult. However, this cannot be guaranteed.

The information we get from this study may help us to support future students in making a successful transition to university study.

What are the possible risks of taking part?

We cannot foresee any risks in this research, but it will take up some of your time, which you might otherwise have spent in studying.

Will my taking part in this study be kept confidential?

The results of this research will be presented in a seminar at the university, at learning and teaching conferences, and in a journal publication.

You will never be identified in any of our findings but we will use the words you generate to describe the qualities of the really good students.

Contact for further information

If you would like any more information, please contact:
    Lin Norton, principal researcher.
    Address of institution
    Telephone number:
    Email:

Consent form template

Title of research project

Name of researcher

1. I confirm that I have read and understand the information sheet for the above study and have had the opportunity to ask questions.   Yes   No
2. I understand that my participation is voluntary and that I am free to withdraw at any time, without giving any reason.   Yes   No
3. I agree to take part in the above study.   Yes   No

   Name of participant:
   Signature:
   Date:
   Name of researcher:
   Signature:
   Date:

Case study of a pedagogical action research study to illustrate some ethical issues

Introduction

This example is taken from a collaborative action research study with a small class of seven postgraduate students taking a module on teaching and learning in higher education as part of an MSc in Applied Psychology. I was keen to explore with them if reflecting on their own learning as we went through the module would help them in a generic sense as postgraduate students, and if it would also help them make more sense of the module by applying some of the theoretical topics to their own situation as learners.

What I have done here is to present an excerpt from the abstract that was accepted for a conference of the Collaborative Action Research Network (CARN) and to annotate it with my reflections on ethical issues [in parentheses]. In this way, I hope to demonstrate with the benefit of hindsight that what originally looked like a clean and straightforward research proposal with no ethical issues was, now I reflect on it, not that straightforward.

Action research and metacognitive awareness in postgraduate students

Norton, L., Aiyegbayo, O., Bhatti, N., de-Petro, V., Doyle, C., Matthews, K. and Parry, T. (2003) 'Action research and metacognitive awareness in postgraduate students', paper presented at the Collaborative Action Research Network conference, Knutsford, 7–9 November 2003.

Abstract

The action research project, which is to be reported, comes from earlier work by Norton and Owens (2003) based on a college-wide, generic skills programme for first-year undergraduate students. As part of that programme, students were asked to complete a number of self-assessment exercises and instruments including Meyer's (2000) Reflections on Learning Inventory (RoLI). They were also required to individually discuss their RoLI profiles with their academic tutor, and write about what they had discovered about themselves as learners and how they thought this fitted the demands of their academic subjects. Initial findings suggest that this process has had the effect of raising students' metacognitive awareness, although the link with academic performance is not yet clear.

[I can see now that I was coming to this study, not only with a strong belief in the value of students reflecting on themselves as learners, but also with a considerable personal investment in previous research studies, I had been involved in].

Set against this theoretical and empirically driven context, the author wanted to use the same process with a small group of seven postgraduate students taking a module in the psychology of teaching and learning as part of an MSc in Applied Psychology. This was a development of the undergraduate programme, since these students were also invited to take part in and be part of an action research project that involved:

1. completing the Reflections of Learning Inventory at the beginning of the module;
2. emailing the module tutor each week with a brief reflective piece about how the topic of that week's session related to their understandings of themselves as learners.

[In action research where the participants are also the co-researchers, there should ideally be some joint consideration of the research design, but in this case the design was entirely mine and I do not recall giving students the chance to change it.

On reflection, this might have been difficult for them to do as I was the one who had the theoretical and the empirical experience here, but had I given them the opportunity they might have come up with equally valid ways of thinking about and recording their own reflections on learning, rather than completing an established inventory, as I asked them to do.

They might also have preferred not to write each week, but keep a journal and send me excerpts when they were ready; but again, I did not give them the opportunity to do this, or even to discuss alternative methods of reflection. What we did discuss was purely a pragmatic matter of what would be the best way to collect the weekly reflections, and we agreed that emailing them to me would serve this purpose.]

In this way, students were encouraged to actively apply their understandings of what had been discussed in each session to their own scores on the RoLI and to reflect on any changes in insight as a result of what they had learned in each session.

[Once again I took the lead and said I would not respond in any way to their emails but just record them. To be fair to myself, I took this decision partly because I did not want to overburden them, and I was taking seriously the ethical issue of asking students to do extra work, which I hoped would enhance their learning but I could not guarantee it.

As I look back on it now, I think what a wasted opportunity for some real tutor–student dialogue on metacognition.]

The author offered to lead the action research project and to accredit all participating students with joint authorship.

[Why did I not empower the students, by offering them the chance to lead if they wanted to?]

Since the author was also one of the researchers and the module tutor, participation was entirely voluntary and had no implications for the assessment of the module. Six of the seven students registered on the module were keen to take part. The seventh student was unable to attend many of the taught sessions and was therefore unable to contribute to the project.

[This is a clear example of what I mean in Chapter 10 when I discuss the difference between taking the necessary pragmatic steps to consider ethical issues and to think ethically.

In such a small class, how hard it must have been for anyone to say no, and although I am sure they trusted me in what I said about it not affecting their assessment in any way, the social pressures of non-participation must have been considerable.]

This paper reports on this initiative and reflects on the outcomes from:

1. the students' perspective as participants in the module and joint action researchers and authors;
2. the first author's perspective as module tutor and lead researcher.

[Since my students were also, quite properly co-authors, they did not have anonymity or confidentiality, but they did have a conference publication to add to their CV. All of them were given the opportunity to attend the CARN conference to co-present and, very pleasingly, one of the students took up this offer, did a fine job at the conference and has since gone on to forge a career as an academic.]

Conclusion

When this research was carried out, there was no institutional requirement to gain ethics approval, and I wonder if there had been how the study would have fared. In the event, I still believe that the students benefited overall, not just in terms of the publication, but also in terms of the desired raising of their learning awareness. Although there were big individual differences, all of them showed evidence in their reflective pieces of some noticeable insights along the way. Nevertheless, this might have been a much better study had I considered the ethical issues more carefully at the time.

Ethics submission template.

Details of applicant(s)

Lead researcher's name:
  Institution:
  Contact details:

Details of study

a. Full title of the research study:
b. Aims and objectives of the research study:

Please state clearly the hypothesis, which this research is intended to test, or the questions it is expected to answer.

c. Brief outline of the research study in non-technical language (approx 150 words).
d. Where will the study take place and in what setting (university, lecture classes, seminar groups etc.).
e. Schedule:
  Proposed starting date:
  Proposed duration:

Recruitment of participants

a. How will the participants in the study be selected, approached and recruited?
b. How many participants will be recruited and of what age group?

Consent

a. Is written consent to be obtained? Yes No
  Please use STANDARD CONSENT FORM.

If no written consent is to be obtained EXPLAIN WHY.

b. Have any special arrangements been made for subjects for whom English is not a first language?   Yes   No   N/A
    If yes, give details:

c. Are the participants in one of the following vulnerable groups?
    Children under 16   Yes   No
    People with learning difficulties   Yes   No
    Other vulnerable groups e.g. mental illness, dementia   Yes   No
    If yes, please complete the details below:
    What special arrangements have been made to deal with the issues of consent, e.g. is parental or guardian agreement to be obtained, and if so in what form?

d. Every participant must be given a written information sheet giving details about the research, separate from the consent form. Please enclose a copy.

Risks and ethical problems

a. Are there any potential hazards to participants
   (physical and/or psychological)?   Yes   No
   If yes, please give details and give the likelihood, and details of precautions taken to meet them and arrangements to deal with adverse events.

b. Is this study likely to cause discomfort or distress to participants?   Yes   No
   If yes, please give details and give the likelihood, and details of precautions taken to meet them and arrangements to deal with adverse events:

Confidentiality

a. Will the study data be held on a computer?   Yes   No
   If yes, will the relevant Data Protection Regulations be observed (e.g. will data be kept under secure conditions so that it will not be accessible, interpretable and used by individuals outside the research study)?   Yes   No

Example of an unsuccessful abstract that was submitted to a conference as a research paper

In this example I reproduce an actual abstract that was submitted to an international conference. At the end I comment in parentheses on why I think it failed.

Abstract

Title: 'The role of personal development planning in enhancing effective learning in higher education'

Aim. This paper reports on a study being carried out in the context of a year one personal development planning (PDP) module delivered on a non-subject-specific basis at a university in the north-west of England. The module incorporates action planning, reflectiveness and meta-learning and includes Meyer's (2000) Reflections on Learning Inventory (RoLI). The study aims to explore students' perceptions of effective studying and to evaluate the effect of PDP on their awareness of meta-learning. It builds on a small pilot study using an open-ended measure called the Ideal *** Inventory to capture students' views about what they think makes a good student. The main findings of this study showed some movement towards meta-learning awareness by the end of the PDP programme (Walters and Norton, 2004).

Method. First-year students have been asked to complete an online constructivist questionnaire that asks them to think of five qualities or abilities they think 'a really good learner' in higher education might have, together with the opposite dimension, i.e. the 'not very good learner'. Students are required to rate themselves against their self-generated scales in semester one and again towards the end of semester two.

Outcomes. The data will be analysed qualitatively, using a process of reiterative content analysis, and quantitatively to ascertain if there are any changes in students' self-ratings. Academic performance measures will also be related to self-ratings.

Significance. This large-scale study will offer a picture of students' perceptions of themselves as learners and their understanding of the concept of meta-learning and how this relates to the success of their studies in year one of their degree course. Implications of our findings and the usefulness of the 'really good learner' inventory will be discussed in the broader terms of enhancing student meta-learning, reflectiveness and success in higher education.

[Comment. It is clear from this abstract that we had not yet collected the data, indeed we said this quite plainly in the extended summary, which was required in addition to the abstract. Another point that went against us was that we referred to the Ideal *** Inventory but we did not make clear that this had a record of publications to give it respectability.

In the event, the reviewing committee's decision was a wise one because this proposal was premature and, in the event, we did not get a large number of students completing both stages.]

Compare this abstract with the one in Appendix K on a very similar research topic: student meta-learning. This was submitted to the same conference two years later and was successful.

Example of a successful abstract that was submitted to a conference as a research paper

Abstract

Title: 'Predicting which students might be academically at risk in higher education'

Aim. This paper reports on findings from work in a university in the UK, using Meyer's (2000) Reflections on Learning Inventory (RoLI) as part of a programme designed to enhance students' meta-learning awareness. The research aims to identify patterns from RoLI scores that might predict which students would be successful and which might be at risk of failure in their studies.

Method. As part of a compulsory module on personal development planning (PDP), all first-year students complete the RoLI, and then are given information on what their scores mean in the context of the expectations of studying for their main academic subjects. In 2002 and 2003, students were asked if they would be willing to submit their RoLI scores for research purposes. There were 230 students from the 2002 cohort and 380 from the 2003 cohort that submitted completed questionnaires, which were matched to the students' records for measures of academic performance, gender and age variables and details of subjects studied.

Outcomes. These data will be explored using factor analysis, multiple regression analysis and structural equation modelling to identify predictive patterns for students who do well and students who may need additional support. Methods of using the RoLI as a diagnostic tool will then be developed, taking into account age, gender and subject, which will enable students at risk of failure to be targeted through institutional student support mechanisms. It will be equally important that if patterns are identified predicting success that this is conveyed to students, thus giving them advice that is evidence based.

Significance. The findings from this research will be discussed in the context of how understanding indicators of success and struggle can be used to build more effective learning environments.

[Comment. Although we were quite straightforward in saying that all the analyses had not been done at the time of writing this abstract, it is clear that we have data from over 600 questionnaires. We used an established and recognised research tool to collect our data.]

This abstract was accepted and the paper duly given:

Norton, L.S. and Norton, J.C.W. (2005) *Predicting which students might be academically at risk in higher education*. Paper presented at the 11th Conference of EARLI, 23–26th August 2005. Nicosia, Cyprus.

Example of a letter to the editor of a journal accompanying a rewritten manuscript

Dear …

I am sending you three copies of my amended manuscript as requested, plus an electronic copy in Word for Windows. I have also enclosed a separate sheet detailing our responses to both referees' comments and criticisms. As you will see, we have paid very careful attention to them and have found their suggestions to be extremely helpful and feel that the paper is now better as a result. I would be grateful if you would pass on our appreciation. (Sometimes authors prefer to put an acknowledgment in their paper if the suggestions have been particularly useful.)

I hope that this amended manuscript will now be suitable for publication and I look forward to hearing from you.

Yours …

Example of a response to reviewers' comments

Manuscript number: XLJ 32

Comment

The problem of student attrition (Referees 1 and 2).

Both referees point out that the fall in student numbers was the main problem, although out of our control. They suggest that following up the non-attenders would have been useful.

Response

We have acknowledged this problem more fully and reported some anecdotal evidence why students did not attend (see page 21 and pages 26–27).

Comment

Analysis of the ASI scores (Referee 1).

The referee suggests that ANOVAs would be more appropriate than sequences of t-tests and that one-tailed tests are not fully justified in the introduction.

Response

The data have been completely reanalysed using two-tailed, three way ANOVAS with two repeated measures, looking firstly at the overall sample (i.e. all those for whom we had pre-ASI and post-ASI scores) and then looking at only those students categorised as consistent attenders of the interventions (see pages 12–14).

Comment

Inter-rater reliability (Referee 1).

The referee says that the inter-rater reliability is low.

Response

Inter-rater reliability on the conceptions of learning transcripts were actually 75% for the pre-course measure and 79% for the post-course measure for the APL students, and 76% for the first attempt and 64% for the second attempt for the university students who had no intervention This was not entirely clear in the manuscript but has now been clarified (see page 11). We acknowledge that the 64% is a little low but it still falls within the acceptable rate.

Comment

Academic performance (Referee 1).

The referee says that the logic of the comparison between attenders and non-attenders hardly allows test improvement to be ascribed to the effect of the teaching. Attenders are different in all sorts of ways (correlated with wanting to attend such courses). Pinning down the specific skills input needs a more sophisticated comparison.

Response

We have taken account of this point on pages 18–19 by drawing out more the distinction between the APL results where there was a benefit and the ISR results where there was no benefit for attenders, which suggests it is the course rather then the characteristics of attenders which is causing the effect.

Comment

Nature of the interventions (Referee 1 and 2).

The referees suggest that more needs to be said about the difference between these two learning interventions and their conceptual basis.

Response

We feel that the differences have already been clearly set out on pages 7–8, but we have added an extra paragraph to summarise the main conceptual differences between the two courses.

Example of a budget for an internally funded research bid

Staffing	Total hours	Hourly rate	Cost
(i) Teaching cover for the lead researcher for supervision of research assistant (one hour per week) and time to write up the study as a journal publication	30	£38*	£1,140.00
(ii) Research assistant (15 hrs for designing and trialling questionnaire; 70 hrs for content analysing pupils' notes and scoring questionnaires; 35 hrs for entering data on computer spreadsheet and analysing data)	120	£10.50*	£1,260.00
(iii) Admin support	–	–	–
TOTAL STAFFING COSTS			
* Includes allowance for 'on costs' (e.g. National Insurance)			£2,400.00

Resources	Cost
(i) Consumable materials (please specify)	
(ii) Equipment (please specify)	
(iii) Photocopying 2000 questionnaires (4 pages at 3p = 12p)	£240.00
(iv) Other (please specify) Qualitative software license for research assistant	£295.00
TOTAL RESOURCES	£535.00

Travel and subsistence	Cost
(i) Travel (please specify) Train travel for 2 return trips (London to Liverpool and reverse) for researcher and research assistant from Liverpool to London for 3 meetings with collaborators. Based on supersaver return train fares (£57.00)	£342.00
(ii) Subsistence (please specify)	
TOTAL TRAVEL AND SUBSISTENCE	£342.00

Other	Cost
Please list: 10 interlibrary loan photocopies of relevant research articles at the full rate of £7.50 each	£75.00
TOTAL OTHER	£75.00

TOTAL FUNDING REQUESTED	£3,352.00

Bibliography

Angelides, P., Evangelou, M. and Leigh, J. (2005) 'Implementing a collaborative model of action research for teacher development', *Educational Action Research*, 13 (2): 275–90.

Angelo, T.A. and Cross, K.P. (1993) Classroom Assessment Techniques: A Handbook For College Teachers, San Francisco: Jossey-Bass.

Asch, S. (1955) 'Opinions and social pressure', *Scientific American*, 193 (5): 31–35.

Barnett, R. (1997) *Higher Education: A Critical Business*. Buckingham: SRHE and Open University Press.

—— (2004) 'Learning for an unknown future', *Higher Education Research and Development*, 23 (3): 247–60.

Bartlett, S. and Burton, D. (2006) 'Practitioner research or descriptions of classroom practice? A discussion of teachers investigating their classrooms,' *Educational Action Research*, 14 (3): 395–405.

Bass, R. (1999) 'The scholarship of teaching: What's the problem?' Inventio. Creative thinking about learning and teaching, 1 (1). Online. Available: http://www.doiiit.gmu.edu/Archives/feb98/rbass.htm (accessed 27 April 2008).

Becher, T. (1989) *Academic Tribes and Territories: Intellectual Enquiry and the Cultures of Disciplines*, Buckingham: Open University Press.

—— (1994) 'The significance of disciplinary differences', *Studies in Higher Education*, 19 (2): 151–61.

Becher, T. and Trowler, P.R. (2001) *Academic Tribes And Territories: Intellectual Enquiry and the Culture of Disciplines*, 2nd edn, Buckingham: SRHE and Open University Press.

BERA (2004) *Revised Ethical Guidelines for Educational Research*. Online. Available.: http://www.bera.ac.uk/publications/pdfs/ETHICA1.PDF?PHPSESSID=7a813daa57da3b947616202ceac5957c (accessed 27 April 2008).

Biggs, J. (1994) 'Student learning research and theory – Where do we currently stand?', in G. Gibbs (ed.) *Improving Student Learning – Theory and Practice*, Oxford: Oxford Centre for Staff Development. Online. Available: http://www.londonmet.ac.uk/deliberations/ocsld-publications/isltp-biggs.cfm (accessed 27 April 2008).

—— (2003) *Teaching for Quality Learning at University. What the Student Does*, 2nd edn, Buckingham: SRHE and Open University Press.

Biggs, J.B. and Collis, K.F. (1982) *Evaluating the Quality of Learning – The SOLO Taxonomy*, 1st edn, New York: Academic Press.

Biggs, J., Kember, D. and Leung, D.P. (2001) 'The revised two-factor Study Process Questionnaire: R-SPQ-2F', *British Journal of Educational Psychology*, 71: 133–49.

Biglan, A. (1973) 'The characteristics of subject matter in different academic areas', *Journal of Applied Psychology*, 57 (3): 195–203.

Boud, D. (1995) *Enhancing Learning through Self-Assessment*, London: RoutledgeFalmer.

Boud, D., Cohen, R and Walker, D. (1993) *Using Experience for Learning*, Buckingham: Open University Press.

Boyer, E. (1990) *Scholarship Reconsidered*, Washington DC: Carnegie Foundation.

Braun, V. and Clarke, V. (2006) 'Using thematic analysis in psychology', *Qualitative Research in Psychology*, 3: 77–101.

Breslow, L., Drew, L., Healey, M., Matthew, B. and Norton, L. (2004) 'Intellectual curiosity: A catalyst for the scholarships of teaching and learning and educational development', in E.M. Elvidge (ed.) (2004) *Exploring Academic Development in Higher Education: Issues of Engagement*, Cambridge: Jill Rogers Associates.

Brockbank, A. and McGill, I. (1998) *Facilitating Reflective Learning in Higher Education*, Buckingham: SRHE and Open University Press.

Brown, G., Bull, J. and Pendlebury, M (1997) *Assessing Student Learning in Higher Education*, London: Routledge.

Brown, E., Gibbs, G. and Glover, C. (2003) 'Evaluation tools for investigating the impact of assessment regimes on student learning', *Bioscience Education eJournal*, 2. Online. Available: http://www.bioscience.heacademy.ac.uk/journal/vol2/beej-2-5.htm (accessed 27 April 2008).

Burchell, H. and Dyson, J. (2005) 'Action research in higher education: Exploring ways of creating and holding the space for reflection', *Educational Action Research*, 13 (2): 291–300.

Button, E. (1994) 'Personal construct measure of self-esteem', *Journal of Constructivist Psychology*, 7: 53–65.

Campbell, A. and Norton, L. (eds) (2007) *Learning, Teaching and Assessing in Higher Education: Developing Reflective Practice*, Exeter: Learning Matters Ltd.

Carr, W. and Kemmis, S. (1986) *Becoming Critical: Knowing Through Action Research*, Lewes: Falmer Press.

—— (2005) 'Staying critical', *Educational Action Research*, 13 (3): 347–59.

Clarke, H., Egan, B., Fletcher, L. and Ryan, C. (2006) 'Creating case studies of practice through appreciative inquiry', *Educational Action Research*, 14 (3): 407–22.

Clegg, F. (1983) *Simple Statistics. A Course Book for the Social Sciences*, Cambridge: Cambridge University Press.

Clough, P. and Nutbrown, C. (2002) *A Student's Guide to Methodology*, London: Sage.

Cohen, J. (1960) 'A coefficient of agreement for nominal scales', *Educational and Psychological Measurement*, 20: 37–46.

Cook, R. and McCallum, S. (2007) 'Talking together, reflecting together and working together: tutor and student reflections on academic discourse, ethical discourse and management education', in A. Townsend (ed.) *Differing Perceptions of the Participative Elements of Action Research*. CARN (The Collaborative Action Research Network) Bulletin, 12: 61–71, Didsbury: Manchester Metropolitan University.

Cotton, T. and Griffiths, M. (2007) 'Action research, stories and practical philosophy', *Educational Action Research*, 15 (4): 545–60.

D'Andrea, V. and Gosling, D. (2000) 'Promoting research in teaching and learning in higher education: Two case studies of multi-disciplinary pedagogic research'. Online. Available: http://www.tlrp.org/pub/acadpub/Dandrea2000.pdf (accessed 27 April 2008).

Davis, S. (n.d.) *A Word from UTS Ethics Manager*. http://www.bell.uts.edu.au/ethics/index_po p3 (accessed 27 April 2008).

Day, C. (1993) 'Reflection: A necessary but not sufficient condition for professional development', *British Educational Research Journal*, 19 (1): 83–93.

—— (2000) 'Effective leadership and reflective practice', *Reflective Practice*, 1 (1): 113–27.

Deem, R. (2001) 'Globalisation, new managerialism, academic capitalism and entrepreneuri-alism', *Comparative Education*, 37 (1): 7–20.

Department for Education and Skills (DfES), (2003) *The Future of Higher Education, London: The Stationery Office*. Online. Available: http://www.dfes.gov.uk/hegateway/strategy/hestrategy/index.shtml (accessed 24 April 2008).

Devlin, M. (2006) 'Challenging accepted wisdom about the place of conceptions of teaching in university teaching', *International Journal of Teaching and Learning*, 18 (2): 112–19.

Dewey, J. (1910) *How We Think*, Amherst, NY: Prometheus Books (1991 edition).

Dunkin, M. and Biddle, B. (1974) *The Study of Teaching*, New York: Holt, Rinehart and Winston.

Elliott, J. (1998) *The Curriculum Experiment: Meeting the Challenge Of Social Change*, Buckingham: Open University Press.

Elton, L. (2001) 'Training for a craft or a profession', *Teaching in Higher Education*, 6 (3): 421–22.

Entwistle, N. (1987) 'A model of the teaching-learning process', in J.T.E. Richardson, M.W. Eysenck, and D. Warren Piper (eds) *Student Learning. Research in Education and Cognitive Psychology*, Milton Keynes: Open University Press and SRHE, Part I, Categories of student learning, Chapter 2, pp. 13–28.

Entwistle, N. J. and Ramsden, P. (1983) *Understanding Student Learning*, London: Croom Helm.

Entwistle, N. and Tait, H. (1990) 'Approaches to learning, evaluations of teaching, and pre-ferences for contrasting academic environments', *Higher Education*, 19: 169–94.

Entwistle, N. and Walker, P. (2000) 'Strategic alertness and expanded awareness within sophisticated conceptions of teaching', *Instructional Science*, 28 (5): 335–61.

Entwistle, N., Hanley, M. and Hounsell, D. (1979) 'Identifying distinctive approaches to studying', *Higher Education*, 8: 365–80.

Ercikan, K. and Roth, W-M., (2006) 'What good is polarizing research into qualitative and quantitative?', *Educational Researcher*, 35 (5): 14–23.

Eraut, M. (1994) *Developing Professional Knowledge and Competence*, London: Falmer Press.

Falchikov, N. (1993) 'Attitudes and values of lecturing staff: tradition, innovation and change', *Higher Education*, 25 (4): 487–510.

Fanghanel, J. (2007) 'Investigating university lecturers' pedagogical constructs in the working context'. York: Higher Education Academy. Online. Available: http://www.heacademy.ac.uk/assets/York/documents/ourwork/research/fanghanel.pdf (accessed 27 April 2008).

Freeman, D. (1998) *Doing Teacher Research; from Inquiry to Understanding*, Pacific Grove: Heinle and Heinle.

Gibbs, G. (1992) *Improving the Quality of Student Learning*, Bristol: Technical and Educational Services Limited.

—— (1996) 'Supporting educational development within departments', *International Journal for Academic Development*, 1 (1): 27–37.

Gibbs, G. and Coffey, M. (2004) 'The impact of training university teachers on their teaching skills, their approach to teaching and the approach to learning of their students', *Active Learning in Higher Education*, 5 (1): 87–100.

Ginns, I., Heirdsfield, A., Attweh, B. and Watters, J.J. (2001) 'Beginning teachers becoming professionals through action research', *Educational Action Research*, 9 (1): 111–33.

Goodnough, K. (2003) 'Facilitating action research in the context of science education; reflections of a university researcher', *Educational Action Research*, 11 (1): 41–63.

Gorard, S. (2004) 'Revisiting a 90-year-old debate: the advantages of the mean deviation', paper presented at the British Educational Research Association annual conference,

University of Manchester, 16–18 September 2004, Education-line. Online. Available: http://www.leeds.ac.uk/educol/documents/00003759.htm (accessed 27 April 2008).

Gorard, S. with Taylor, C. (2004) *Combining Methods in Social and Educational Research*, Maidenhead: Open University Press.

Gordon, G., D'Andrea, V., Gosling, D. and Stefani, L. (2003) 'Building capacity for change: research on the scholarship of teaching'. Report to HEFCE. Online. Available: http://www.hefce.ac.uk/pubs/RDreports/2003/rd02_03/rd02_03.doc (accessed 27 April 2008).

Gravett, S. (2004) 'Action research and transformative learning in teaching development', *Educational Action Research*, 12 (2): 259–72.

Great Britain (1998) *Data Protection Act*, Norwich: HMSO. Online. Available: http://www.opsi.gov.uk/acts/acts1998/ukpga_19980029_en_1 (accessed 30 July 2008).

Grinyer, A. (2004) 'The anonymity of research participants: Assumptions, ethics and practicalities', *Social Research Update*, 36 (1–6).

Habermas, J. (1970) *Toward a Rational Society: Student Protest, Science, and Politics*, trans. J.J. Shapiro, Boston, MA: Beacon Press.

—— (1972) *Knowledge and Human Interests*, trans. J.J. Shapiro, Boston, MA: Beacon Press.

—— (1974) *Theory and Practice*, trans. J. Viertel, Boston: Beacon Press.

Hammersley, M. (1998) 'Telling tales about educational research: A response to John K. Smith', *Educational Researcher*, 27 (7): 18–21.

Hammersley-Fletcher, L. and Orsmond, P. (2005) 'Reflecting on reflective practices within peer observation', *Studies in Higher Education*, 30 (2): 213–24.

Hannay, L.M., Telford, C. and Seller, W. (2003) 'Making the conceptual shift: teacher performance appraisal as professional growth', *Educational Action Research*, 11 (1): 121–37.

Hargreaves, D. (1996) *Teaching as a Research Based Profession: Possibilities and Prospects*, London: Teacher Training Agency.

Harrington, K., Elander, J., Lusher, J., Norton, L., Aiyegbayo, O., Pitt, E., Robinson, H. and Reddy, P. (2006) 'Using core assessment criteria to improve essay writing', in C. Bryan and K. Clegg (eds) *Innovative Assessment in Higher Education*, London: Routledge, Chapter 9, pp. 110–19.

Hartmann D. (1977) 'Considerations in the choice of interobserver reliability estimates', *Journal of Applied Behaviour Analysis*, 10 (1): 103–16.

Hativa, N. and Birenbaum, M. (2000) 'Who prefers what? Disciplinary differences in students' preferred approaches to teaching and learning styles', *Research in Higher Education*, 41 (2): 209–36.

Hattie, J. and Marsh, H.W. (1996) 'The relationship between research and teaching: A meta-analysis', *Review of Educational Research*, 66 (4): 507–42.

—— (2004) 'One journey to unravel the relationship between research and teaching', paper presented at the International Colloquium on Research and teaching: Closing the divide? Marwell Conference Centre, Colden Common, Winchester, Hampshire, 18–19 March 2004. Online. Available: http://portal-live.solent.ac.uk/university/rtconference/2004/resources/hattie_marsh_paper.pdf (accessed 27 April 2008).

Healey, M. (2000) 'Developing the scholarship of teaching in higher education: A discipline-based approach', *Higher Education Research and Development*, 19 (2): 169–88.

—— (2005) 'Linking research and teaching to benefit student learning', *Journal of Geography in Higher Education*, 29 (2): 183–201.

HEFCE (2008) 'Outcomes of the Research Excellence Framework consultation'. Online. Available: http://www.hefce.ac.uk/Research/assessment/reform/ (accessed 27 April 2008).

Heywood, J. (2000) *Assessment in Higher Education. Student Learning, Teaching, Programmes and Institutions*, New York: Wiley and Sons.

Hofer, B.K. (2000) 'Dimensionality and disciplinary differences in personal epistemology', *Contemporary Educational Psychology*, 25 (4): 378–405.

—— (2004) 'Exploring the dimensions of personal epistemology in differing classroom contexts: Student interpretations during the first year of college'. *Contemporary Educational Psychology*, 29 (2): 129–63.

Hounsell, D. (2002) 'Does research benefit teaching? And how can we know?', *Exchange*, 3: 6–7. Online. Available: http://www.exchange.ac.uk/files/eissue3.pdf (accessed 26 April 2008).

House, A., House, B. and Campbell, M. (1981) 'Measures of interobserver agreement. Calculation formulas and distribution effects', *Journal of Behavioral Assessment*, 3 (1): 37–57.

Hughes, I. (2006) 'The findings of an assessment audit: An NTFS project report'. *Bioscience Education eJournal*, 7. Online. Available: http://www.bioscience.heacademy.ac.uk/journal/vol7/beej-7-1.htm (accessed 27 April 2008).

Hutchings, P. (ed.) (2002) *Ethics of Inquiry, Issues in the Scholarship of Teaching and Learning*, Menlo Park, CA: The Carnegie Foundation for the Advancement of Teaching.

Hyland, T. and Johnson, S. (1999) 'Of cabbages and key skills: Exploding the mythology of core transferable skills in post-school education', *Journal of Further and Higher Education*, 22 (2): 163–72.

Jenkins, A. (2004) *A Guide to the research Evidence on Teaching-Research Relations, York: Higher Education Academy*. Online. Available: http://www.heacademy.ac.uk/assets/York/documents/ourwork/research/id383_guide_to_research_evidence_on_teaching_research_relations.pdf (accessed 27 April 2008).

Kane, R., Sandretto, S. and Heath, C. (2002) 'Telling half the story: A critical review of research on the teaching beliefs and practices of university academics', *Review of Educational Research*, 72: 177–228.

Kelly, G.A. (1955) *A Theory of Personality: The Psychology of Personal Constructs*, New York: W. W. Norton.

Kember, D. (1997) 'A reconceptualisation of the research into university academics' conceptions of teaching', *Learning and Instruction*, 7 (3): 255–75.

—— (2000) *Action Learning and Action Research. Improving the Quality of Teaching and Learning*, London: Kogan Page.

Kember, D. and Gow, L. (1992) 'Action research as a form of staff development', *Higher Education*, 23: 297–310.

Kember, D., Leung, D.Y.P., Jones, A., Yuen Loke, A., McKay, J., Sinclair, K., Tse, H., Webb, C., Wong, F.K.Y., Wong, M. and Yeung, E. (2000) 'Development of a questionnaire to measure the level of reflective thinking', *Assessment and Evaluation in Higher Education*, 25 (4): 381–95.

Kemmis, S. (1993) 'Action research and social movement: A challenge for policy research', Education Policy Analysis Archives (EPAA), 1 (1). Online. Available: http://epaa.asu.edu/epaa/v1n1.html (accessed 27 April 2008).

King, P.M. and Kitchener, K.S. (1994) *Developing Reflective Judgment: Understanding and Promoting Intellectual Growth and Critical Thinking in Adolescents and Adults*, San Francisco, CA: Jossey-Bass.

Kivinen, O. and Ristelä, P. (2002) 'Even higher learning takes place by doing: From postmodern critique to pragmatic action', *Studies in Higher Education*, 27 (4): 419–30.

Knight, P.T. (2002) *Being a Teacher in Higher Education*, Buckingham: SRHE and Open University Press.

Knight, P.T. and Trowler, P.R. (2000) 'Department-level cultures and the improvement of learning and teaching', *Studies in Higher Education*, 25 (1): 69–83.

Kreber, C. (2002a) 'Controversy and consensus on the scholarship of teaching', *Studies in Higher Education*, 27 (2): 151–67.

—— (2002b) 'Teaching excellence, teaching expertise and the scholarship of teaching', *Innovative Higher Education*, 27: 5–23.

—— (2005) 'Charting a critical course on the scholarship of university teaching movement', *Studies in Higher Education*, 30 (4): 389–406.

Kreber, C. and Cranton, P.A. (2000) 'Exploring the scholarship of teaching', *Journal of Higher Education*, 71: 476–96.

Land, R. (2006) 'Paradigms lost: Academic practice and exteriorising technologies', *E-Learning*, 3 (1): 100–110. Online. Available: http://www.wwwords.co.uk/pdf/viewpdf.asp?j=eleaandvol=3andissue=1andyear=2006andarticle=10_Land_ELEA_3_1_webandid=86.156.163.251 (accessed 27 April 2008).

Landis, J.R. and Koch, G.G. (1977) 'The measurement of observer agreement for categorical data', *Biometrics*, 3 (1): 159–74.

Lather, P. (1991) *Getting Smart: Feminist Research and Pedagogy with/in the Postmodern*, New York: Routledge.

Ledwith, M. (2007) 'On being critical: Uniting theory and practice through emancipatory action research', *Educational Action Research*, 15 (4): 597–611.

Leitch, S. (2006) 'Leitch Review of Skills, Prosperity for all in the global economy – World class skills. Final report', London: HM Treasury. Online. Available.: http://www.hm-treasury.gov.uk/media/6/4/leitch_finalreport051206.pdf (accessed 27 April 2008).

Lewin, K. (1951) *Field Theory in Social Science; Selected Theoretical Papers*, edited by D. Cartwright, New York: Harper and Row.

Lewin, K. and Lewin, G.W. (eds) (1948) *Resolving Social Conflicts; Selected Papers on Group Dynamics*, New York: Harper and Row.

Lindblom-Ylänne, S. (2003) 'Broadening an understanding of the phenomenon of dissonance', *Studies in Higher Education*, 28: 63–77.

Lindsay, R., Breen, R. and Jenkins, A. (2002a) 'Evidence-based management and action-at-a-distance', *Psychology Teaching Review*, 10 (1): 20–30.

Lindsay, R., Breen, R. and Paton-Saltzberg, R. (2002b) 'Pedagogic research and evidence-based management', *Psychology Teaching Review*, 10 (1): 20–30.

McKernan, J. (1991) *Curriculum Action Research. A Handbook of Methods and Resources for the Reflective Practitioner*, London: Kogan Page.

McNiff, J. (1993) *Teaching as Learning: An Action Research Approach*, London: Routledge.

Malcolm, J. and Zukas M. (2001) 'Bridging pedagogic gaps: Conceptual discontinuities in higher education', *Teaching in Higher Education*, 6 (1): 33–42.

Martin, E. and Balla, M. (1991) 'Conceptions of teaching and implications for learning,' *Research and Development in Higher Education*, 13: 298–304.

Martin, E. and Lueckenhausen, G. (2005) 'How university teaching changes teachers: Affective as well as cognitive challenges', *Higher Education*, 49 (3): 389–412.

Martin, E. and Ramsden, P. (1993) 'An expanding awareness: How lecturers change their understanding of teaching', *Research and Development in Higher Education*, 15: 148–55.

Martin, E., Prosser, M., Trigwell, K., Ramsden, P. and Benjamin, J. (2000) 'What university teachers teach and how they teach it', *Instructional Science*, 28: 387–412.

Marton, F. (1994) 'Phenomenography', in T. Husen and T. N. Postlethwaite (eds) *The International Encyclopedia of Education*, 2nd edn, Oxford: Pergamon, volume 8, pp. 4424–29.

Marton, F. and Säljö, R. (1976) 'On qualitative differences in learning. I: Outcome and process', *British Journal of Educational Psychology*, 46: 4–11.

Marton, F., Dall'Alba, G. and Beaty, E. (1993) 'Conceptions of Learning', *International Journal of Educational Research*, 19: 277–300.

Masters, J. (1995) 'The history of action research', in I. Hughes (ed.) *Action Research Electronic Reader*. The University of Sydney. Online. Available: http://www.scu.edu.au/schools/gcm/ar/arr/arow/rmasters.html (accessed 27 April 2008).

Meyer, J.H.F. (1995) 'A quantitative exploration of conceptions of learning', *Research and Development in Higher Education*, 18: 545–50.

—— (2000) 'An overview of the development and application of the Reflections on Learning Inventory (RoLI©)', paper presented at the RoLI© Symposium, Imperial College, London, July 25, 2000.

—— (2004) 'An introduction to the RoLI©', *Innovations in Education and Teaching International*, 41 (4): 491–97.

Mezirow, J. (ed.) (2000) *Learning as Transformation: Critical Perspectives on a Theory in Progress*, San Francisco, CA: Jossey-Bass.

Milgram, S. (1974) *Obedience to Authority*, New York: Harper and Row.

National Committee of Inquiry into Higher Education (1997), *Higher Education in the Learning Society, Report of the National Committee*, Norwich: HMSO [The Dearing report].

Neumann, R., Parry, S. and Becher, T. (2002) 'Teaching and learning in their disciplinary contexts: A conceptual analysis', *Studies in Higher Education*, 27 (4): 405–17.

Newman, J.H. (1976) *The Idea of a University Defined and Illustrated by John Henry Newman*, edited with an introduction and notes by I.T. Ker, Oxford English Texts, Oxford: Clarendon Press.

Newman, M. (2004) 'A pilot systematic review and meta-analysis on the effectiveness of problem based learning', published on behalf of the Campbell Collaboration Systematic Review Group on the effectiveness of problem-based learning. Online. Available: http://www.ltsn-01.ac.uk/docs/pbl_report.pdf (accessed 27 April 2008).

Nicholls, G.M. (2000) 'Professional development, teaching and lifelong learning: Is there a connection?', International Journal of Lifelong Learning and Adult Education, 19 (4): 370–77.

—— (2005) 'New lecturers' constructions of learning, teaching and research in higher education', Studies in Higher Education, 30 (5): 611–25.

Nixon, J. (2001) 'Not without dust and heat: The moral bases of the "new" academic professionalism', *British Journal of Educational Studies*, 29 (2): 173–86.

Norton, L.S. (1990) 'Essay writing: What really counts?', *Higher Education*, 20 (4): 411–42.

—— (2001a) *The Ideal *** Inventory. A useful tool for pedagogical research in higher education.* Online. Available: http://www.heacademy.ac.uk/assets/York/documents/resources/resourcedatabase/id495_ideal_inventory_norton.pdf (accessed 27 April 2008).

—— (2001b) 'Researching your teaching: The case for action research', *Psychology Learning and Teaching*, 1 (1): 21–27.

—— (2004) *Psychology Applied Learning Scenarios (PALS). A Practical Introduction to Problem-Based Learning Using Vignettes for Psychology Lecturers. A tutor pack funded by LTSN Psychology.* York: Higher Education Academy. Online. Available: http://www.psychology.heacademy.ac.uk/docs/pdf/p20040422_pals.pdf (accessed 27 April 2008).

—— (2008) 'Pedagogical research in higher education. Ethical issues facing the practitioner-researcher', in A. Campbell and S. Groundwater-Smith (eds) *An Ethical Approach to Practitioner Research. Dealing with Issues and Dilemmas in Action Research*, London: Routledge, chapter 12, pp. 162–71.

Norton, B. (J.C.W.), Norton, L., Thomas, S., Griffiths, T., Walters, D., Perrin, S. and Owens, T. (2003) 'Building confidence in using information resources: A core academic skill', paper presented at European Association for Research in Learning and Instruction, 10th biennial conference, Padova, Italy, August 26–30, 2003.

Norton, L.S. and Aiyegbayo, O. (2005) 'Becoming an excellent teacher: Factors that influence new university lecturers' beliefs about learning and teaching', paper presented at the 5th international conference on the Scholarship of Teaching and Learning (SoTL), London, 12–13 May, 2005.

Norton, L., Aiyegbayo, O., Bhatti, N., de-Petro, V., Doyle, C., Matthews, K. and Parry, T. (2003) 'Action research and metacognitive awareness in postgraduate students', paper presented at the Collaborative Action Research Network conference, Knutsford, 7–9 November 2003.

Norton, L., Brunas-Wagstaff, J. and Lockley, S. (1999) 'Learning outcomes in the traditional coursework essay: Do students and tutors agree?', in C. Rust (ed.) *Improving Student Learning. Improving Student Learning Outcomes*, Oxford: The Oxford Centre for Staff and Learning Development, Part IV, chapter 21. pp. 240–48.

Norton, L., Clifford, R., Hopkins, L., Toner, I. and Norton, J.C.W. (2002) 'Helping psychology students write better essays', Psychology Learning and Teaching, 2 (2): 116–26. Online. Available: http://www.psychology.heacademy.ac.uk/docs/pdf/p20030617_22norton.pdf (accessed 27 April 2008).

Norton, L.S. and Crowley, C.M. (1995) 'Can students be helped to learn how to learn? An evaluation of an approaches to learning programme for first year degree students', *Higher Education*, 29: 307–28.

Norton, L.S. and Hartley, J. (1986) 'What factors contribute to good examination marks? The role of note-taking in subsequent examination performance', *Higher Education*, 15: 355–71.

Norton, L. Horn, R. and Thomas, S. (1997) 'Innovatory courses: Matching lecturers' objectives with students' perceptions and academic performance', in C. Rust and G. Gibbs (eds) Improving Student Learning. Improving Student Learning through Course Design. Oxford: The Oxford Centre for Staff and Learning Development, Part X, Chapter 30, pp. 331–43.

Norton, L., Kahn, P., van Arendsen, J. and Walters, D. (2001) 'Reflective thinking about the study of psychology, mathematics and music at degree level: Does it change over the first year?', in C. Rust (ed.) *Improving Student Learning. Improving Student Learning Strategically*, Oxford: The Oxford Centre for Staff and Learning Development, Part 2, chapter 11, pp. 120–31.

Norton, L.S., Morgan, K. and Thomas, S. (1995) '"The ideal self inventory': A new measure of self esteem', *Counselling Psychology Quarterly*, 8 (4): 305–10.

Norton, L.S. and Norton, B. (2000) 'Information skills: Do we help our students enough?', in C. Rust (ed.) *Improving Student Learning. Improving Student Learning through the Disciplines*, Oxford: The Oxford Centre for Staff and Learning Development, Part III, chapter 27, pp. 283–93.

Norton, L.S., Norton, J.C.W. and Thomas, S. (2004) 'Encouraging psychology students to use more journal papers', paper presented at the Psychology Learning and Teaching conference (PLAT 2004), University of Strathclyde, 5–7 April 2004.

Norton, L.S. and Owens, T. (2003) 'Encouraging metalearning in first year undergraduates', Symposium paper presented at the European Association for Research in Learning and Instruction, 10th biennial conference, Padova, Italy, August 26–30, 2003.

Norton, L.S., Scantlebury, E. and Dickins, T.E. (1999). 'Helping undergraduates to become more effective learners: An evaluation of two learning interventions'. Innovations in Education and Training International (IETI), 36 (4): 273–284.

Nyquist, J.D. and Wulff, D.H. (1996) *Working Effectively with Graduate Assistants*, Thousand Oaks, CA: Sage.

Orne, M.T. (1962) 'On the social psychology of the psychological experiment: With particular reference to demand characteristics and their implications', *American Psychologist*, 17: 776–83.

Parker, S. (1997) *Reflective Teaching in the Postmodern World: A Manifesto for Education in Postmodernity*, Buckingham: Open University Press.

Perrin, S., Busby, R. and Norton, B. (2003) 'Listening and learning: Student and staff perceptions of oral assessment in American studies'. Online. Available: http://www.llas.ac.uk/prf.aspx#as1 (accessed 27 April 2008).

Perry, W.G. (1970) *Forms of Intellectual and Ethical Development in the College Years: A Scheme*, New York: Holt, Rinehart and Winston.

Peters, J. (2004) 'Teachers engaging in action research: Challenging some assumptions', *Educational Action Research*, 12 (4): 535–55.

Ponte, P. (2002) 'How teachers become action researchers and how teacher educators become their facilitators', *Journal for Educational Action Research*, 10: 399–422.

Postareff, L. (2007) *Teaching in Higher Education. From Content-Focused to Learning-Focused Approaches to Teaching*, Helsinki: Helsinki University.

Prosser, M. and Trigwell, K. (1999) *Understanding Learning and Teaching. The Experience in Higher Education*, Buckingham: Society for Research into Higher Education and The Open University Press.

Prosser, M., Trigwell, K. and Taylor, P. (1994) 'A phenomenographic study of academics' conceptions of science teaching and learning', *Learning and Instruction*, 4: 217–31.

Ramsden, P. (1998) *Learning to Lead in Higher Education*, London: Routledge.

—— (1991) 'A performance indicator of teaching quality in higher education: The course experience questionnaire', *Studies in Higher Education*, 16 (2): 129–50.

—— (1992) *Learning to Teach in Higher Education*, London: Routledge.

—— (2003) *Learning to Teach in Higher Education*, 2nd edn, London: RoutledgeFalmer.

Ramsden, P. and Entwistle, N.J. (1981) 'Effects of academic departments on students' approaches to studying', *British Journal of Educational Psychology*, 51: 368–83.

Rees, G., Baron, S., Boyask, R. and Taylor, C. (2007) 'Research capacity building, professional learning and the social practices of educational research', *British Educational Research Journal*, 33 (5): 761–79.

Revans, R.W. (1971) *Developing Effective Managers: A New Approach to Business Education*, London: Longman.

Richardson, J.T.E. (1990) 'Reliability and replicability of the Approaches to Studying questionnaire', *Studies in Higher Education*, 15: 155–68.

—— (2007) Comparative Review of British, American and Australian National Surveys of Undergraduate Students, York: Higher education Academy. Online. Available: http://www.heacademy.ac.uk/assets/York/documents/ourwork/research/National_Survey_Comparative_Review_Feb_2007.doc (accessed 27 April 2008).

Rönnerman, K. (2003) 'Action research: Educational tools and the improvement of practice', *Educational Action Research*, 11 (1): 9–21.

Roulston, K., Legette, R., Deloach, M. and Buchalter Pitman, C. (2005) 'What is "research" for teacher-researchers?', *Educational Action Research*, 13 (2): 169–89.

Rowland, S. (2003) 'Teaching for democracy in higher education', *Teaching in Higher Education*, 8 (1): 89–101.

Säljö, R. (1979) 'Learning about learning', *Higher Education*, 8: 443–51.

Saloman, G. (1991) 'Transcending the qualitative–quantitative debate: The analytic and systemic approaches to educational research', *Educational Researcher*, 20 (6): 10–18.

Samuelowicz, K. and Bain, J.D. (2001) 'Revisiting academics' beliefs about teaching and learning', *Higher Education*, 41: 299–325.

Schön, D.A. (1983) *The Reflective Practitioner*, New York: Basic Books.

Seider, S.N. and Lemma, P. (2004) 'Perceived effects of action research on teachers' professional efficacy, inquiry mindsets and the support they received while conducting projects to intervene in student learning', *Educational Action Research*, 12 (2): 219–37.

Shevlin, M., Banyard, P., Davies, M.N.O. and Griffiths, M. (2000) 'The validity of student evaluation of teaching in higher education: Love me, love my lectures?', *Assessment and Evaluation in Higher Education*, 25 (4): 397–405.

Shulman, L.S. (1986) 'Those who understand: Knowledge growth in teaching', *Educational Researcher*, 15 (2): 4–14.

—— (2002) 'Foreword: The ethics of teaching and scholarship', in P. Hutchings (ed.) *Ethics of Inquiry, Issues in the Scholarship of Teaching and Learning*, Menlo Park, CA: The Carnegie Foundation for the Advancement of Teaching.

Smith, J.K. (1986) 'Closing down the conversation: The end of the quantitative–qualitative debate among educational inquirers', *Educational Researcher*, 15 (1): 4–12.

Smith, M.K. (1996; 2001, 2007) 'Action research', The Encyclopedia of Informal Education. Online. Available: www.infed.org/research/b-actres.htm (accessed 26 April 2008).

Smith, P. (2008) Personal communication.

Sotto, E. (2007) *When Teaching Becomes Learning. A Theory and Practice of Teaching*, London: Continuum International Publishing Group.

Staniforth, D. and Harland, T. (2003) 'Reflection on practice; collaborative action research for new academics', *Educational Action Research*, 11 (1): 79–91.

Stark, S. (2006) 'Using action learning for professional development', *Educational Action Research*, 14 (1): 23–43.

Stead, V., Mort, M and Davies, J. (2001) 'Theory generation and practice improvement: A mental health service perspective', *Educational Action Research*, 9 (1): 61–77.

Stenhouse, L. (1971) 'The Humanities Curriculum Project: The rationale', *Theory into Practice*, 10 (3): 154–62.

—— (1975) An Introduction to Curriculum Research and Development, London: Heinemann.

Steward, S., Norton, L.S., Evans, I. and Norton, J.C.W. (2003) 'Lecturers! What are you assessing?' Paper presented at the Learning and Skills Research Network annual conference 'Research for all' GMB National College, Manchester, 6 June, 2003.

Strauss, A. and Corbin, J. (1990) *Basics of Qualitative Research: Grounded theory Procedures and Techniques*, Sage Publications.

Tait, H., Entwistle, N.J., and McCune, V. (1998) 'ASSIST: A reconceptualisation of the Approaches to Studying Inventory', in C. Rust (ed.) *Improving Student Learning: Improving Students as Learners* (pp. 262–71). Oxford: Oxford Centre for Staff and Learning Development.

Tight, M. (2003) *Researching Higher Education*, Maidenhead: SRHE and Open University Press.

Titchen, A. and Manley, K. (2006) 'Spiralling towards transformational action research: Philosophical and practical journeys', *Educational Action Research*, 14 (3): 333–56.

Trigwell, K. and Prosser, M. (2004) 'Development and use of the Approaches to Teaching Inventory', *Educational Psychology Review*, 16 (4), 409–24.

Trigwell, K., Martin, E., Benjamin, J. and Prosser, M. (2000) 'Scholarship of teaching: A model', *Higher Education Research and Development*, 19: 155–68.

Trigwell, K. and Shale, S. (2004) 'Student learning and the scholarship of university teaching', *Studies in Higher Education*, 29: 523–36.

Van Valey, T.L. (2001) 'Recent changes in higher education and their ethical implications', *Teaching Sociology*, 29 (1): 1–8.

Wahlstrom, K.L. and Ponte, P. (2005) 'Examining teachers' beliefs through action research; guidance and counselling/pastoral care reflected in the cross-cultural mirror', *Educational Action Research*, 13 (4): 543–61.

Walters, D. and Norton, L. (2004) Personal development planning: Promoting excellent learning? Paper presented at the ILTHE annual conference, University of Hertfordshire, 29 June–1 July.

Watson, J.S. and Wilcox, S. (2000) 'Reading for understanding: Methods of reflecting on practice', *Reflective Practice*, 1 (1): 57–67.

Whitehead, J. (2000) 'How do I improve my practice? Creating and legitimating an epistemology of practice', *Reflective Practice*, 1 (1): 91–104.

Williamson, T. (2002) 'Ideal *** Inventory: Is there an 'ideal' accounting and finance i) programme, ii) student?', presentation given at ILT North West Members' Forum, Manchester Metropolitan University, April 2002.

Winkler, G. (2001) 'Reflection and theory: Conceptualising the gap between teaching experience and teacher expertise', *Educational Action Research*, 9 (3): 437–49.

Wood, P.K. (1997). 'A secondary analysis of claims regarding the Reflective Judgment interview: Internal consistency, sequentiality and intra-individual differences in ill-structured problem solving', *Higher Education: Handbook of theory and research*, Edison, N.J.: Agathon, pp. 245–314.

Woolhouse, M. (2005) 'You can't do it on your own: Gardening as an analogy for personal learning from a collaborative action research group', *Educational Action Research*, 13 (1): 27–41.

Yorke, M. and Knight, P. (2003) *Using Educational Research in Course Design and Delivery: Employability and Transferable Skills*. Online. Available: http://66.102.1.104/scholar?hl=ena ndlr=andq=cache:nPhz972Q3_YJ:www.open.ac.uk/vqportal/Skills-Plus/documents/ Notesoneducationalres.pdf+Yorke+Knight+2003 (accessed 27 April 2008).

Zaman, M.Q. uz (2004) Review of the Academic Evidence on the Relationship between Teaching and Research in Higher Education, London: Department for Education and Skills. Online. Available: http://www.dfes.gov.uk/research/data/uploadfiles/RR506.pdf (accessed 27 April 2008).

Index

266   Index

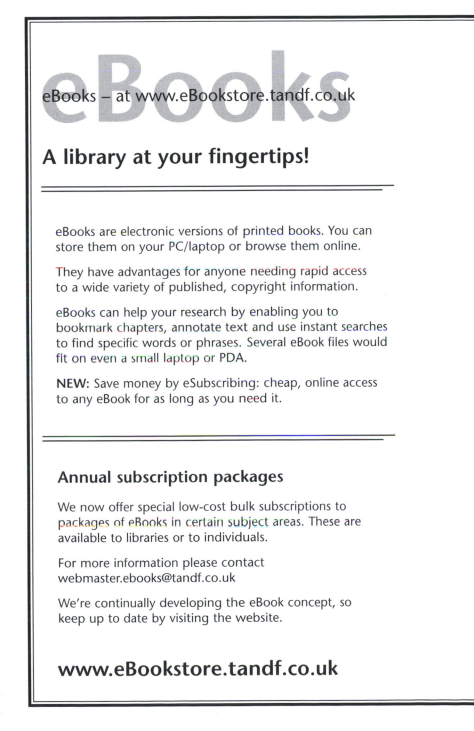

Made in the USA
San Bernardino, CA
09 October 2013